RABBI MOSHE HEINEMANN
6109 Gist Avenue
Baltimore, MD 21215
Tel. (410) 358-9828
Fax. (410) 358-9838

משה היינעמאן
אב"ד ק"ק אגודת ישראל
באלטימאר
טל. 764-7778 (410)
פקס 764-8878 (410)

בס"ד

באתי בשורות אלו להגיד לאיש ישרו ולהכיר טובה להרב ר' נתן מילער שליט"א מחשובי אברכים בכולל עבודת לוי, על יד הישיבה הקדושה נר ישראל בבאלטימאר, שתרם מזמנו היקר ומכחותיו הבלתי עיפים לסדר פסקי דינים שהשבתי לבני הישיבה ברבות השנים וסדרם להעלותם על מזבח הדפוס בבינה ובהשכל וגם יגע ומצא את המקור שממנו שאבתי הפנינים האלו וגם טרח ועמל הרבה שיהא הכל בסדר נכון וקל להבין.

ראיתי את הספרים שחיבר הרב ר' נתן הנ"ל בשמי ועברתי בין בתריהם וראיתי שהם הם הדברים שאמרתי בהגידי שיעורים לפני בני הישיבה היקרים במוצאי שבתות וגם אני מכיר טובה להישיבה נר ישראל הנ"ל שנתנה לי האפשרות להפיץ דיני התורה ברבים לתלמידים הגונים ומחבבים תורת השי"ת.

אין כוונת החיבורים האלו לפרש כל הדינים של הענינים שהם עסוקים בהם, אלא הם תשובות להשאלות אשר שאלוני והם מקצת הלכות נהוגות אצלנו מפי רבותינו לפיכך נקראים שם החיבורים האלו "מה נאמר" שמה נאמר בהלכה מעצמנו כי אם דברים המובאים, המוזכרים בהגמרא, בראשונים, אחרונים ובפוסקים. ויהי רצון מלפני אבינו שבשמים שיהא בחיבורים אלו "מה נאמר" תועלת לאחינו בית ישראל עד בוא הזמן של מלאה הארץ דעה את השם כמים לים מכסים.

ועל זה בעה"ח בשני בשבת לסדר זה הדבר אשר צוה ד' תעשו, באיסרו חג הפסח, שלשה ועשרים יום לחדש ניסן, שמנה ימים למב"י, שנת חמשת אלפים ושבע מאות ושמנים ואחת לבה"ע

משה בן הזכר ר' ברוך גדליה למשפחת היינעמאן החונ"פ מתא באלטימאר

Please note this קונטרוס was compiled based on the שיעורים of Rav Heinemann שליט"א, given at Yeshivas Ner Yisroel of Baltimore. Recordings of the שיעורים were provided by the Audio Library of Yeshivas Ner Yisroel. Although the קונטרוס was reviewed and revised by the Rav, any questions or errors are due to my חסרונות alone.

May this collection of insights and stories gathered from Rav Heinemann's שיעורים serve as a springboard for a more profound understanding of רצון ה', a greater level of השראת השכינה, and a tremendous קידוש שם שמים.

With boundless gratitude to the רבונו של עולם, the Rav, R' Yechiel Schreck for reviewing the content, the Yeshiva, and my family – especially my wife

נתן יוסף מיללער

לזכות רפואה שלימה דניאל יצחק בן דבורה

לעילוי נשמת הרב שעפטיל מאיר בן הרב נפתלי הלוי ז"ל
נתבקש בישיבה של מעלה בכ"ח שבט שנת תשפ"א לפ"ק

ולעילוי נשמת רפאל ישראל חיים בן מרדכי אריה פארעצקי ז"ל
עלתה נשמתו השמימה בט"ו אב שנת תשע"ט לפ"ק

For Comments, Questions, or Suggestions, please email:
60SecondSpark@gmail.com

Table of Contents

Chapter 1: Shonim Iyar 5778

Q1: How exact must *tefillin* be placed in the center of the head?

A: The Gemara says that when the Kohen Gadol wore the *tzitz*, it would have to sit *b'makom tefillin*.[1] The Gemara then asks how he wore his *tefillin* if they both needed to be in the same spot? The Gemara answers, "There is enough space on the head to put on two pairs of *tefillin*," one in front of the other. Therefore, you can have both the *tzitz* and the *tefillin* *b'makom tefillin*.[2] That's the *poshut pshat* of the Gemara. The Avnei Nezer says you could wear two pairs of *tefillin* side by side, next to one another. Evidently, בֵּין עֵינֶיךָ [3] isn't exact because otherwise you can't have both pairs of *tefillin* exactly in the center if they are sitting next to one another. Even though most *meforshim* don't have this understanding in the Gemara, there's no proof to say they disagree with what the Avnei Nezer implies that they don't need to be exactly in the middle either. It's a *hiddur* to make your *tefillin* as precise as you can in the middle,[4] but it's impossible to make it exactly in the center. Chazal say on the *posuk*[5] 'Moshe took half of the blood and put it on the *Mizbei'ach*' – "who decided this was half the blood? An

---

[1] Zevachim (19b) - תנא שערו היה נראה בין ציץ למצנפת ששם מניחין תפילין

[2] Zevachim (19a) - בעי רבי זירא תפילין מהו שיחוצו אליבא דמאן דאמר לילה לאו זמן תפילין הוא לא תבעי לך כיון דלילה חייצי יום נמי חייצי כי תיבעי לך למ"ד לילה זמן תפילין מאי מצוה דגופיה חייץ או לא חייץ איגלגל מילתא ומטא לקמיה דרבי אמי א"ל תלמוד ערוך הוא בידינו תפילין חוצצות

[3] Devarim (6:8) - וּקְשַׁרְתָּם לְאוֹת עַל־יָדֶךָ וְהָיוּ לְטֹטָפֹת בֵּין עֵינֶיךָ

[4] Shulchan Aruch OC (27:10) - צריך שיהיה הקשר מאחורי הראש למעלה בעורף צריך לכוין הקציצה שתהא באמצע כדי שתהא כנגד בין העינים וגם הקשר יהיה באמצע העורף ולא יטה לכאן או לכאן

[5] Shemos (24:6) - וַיִּקַּח מֹשֶׁה חֲצִי הַדָּם וַיָּשֶׂם בָּאַגָּנֹת וַחֲצִי הַדָּם זָרַק עַל־הַמִּזְבֵּחַ

angel took half the blood."[6] The straightforward understanding is that you have to take the blood as it's coming out of the animal – but how do you know when half the blood has poured out? Therefore, an angel must have done it. Nonetheless, the general rule by all the *mitzvos* of the Torah is that they don't have to be exact - other than *arbayim se'ah* of a *mikvah*. If the *halacha* would be that you need exactly 40 *se'ah* in a *mikvah*,[7] then the obligation wouldn't be for the measurement to be exactly 40 *se'ah*. That would be impossible. I have a friend who is a *battim macher* who received a request to make *battim* which are exactly square on all sides even when measured with a micrometer for the price of $10,000.[8] He took on the request, successfully made the perfectly square *tefillin*, and handed them to the person who had made the request. When the buyer checked the *tefillin* with a micrometer, he saw they were 1/100 of an inch off and asked the *battim macher* what happened. "What time of the day did you measure and where did you measure the *battim*?" The man said when and where he checked them, and the *battim macher* took the *tefillin* to the window, opened the window, and after ten minutes said, "Now measure them." They were exactly square. Leather - which *tefillin* are made from - is a living thing. A humid and moist atmosphere will expand the leather, while a colder climate will make the leather contract. Even though the *tefillin* were made exactly square in the *battim macher*'s facility, it's impossible that the *tefillin* would remain exactly

---

[6] Vayikra Rabba (6:5) - מִי חִלְּקוֹ, מַלְאָךְ בָּא וְחִלְּקוֹ

[7] Yoma (31a) - ותניא ורחץ בשרו במים במי מקוה כל בשרו מים שכל גופו עולה בהן וכמה הן אמה על אמה ברום ג' אמות ושיערו חכמים מי מקוה ארבעים סאה

[8] Shulchan Aruch OC (32:39) - תפילין בין של ראש בין של יד הלכה למשה מסיני שיהיו מרובעות בתפרן ובאלכסונן דהיינו שיהיה ריבוען מכוון ארכו כרחבו כדי שיהא להם אותו אלכסון שאמרו חז"ל כל אמתא בריבועא אמתא ותרי חומשי באלכסונא וצריך לרבע מקום מושבן וגם הבתים: הגה אבל על גובה הבתים אין להקפיד אם הוא יותר מרחבן וארכן עשאן מרובעות ואחר זמן נתקלקל ריבוען יש מי שאומר שצריך לרבען

square in every location. The Aruch HaShulchan[9] says if the *tefillin* look square then that's good enough. They don't need to be fully square. Even though the top and bottom of the *tefillin* must be square, and even if all sides are equal, the *tefillin* may not be kosher if it is a rhombus. How do we make sure it is not a rhombus? The Shulchan Aruch says the diagonal must also be the diagonal of the square. Chazal say the diagonal of a square is 1 and $\frac{2}{5}$ of the side. Rav Moshe[10] says in actuality, it's not exactly 1 and $\frac{2}{5}$, rather it's close to 1 and $\frac{2}{5}$. The difference between exactly the diagonal of a

---

[9] Aruch HaShulchan OC (32:75) - ודע שאף אם נאמר שאי אפשר לצמצם בידי אדם לעשות ריבוע ממש מכל מקום התורה אמרה עשה כפי מה שביכולתך לצמצם ובזה תקיים המצוה. וכן אמרו חכמינו ז"ל בבכורות (יז:) לענין מידות המזבח וכלי בית המקדש שאמרה תורה מידה וזה לשון הגמרא: רחמנא אמר עביד ובכל היכי דמצית למיעבד ניחא ליה עיין שם והכא נמי בתפילין כן הוא

[10] Igros Moshe YD (3:120:5) - ולעניו ריבוע התפילין שאין למדוד במיקראסקאפ ברור ופשוט, וגם מה שכתבתי הכרח מהא דחשבון תרי חומשי באלכסונא אינו מדויק והכוונה שאף זה הוא ריבוע הכשר לכתחלה אף למהדרין ביותר וגם כשר ומהודרין אף אם יזדמן ריבוע אמתי ממש, וכן כאן שהלכה דא"א לצמצם ובכל דבר שאמרה תורה מדה הכשירה תורה אף לכתחלה כהמדה שמודדין האינשי כמפורש בבכורות דף י"ז וא"כ בהכרח שכשר בין משהו יותר מהאמת שגליא כלפי שמיא ובין שהוא משהו פחות ובודאי כשיזדמן שהוא מצמצם כדכתבתי ולא שייך למיפלג ע"ז כי הרי אף התנאים ואמוראים לא יכלו לצמצם, וגם על בצלאל ואהליאב וכל חכם לב אמר הגמ׳ בבכורות שלמ"ד א"א לצמצם גם בהם אפשר שלא היה מצומצם והיה כשר משום דזה גם כן הכשירה תורה ואין זה ענין חריפות ובקיאות אלא שהוא דבר מוכרח, ולכן כתבתי שהוא פלא מה שאמר אחד שהגרי"ז הלוי זצ"ל היה סבור שיש מעלה כשימדדו ריבוע דתפילין במיקראסקאפ, אך אם הוא אמת יש אולי לתרץ דחשש שמא עושי הבתים לא טרחו כפי יכלתם למדוד היטב שא"כ ליכא אף מדה דהאינשי שהם אף שא"א לצמצם והתורה הכשירה כל היכא דמצית למעבד הרי צריך למדוד כל היכי דמצי בכל הטירחא וראיית העין שאפשר ולא יוכשר כשיתעצלו לטרוח ולעיין היטב שזה הא אינו אמת אף למדת האינשי שלכן החמיר למדוד במיקראסקאפף שזה שייך להחמיר לחוש לזה אף שלדינא אין מחוייבין לחשוש דסומכין על האומדנא דמומחין

square and 1 and $\frac{2}{5}$ is the amount of leeway which Chazal said you are allowed to have. If it's less than that, it is kosher even though it is not a true square. Evidently, it does not need to be exact as long as it appears square.

Q2: May one stack *seforim* to use as a *shtender*? What if they're already stacked?

A: Generally, a person is not allowed to use a *sefer* for his own needs. However, if you're using a *sefer* to make it easier to learn, then it's helping you learn and it would be permitted. If you're just using another *sefer* to allow you to put your phone on it, that's not permitted because it's a *bizayon.* This *shailah* is brought in the Kitzur Shulchan Aruch where you want to learn a *sefer* but the sun is glaring and making it difficult to read. The Kitzur Shulchan Aruch[11] says it's permitted to use another *sefer* to block out the sun to allow you to learn.

Q3: What is a *tinok shenishba*?

A: That's a good question because there's not one standard answer for this. It depends on the circumstances regarding where we're applying the concept. *Tinok shenishba* means that a baby was taken as a captive among the non-Jews, was brought up by them, and he never knew anything about Yiddishkeit.[12] Even if he knew he was a *yid,* he didn't know any practices of Judaism, so there's no claim against him for not performing any *mitzvos.* How is he supposed to know what to do if he never saw it? The *halacha* regarding a *tinok*

---

[11] Kitzur Shulchan Aruch (28:9) - אָסוּר לְהִשְׁתַּמֵּשׁ בְּסֵפֶר לַהֲנָאָתוֹ כְּגוֹן לְהַעֲמִידוֹ לְהָגֵן מִפְּנֵי הַחַמָּה אוֹ כְּדֵי שֶׁלֹּא יִרְאֶה חֲבֵרוֹ מַה שֶּׁהוּא עוֹשֶׂה אֲבָל אִם הַשֶּׁמֶשׁ זוֹרַחַת עַל הַסֵּפֶר שֶׁהוּא לוֹמֵד בּוֹ מֻתָּר לְהָגֵן בְּסֵפֶר אַחֵר כֵּיוָן שֶׁאֵינוֹ עוֹשֶׂה לַהֲנָאָתוֹ וְכֵן לְהַנִּיחַ סֵפֶר תַּחַת סֵפֶר שֶׁהָיָה לוֹמֵד בּוֹ כְּדֵי לְהַגְבִּיהוֹ לְצֹרֶךְ הַלִּמּוּד יֵשׁ לְהַתִּיר

[12] Shabbos (68b) - כיצד תינוק שנשבה לבין הגוים וגר שנתגייר בין הגוים ועשה מלאכות הרבה בשבתות הרבה אינו חייב אלא חטאת אחת וחייב על הדם אחת ועל החלב אחת ועל עבודה זרה אחת ומונבז פוטר

shenishba in general is that he's not considered responsible for his actions,[13] not an עבריין, and yet is still considered a *yid* regarding certain *halachos* like counting him towards a *minyan* even if you hold that someone who desecrates Shabbos is not *mitztaref* to a *minyan*.[14] We don't say his testimony is believed because he doesn't know there's an *issur* to lie. There was a *choshuv* Rav and big posek here in Baltimore whose name was Rav Yitzchok Sternhell. He started Yeshivas Kochav Yitzchok, based on the name of his *sefer* Kochav Yitzchok which was three *chalakim* of *teshuvos*. Also, Sternhell means "light of the star." He was *moser nefesh* in Baltimore at a time before Rav Yosef Tendler came and established *Cholov Yisroel*. When the Yeshiva was in Baltimore City, there was no *Cholov Yisroel* because the city made a law that you cannot have *Cholov Yisroel*. How did they get away with such a discriminatory law? They said all milk sold in the city of Baltimore must stand 48 hours after pasteurization and be retested to ensure pasteurization was effective. They claimed it was a health law, but it was really pushed by the three major milk companies – Borden, Sheffield, and Greenspring. They wanted to ensure they had no competition from the outside and made this law which wasn't required anywhere else. Consequently, all the milk in Baltimore city had to be stored for 48 hours and required massive silos which held at least 100,000 gallons and refrigerated at 34 degrees until it would be retested and sold. Since the Yeshiva was visited on a constant basis from the Board of Health, they had no choice

---

[13] Rambam Mamrim (3:3) - אֲבָל בְּנֵי הַתּוֹעִים הָאֵלֶּה וּבְנֵי בְנֵיהֶם שֶׁהִדִּיחוּ אוֹתָם אֲבוֹתָם וְנוֹלְדוּ בֵּין הַקָּרָאִים וְגִדְּלוּ אוֹתָם עַל דַּעְתָּם. הֲרֵי הוּא כְּתִינוֹק שֶׁנִּשְׁבָּה בֵּינֵיהֶם וְגִדְּלוּהוּ וְאֵינוֹ זָרִיז לֶאֱחֹז בְּדַרְכֵי הַמִּצְוֹת שֶׁהֲרֵי הוּא כְּאָנוּס וְאַף עַל פִּי שֶׁשָּׁמַע אַחַר כָּךְ [שֶׁהוּא יְהוּדִי וְרָאָה הַיְהוּדִים וְדָתָם הֲרֵי הוּא כְּאָנוּס שֶׁהֲרֵי גִּדְּלוּהוּ עַל טָעוּתָם] כָּךְ אֵלּוּ שֶׁאָמַרְנוּ הָאוֹחֲזִים בְּדַרְכֵי אֲבוֹתָם הַקָּרָאִים שֶׁטָּעוּ. לְפִיכָךְ רָאוּי לְהַחֲזִירָן בִּתְשׁוּבָה וּלְמָשְׁכָם בְּדִבְרֵי שָׁלוֹם עַד שֶׁיַּחְזְרוּ לְאֵיתָן הַתּוֹרָה

[14] Mishna Berura (55:46) - כתב הפמ"ג דוקא עבירה שעבר לתיאבון אבל להכעיס אפילו בדבר אחד או שהוא מומר לע"ג או לחלל שבת בפרהסיא דינו כעכו"ם ואינו מצטרף

other than comply with this law and not have *Cholov Yisroel*. Throughout the United States, there was no law preventing *Cholov Yisroel*, but no one sold *Cholov Yisroel* in America betause there were hardly any *yidden* living in the county at that time. Consequently, Rav Sternhell made an arrangement with a *Cholov Yisroel* company in upstate New York to deliver milk to an unknown address where he would ship it to his house, bringing in 200 quarts of *Cholov Yisroel* milk per week. Anyone who wanted *Cholov Yisroel* milk could purchase it from the Rav. He wasn't making a profit on the milk and did this for years. That's how I got to know Rav Sternhell. Later on, Rav Tendler came to Baltimore. Not only did he make *Cholov Yisroel* available on a wider scale, he also fought the law at the same time. He said this law had no health benefits and that it was only enacted to prevent others from creating a milk business since no one has ever tested pasteurized milk and found it wasn't effective. The outside competitive milk companies helped Rav Tendler finance the lawsuit as he spearheaded the fight for *Cholov Yisroel*. He made the milk available at a certain place outside the city, maybe unofficially in the city, and made Rav Sternhell very happy with no longer needing to put himself at risk of being imprisoned, and it made the Rebbetzin happy that she wouldn't have to wash the floors as frequently from people tracking snow and dirt in the house when they came to purchase milk. As long as it was necessary, Rav Sternhell and his Rebbetzin went along with it. However, before he gave up the *Cholov Yisroel* endeavor, Rav Sternhell asked me to show him Rav Tendler's milk farm to ensure it met his specifications. At that time, Rav Tendler's farm was in Lancaster, Pennsylvania and it was in the Amish Country. As we were driving along, Rav Sternhell saw someone who looked like *Chassidish yid* walking along the street with a hat and beard as the Satmar Chassidim do. Then we saw another Satmar *chassid*. At that point, Rav Sternhell wanted to speak with them, and started speaking with them in German. The Amish are called Pennsylvania Dutch, really they are Pennsylvania Deutsch – which means German. In fact, Rav Sternhell was a Rav in Salzburg before the war and was in Rav Breuer's Yeshiva in Frankfurt for a year or two despite coming from Hungary. Rav Sternhell and this Amish man spoke for three quarters of an hour as the individual was explaining to Rav Sternhell all about the Amish religion and the basic belief of the Amish is that they need to remain apart from the rest of the people. Therefore, they don't drive cars or use electrical equipment in order to maintain their distance. They have a *machlokes haPoskim* whether they're allowed to use a diesel-powered washing machine since that's different than what everyone else uses, but the *machmirim* say they need to wash clothing by hand like they used to do. The whole conversation was very interesting. In fact, women need to have their hair covered at all times, and need to wear a second covering on their heads when they *daven*. Also, a person cannot have a beard until he has a child and cannot have a mustache until having a second child. There are all kinds of *halachos* which they have and are very interesting. They have *geirim* who increase the community about 3% each year, and all do well in business despite not being able to use electricity. Houses have always cost about two years of wages. If you don't have so much money, you buy a cheaper house. If you earn more, then you can purchase a larger home. Although you might be able to make 20 planks out of a tree which costs 10 dollars, you still have to pay the price of the machine required to cut the raw materials. There's no question the Amish believe in the Ribbono Shel Olam. Although they are not allowed to have a Rabbi, they are allowed to have Chachamim. After the whole discussion, neither Rav Sternhell nor myself felt a desire to become Amish. We respected the Amish for adhering steadfast for their religion but didn't feel it had anything to do with us. We didn't say, "That's old fashioned!" or "It's not practical." Therefore, if you find a *tinok shenishba* and tell him about Shabbos, wearing *tzitzis* and *tefillin*, if he thinks to himself, "What does that have to do with me? I wasn't brought up to believe in any of this," that is a true *tinok shenishba*. Even if he's exposed to Yiddishkeit, he doesn't think he has anything to do with it. However, if he thinks "that's old fashioned" or "this is not practical," then evidently he harbors a feeling in himself that, "I don't have to do this because it's not in line with what I want to do." He is making an excuse to himself why he is not going to be intimidated by this person. That is someone who is not a *tinok shenishba.* There are different kinds of people who aren't frum. Rav Elyashiv says there is no such thing nowadays as someone who is a *tinok shenishba*. Rav Moshe[15] follows the same line of thinking, but doesn't go that far. Rather, Rav Moshe says every *yid* knows about Chanuka as even post offices say "Happy Chanuka." There is no *yid* in America, and certainly Israel, who doesn't know about Pesach. People walk around the foodstores where the label "Passover Food" is prominently displayed. Essentially every place in the world has been exposed to Yiddishkeit as Chabad has places everywhere. It's very good – being involved in *kashrus* myself, I can say it's very useful to have a Chabad House in the middle of Yehuppitsville, Ethiopia. There are Jews who belong to a Reform Hebrew congregation in Baltimore. They don't keep too much. In fact, I heard one of the assistant Rabbis got married to another man where the regular rabbi, a woman, was *mesader kiddushin*. They are holding on a very low *madrega* of

---

[15] Igros Moshe OC (5:28:22) - והתיקון שיש בעירוב למחללי שבת במזיד בפרהסיא הרי פליגי תנאי בזה דלרשב"ג הא אין צורך דהא אמר בפ"ה דמעשר שני מ"א שאין מציינין על ערלה ונטע רבעי בשאר שני שבוע דהלעיטהו לרשע וימות ובירושלמי דמאי פ"ג ה"ה איתא שגם ר' יוסי סובר כן ומשמע שהלכה כן דהא הלכה כרשב"ג במשנתינו. וגם הא רוב המחללין שבת הם כופרין בכל התורה כולה שאולי כו"ע מודו שליכא חיוב ואף לא מצווה להשתדל לתקן עירובין בשבילם. אך שאולי בשביל אלו שאין יודעין כלום דרשעותן ואף הכפירה שלהן בא להם מצד שחנכום כן אבותיהם הרשעים יש איזה מעלה ואולי גם מצווה לתקן עירובין שלא יעברו גם על איסור הוצאה שבידינו למנוע אותו בתיקון העירובין מאחר שיש לדונו כשוגג. אף שאינו שוגג ממש דאף שאביו חנכו לרשעותו ולכפירתו הא עכ"פ רואה ויודע משומרי תורה ומצוות ויודע שאיכא גדולים ובעלי דעת וחכמה יותר מאביו שלכן נוטה יותר לומר שליכא חיוב למונעו מעבירה. ובפרט להש"ך יו"ד סימן קנ"א סק"ו, להדגמ"ר שביאר טעמו ומשמע שהסכים עמו לדינא דהא משמע שמתירין למכור דברים אסורים לכל ישראל מומר, אפילו לבן המומר כשיכול לקנות במקום אחר

anything. As a matter of fact, they did a *tova* for the descendents of Cham who needed a place of worship, so the congregation allowed the group to use their temple for Sunday services. However, this group stopped praying at this congregation once they heard the Rabbi allowed *mishkav zachor* because how could you pray in a temple which allows that? These Jews who drive to temple on Shabbos see a lot of *yidden* walking back home from *shul.* Do they think all those *yidden* just missed the bus so they're walking home? No, they know Orthodox Jews don't drive on Shabbos. Is the Ribbono Shel Olam Orthodox, Conservative, or Reform? It's a *davar poshut* that before the Reform came around, He was Orthodox. What made Him change just became a Reform temple was constructed? I think it's a poor argument to say He changed once the Reform movement started.

Q4: May one rely on a Chabad *mashgiach*?

A: We know we can rely on them most of the time to take care of the *kashrus*. Rav Aharon Feldman says there are three types of Lubavitchers. One is the non-*mashiach* individuals who are regular *yidden* who are just from Lubavitch, like other *yidden* are from Latvia or Satmar. It's hard to find two *yidden* exactly on the same page. These Lubavitchers are fine *yidden* and there's no problem with that. Then there are those who believe the Rebbe created them, and that's *apikorsus* which you cannot rely on for *kashrus*. The third group of people are those who believe the Rebbe is *mashiach* which requires us to have *rachmanus* on them. We find Rebbi Akiva thought Bar Kochba was the *mashiach* until after he was killed in war.[16] Evidently,

---

[16] Eicha Rabba (2:4) - אָמַר רַבִּי יוֹחָנָן רַבִּי הָיָה דוֹרֵשׁ דָּרַךְ כּוֹכָב מִיַּעֲקֹב אַל תִּקְרֵי כּוֹכָב אֶלָּא כּוֹזָב. רַבִּי עֲקִיבָא כַּד הֲוָה חָמֵי לֵיהּ לְהָדֵין בַּר כּוֹזִיבָא הֲוָה אָמַר הַיְינוּ מַלְכָּא מְשִׁיחָא אָמַר לֵיהּ רַבִּי יוֹחָנָן בֶּן תּוֹרְתָא עֲקִיבָא יַעֲלוּ עֲשָׂבִים בִּלְחָיֶיךָ וַעֲדַיִן אֵינוֹ בָּא. אָמַר רַבִּי יוֹחָנָן הַקֹּל קוֹל יַעֲקֹב קוֹל אַדְרִיָּאנוּס קֵיסָר הָרַג בְּבֵיתָר שְׁמוֹנִים אֶלֶף רִבּוֹא בְּנֵי אָדָם וּשְׁמוֹנִים אֶלֶף תּוֹקְעֵי קְרָנוֹת הָיוּ צָרִין עַל בֵּיתָר וְהָיָה שָׁם בֶּן כּוֹזִיבָא וְהָיוּ לוֹ מָאתַיִם אֶלֶף מְקֻטְּעֵי אֶצְבַּע

mashiach is a live person. If someone wants to believe the Rebbe is *mashiach*, it's a pity on them that they can believe such a thing. The Rebbe was a *gadol b'yisroel* - no question about that - and just because it's a pity on them that they believe he's still *mashiach* doesn't mean we can't necessarily trust them if they're healthy with other elements of Yiddishkeit. If someone believes a fire hydrant is *mashiach,* that means he has a few screws loose, but we don't say he's no longer trustworthy for anything. It could be argued that it's not *poshut* that the fire hydrant isn't *mashiach* – fire is a tremendous power which can destroy entire cities, but this hydrant can put out the destructive force of fire. If it has strength to save the whole city, then maybe it can be *mashiach* too. However, we will only accept the *mashiach* if we are instructed by the gedolei Yisroel that this person is the *mashiach* or if he conforms to all the specifications that the Rambam[17] writes of how to identify the *mashiach.* Once the Rebbe passed away, it became pretty clear that he can no longer be the *mashiach* even though we still respect Lubavitchers who are *ehrliche yidden* and keep the Torah with all its mitzvos, and we can *daven* with them and be included in all their Torah endeavors.

שָׁלְחוּ לוֹ חֲכָמִים עַד מָתַי אַתָּה עוֹשֶׂה לְיִשְׂרָאֵל בַּעֲלֵי מוּמִין אָמַר לָהֶם וְהֵיאַךְ יִבָּדְקוּ אָמְרוּ לוֹ כָּל מִי שֶׁאֵינוֹ עוֹקֵר אֶרֶז מִלְּבָנוֹן אַל יִכָּתֵב בְּאִסְטְרַטְיָא שֶׁלְּךָ. וְהָיוּ לוֹ מָאתַיִם אֶלֶף מִכָּאן וּמִכָּאן וּבְשָׁעָה שֶׁהָיוּ יוֹצְאִין לַמִּלְחָמָה הָיוּ אוֹמְרִים לָא תִסְעוֹד וְלָא תַסְכֵּיף הֲדָא הוּא דִכְתִיב: הֲלֹא אַתָּה אֱלֹקִים זְנַחְתָּנוּ וְלֹא תֵצֵא אֱלֹהִים בְּצִבְאוֹתֵינוּ. וּמֶה הָיָה עוֹשֶׂה בֶּן כּוֹזִיבָא הָיָה מְקַבֵּל אַבְנֵי בַּלִּיסְטְרָא בְּאֶחָד מֵאַרְכּוּבוֹתָיו וְזוֹרְקָן וְהוֹרֵג מֵהֶן כַּמָּה נְפָשׁוֹת וְעַל זֶה אָמַר רַבִּי עֲקִיבָא כָּךְ

[17] Rambam Melachim (11:5) - ואם לא הצליח עד כה או נהרג בידוע שאינו זה שהבטיחה עליו תורה והרי הוא ככל מלכי בית דויד השלמים הכשרים שמתו. ולא העמידו הקדוש ברוך הוא אלא לנסות בו רבים שנאמר ומן המשכילים ייכשלו לצרוף בהן ולברר וללבן עד עת קץ כי עוד למועד

Q5: May one read Reform works for entertainment, like the Animal Right's Haggada?

A: You should have nothing to do with them. I just got a book in the mail called, "Sid Roth." I glanced at it and saw it was *mamash apikorsus*, so I took a blowtorch and burned it page by page. It didn't burn so easily, and it took about 15 minutes. There's a *machlokes* whether *biur chametz* is with only fire, or anything else is acceptable. Rav Yehuda says only burning works.[18] Since this book had the Ribbono Shel Olam's name in it, it wasn't so simple that anything other than burning would be OK. Rav Moshe[19] writes that the Ribbono Shel Olam is happy to have His name burned in order to have no connection to *apikorsus*. A Torah written by a *min* is someone who Rashi[20] explains is bound to *avodah zara* where every time he writes the Shem Hashem, he thinks of the *avoda zara*. Here, when the author writes "G-d," they have Hashem in mind.[21] Burning such a book is an honor for Hashem.[22] You could throw it out too, but I was happy I burned it. Rav Chaim Volozhiner[23] says today there is no point in openly fighting *apikorsus* based on the *makkah* of *tzefardea*. Rashi[24] explains there was one frog which was hit and produced another 20 frogs. The Steipler asks what

---

[18] Pesachim (21a) - רבי יהודה אומר אין ביעור חמץ אלא שריפה וחכמים אומרים אף מפרר וזורה לרוח או מטיל לים

[19] Igros Moshe YD (3:116:3)

[20] Rashi Gittin (45b) - האדוק בעבודת כוכבים כגון כומר

[21] Gittin (45b) - הא דתניא ישרף ר"א היא דאמר סתם מחשבת עובד כוכבים לעבודת כוכבים

[22] Shulchan Aruch YD (281:1) - סֵפֶר תּוֹרָה שֶׁכְּתָבוֹ אֶפִּיקוֹרוֹס יִשָּׂרֵף

[23] See M'Shulchan Gavoha (Shemos p.58) - רבי איצל'ה מוולוז'ין בשם אביו הגאון רבי חיים: הדרך להאבק נגד הכתות והתנועות החדשות שקמו לישראל בדורות האחרונים אסור לה שתהא בדרך של תגרה ומלחמה גלויה כי עצם ההתנצחות הפומבית וההתגרות המוגזמת מביאה להתחזקות יתר של הצד שכנגד. ולא עוד אלא שהזהיר הגר"ח כי כל המתגרה יותר מדי עם המתחדשים לא תהיה לו תקומה

[24] Rashi Shemos (8:2) - צְפַרְדֵּעַ אַחַת הָיְתָה וְהָיוּ מַכִּין אוֹתָהּ וְהִיא מַתֶּזֶת נְחִילִים נְחִילִים

was the logic of these people that they kept on hitting it and bringing more frogs? He explains that when a person is angry, he no longer thinks rationally. Nowadays, people are angrily disproving that the Ribbono Shel Olam doesn't exist and won't think logically anymore. Sometimes if you start a war with these people, they will spread even more *apikorsus*. When I was in the Yeshiva in Lakewood and travelled there by bus, a lady sat next to me and started asking about what I did in Lakewood. "I go to a Rabbinic seminary." She asked, *"Do you want to be a rabbi?"* I replied, "I don't know – maybe, I'm not sure, but I want to study Jewish Law." *What kind of rabbi will you be – Orthodox or Conservative?* "Orthodox." *Why not become Conservative? They make much more money.* "I understand that makes sense, but the only problem is that G-d is Orthodox, therefore I have to be Orthodox." *How do you know He's Orthodox?* "Before the Reform started, and before the Conservative started in the 1920s, G-d was Orthodox, so why would He change His faith just because someone opened up a recent temple?"

Q6: What should you do if a missionary contacts you to preach to you?

A: Just tell him that you're not interested. The woman I spoke to on the bus wasn't a missionary. She was just trying to understand why I wouldn't want to make more money as a Conservative rabbi.

Q7: Is there an *issur* of *lo yilbash* to look into a mirror?

A: The Shulchan Aruch[25] says not to look into a mirror to see how handsome you are, or if your hat needs to be straightened, or hair needs to be combed, etc. since those are *maaseh nashim*. However, you may look into a mirror if you need it – like helping you remove something stuck between

---

[25] Shulchan Aruch YD (156:2) - אָסוּר לְאִישׁ לְהִסְתַּכֵּל בְּמַרְאָה מִשּׁוּם לֹא יִלְבַּשׁ גֶּבֶר אֶלָּא אִם כֵּן מִשּׁוּם רְפוּאָה כְּגוֹן שֶׁחוֹשֵׁשׁ בְּעֵינָיו אוֹ שֶׁמְּסַפֵּר עַצְמוֹ אוֹ אִם מִסְתַּפֵּר מִן הָעוֹבֵד כּוֹכָבִים בֵּינוֹ לְבֵינוֹ

your teeth or if you need to know where to put a *refuah* on a boil. There used to be a time on the New York subway that every vending machine had a mirror to get women to buy something since they're standing there already. However, it's not the *derech* of men to look into a mirror unless he needs to check if he's shaving correctly or the like.[26] I don't know if women look in the mirror as much as they used to, and anything which is the *derech* for both men and women to do is not forbidden as *lo yilbash*.[27]

Q8: Is a multi-layer trifle considered a *ta'aruvos* regarding *ikar v'tofel*?

A: Yes. Usually, the multi-layer is one layer of cake, then another layer of filling, another of cake, then almond or another filling. The *ikar* would be *mezonos*.

Q9: What is the *beracha* on sushi?

A: What's the *beracha* you make on *kugel*? It's the same answer. Both depend on the ingredients. My thinking is that the primary ingredient in sushi is the rice because all sushi – whether fish, chicken, vegetable – has rice. However, often the other ingredients in sushi are more than the rice, so you would make a *beracha* on the *ikar*. Nonetheless, I don't think you can call something sushi if it doesn't have rice.

Q10: If you open an oven door on Shabbos, must you remove all the food from inside?

A: If someone opens the door to an oven and it's not on, then you don't need to remove all the food from the oven, whether

---

[26] Rema YD (156:2) - וְיֵשׁ אוֹמְרִים הָא דְּאָסוּר לִרְאוֹת בְּמַרְאָה הַיְנוּ דַּוְקָא בְּמָקוֹם דְּאֵין דֶּרֶךְ לִרְאוֹת בְּמַרְאָה רַק נָשִׁים וְאִית בֵּיהּ מִשּׁוּם לֹא יִלְבַּשׁ גֶּבֶר אֲבָל בְּמָקוֹם שֶׁדֶּרֶךְ הָאֲנָשִׁים לִרְאוֹת גַּם כֵּן בְּמַרְאָה מֻתָּר. וַאֲפִלּוּ בְּמָקוֹם שֶׁנָּהֲגוּ לְהַחְמִיר אִם עוֹשֶׂה לִרְפוּאָה שֶׁמֵּאִיר עֵינָיו אוֹ שֶׁעוֹשֶׂה לְהָסִיר הַכְּתָמִים מִפָּנָיו אוֹ נוֹצוֹת מֵרֹאשׁוֹ שָׁרֵי וְכֵן נָהֲגוּ

[27] Devarim (22:5) - לֹא־יִהְיֶה כְלִי־גֶבֶר עַל־אִשָּׁה וְלֹא־יִלְבַּשׁ גֶּבֶר שִׂמְלַת אִשָּׁה כִּי תוֹעֲבַת ה' אֱלֹקֶיךָ כָּל־עֹשֵׂה אֵלֶּה

the oven is on Shabbos mode or not. However, if the oven is on then you must remove all the food from the oven at one time - even if it's on Shabbos mode - because the oven has a thermostat which will be affected by you opening the oven door. Either the oven will go on because you took out the food, or the oven will remain on for longer since you opened the door. Therefore, you are causing the fire to burn longer than if you had not opened the door.[28] So then what's the *heter* to open the oven in the first place? The *heter* is based on the fact that it's a *grama* since the oven doesn't turn on right away. *Grama* is only permitted *b'makom p'seida,*[29] like the case in the Gemara where one of the candles fell on the table and might burn down the house – then you are allowed to fill a few utensils with water and surround the candle with them so that the fire will burst the containers of water and extinguish the flames.[30] Also, Rav Shlomo Zalman[31] says you only need a *makom p'seida* for *grama* by an *issur d'oraysa*. If it's a *d'rabanan* then you don't need a *hefsed* to be lenient. As far as you're concerned, you don't want the oven fire to go on after you open the door since it's a waste of gas or electricity as well as the fact that it will heat up the house in the summer. *Melacha sh'aino tzarich lgufo* is only *mid'rabanan* according to most Rishonim except the

---

[28] Mishna Berura (320:53) - דפסיק רישא הוא אסור מדרבנן אבל חיובא ליכא בפסיק רישא דלא ניחא ליה לכו"ע וכ"ז הוא לענין שבת דבעינן שיהא מלאכת מחשבת אבל לענין שארי איסורי תורה דעת הרא"ש דפ"ר דלא ניחא ליה לכו"ע אסור ואיסורו הוא מן התורה

[29] Shulchan Aruch OC (334:22) - תיבה שאחז בה האור יכול לפרוס עור של גדי מצדה האחת שלא תשרף ועושים מחיצה בכל הכלים להפסיק בין הדליקה אפי' כלי חרס חדשים מלאים מים שודאי יתבקעו כשתגיע להם הדליקה דגרם כיבוי מותר. הגה במקום פסידא

[30] Shabbos (120a) - רבי שמעון בן ננס אומר פורסין עור של גדי על גבי שידה תיבה ומגדל שאחז בהן את האור מפני שהוא מחרך ועושין מחיצה בכל הכלים בין מלאין בין ריקנים בשביל שלא תעבור הדליקה רבי יוסי אוסר בכלי חרס חדשים מלאין מים לפי שאין יכולין לקבל את האור והן מתבקעין ומכבין את הדליקה

[31] See Minchas Shlomo (1:10)

Rambam,[32] which most *Poskim* don't follow *l'halacha*.[33] Therefore, if you remove everything from the oven at one time, then you're only causing a *grama* on a *d'rabanan*. However, if food remains in the oven, then it's a *grama* on a *d'oraysa* since you want the food to remain in the oven to keep it hot.

Q11: Is it permitted to open a refrigerator on Shabbos?

A: A refrigerator is generally *d'rabanan* since it's electric power which is *d'rabanan* versus electric heat or light which is *d'oraysa*. Refrigerators used to work that about every hour for five minutes, the heat would turn on to defrost the coils which became covered with ice and prevented the cold air from circulating. It didn't matter whether you opened the door or not. Now there's a law which requires the companies to write how much power each device uses per year, "$169 a year for electricity." Once that became a requirement, companies wanted to use as little electricity as possible and questioned why refrigerators needed to run on this constantly steady cycle. They reasoned that refrigerators only needed the heat to turn on based on the frequency of use. Consequently, during the night the refrigerators need significantly less heat since the coils aren't working as much to produce cool air with the door hardly being opened. The same thing is true with people having different schedules

---

[32] Rambam Shabbos (1:7) - כָּל הָעוֹשֶׂה מְלָאכָה בְּשַׁבָּת אַף עַל פִּי שֶׁאֵינוֹ צָרִיךְ לְגוּפָהּ שֶׁל מְלָאכָה חַיָּב עָלֶיהָ כֵּיצַד הֲרֵי שֶׁכִּבָּה אֶת הַנֵּר מִפְּנֵי שֶׁהוּא צָרִיךְ לַשֶּׁמֶן אוֹ לַפְּתִילָה כְּדֵי שֶׁלֹּא יֹאבַד אוֹ כְּדֵי שֶׁלֹּא יִשָּׂרֵף אוֹ כְּדֵי שֶׁלֹּא יִבָּקַע חֶרֶשׂ שֶׁל נֵר מִפְּנֵי שֶׁהַכִּבּוּי מְלָאכָה וַהֲרֵי נִתְכַּוֵּן לְכַבּוֹת וְאַף עַל פִּי שֶׁאֵינוֹ צָרִיךְ לְגוּף הַכִּבּוּי וְלֹא כִּבָּה אֶלָּא מִפְּנֵי הַשֶּׁמֶן אוֹ מִפְּנֵי הַחֶרֶשׂ אוֹ מִפְּנֵי הַפְּתִילָה הֲרֵי זֶה חַיָּב וְכֵן הַמַּעֲבִיר אֶת הַקּוֹץ אַרְבַּע אַמּוֹת בִּרְשׁוּת הָרַבִּים אוֹ הַמְכַבֶּה אֶת הַגַּחֶלֶת כְּדֵי שֶׁלֹּא יִזּוֹקוּ בָּהֶן רַבִּים חַיָּב וְאַף עַל פִּי שֶׁאֵינוֹ צָרִיךְ לְגוּף הַכִּבּוּי אוֹ לְגוּף הַהַעֲבָרָה אֶלָּא לְהַרְחִיק הַהֶזֵּק הֲרֵי זֶה חַיָּב וְכֵן כָּל כַּיּוֹצֵא בָּזֶה

[33] Mishna Berura (334:84) - דכיבוי שחייב מן התורה הוא דוקא כשמכבה לעשות פחמין אבל סתם כיבוי הוי מלאכה שאינה צריכה לגופה והוא רק איסור דרבנן ובמקום הזיקא דרבים שיוכלו להנזק בגופן לא גזרו

throughout the day. Therefore, the companies based the heating element's use on how often the compressor turns on or how often the refrigerator door is opened. Every time you open the door, you are causing the heating element to turn on earlier which is a *grama d'oraysa*. Light without heat isn't considered fire *d'oraysa*. Therefore, the lights which truckers use when pulled over on the side of the road are only *d'rabanan* since the light doesn't give off heat. Only the combination of heat and light is *havara d'oraysa*. I once asked Rav Moshe whether it's permitted to remove a sweater on Shabbos if it will spark static electricity, and he said it's nothing since it's light without heat.[34] The company said the heating coil was only heat without light, so I asked them to send me one to check. As they claimed, I plugged in the coil and didn't see it light up. However, I reinvestigated it by plugging in the coil while staying in a closet without any windows. It was clearly lighting up without any external light affecting it. Therefore, opening up such a refrigerator would be *assur mid'rabanan* because of the *grama*. You can open the fridge with a *shinui* like opening by pulling a towel inserted through the handle of the door or with the back of your hand. Opening with your left hand doesn't work

---

[34] See Tzitz Eliezer (7:10) - נלפענ״ד ברור דבכגון נידוננו כו״ע יודו דאין בזה משום ליתא דאיסורא כלל כי שונים ניצוצות אלה תכלית שינוי מניצוץ היוצא מן האבנים או מן החשמל כבשעת צילצול בטליפון או הפעלת המאוורר דבשם אילו היה באותה שעה איזה אחיזה באבק שריפה היה בכחו של הניצוץ להדליקו דטמון בחובו כח האשיי אבל בנידוננו אין במראות ההברקות הנראין שום חומר אשיי והמה ברקי־אור מופשטים בלבד שאין בכחם להבעיר שום אבק שריפה שיאחזו בהם באותה שעה ואור הברקתם דומים כמעט לסוג האור שנמצאים בכמה ממחוגי השעונים המאירים בחשיכה ורק בכאן הם סוגי אלקטרונים זעירי אנפין הנוצרים ע״י התחברות עם כחות מנוגדים באופן שאין בהם מכח האשיי כלל ועל כן ברור שאין שום חשש בלבישתן של כתנות אלה בשבת ואין כל איסור מהולדת מראות הברקה אלה מדי בואם במגע עם בגדי צמר שמלובש בהט ובפרט שגם אינם נראים כלל אפילו לעינים ורק באישון לילה ואפילה וגם אינו מכוון להולידם כלל ואין לו כל ענין בהם ויכולים איפוא בשופי ללובשם בשבת אפילו מתחת ומעל לבגד צמר. Cf. Chazon Ish OC (50:5)

because you open up the fridge during the week with the right hand or left hand. You might have *Poskim* to rely on to open such a refrigerator without a *shinui*, but *b'pashtus* you're transgressing an *issur d'rabanan*.

Q12: When one looks at his *tzitzis* to fulfill the mitzvah of וּרְאִיתֶם אֹתוֹ,[35] should he be *mechaven* for the *sefiros*?

A: I don't know what it means to be *mechaven* for the *sefiros*.[36] You don't have to be *mechaven* for them even if you know what they are. *Sefiros* are complicated – they are *hanhagos* the Ribbono Shel Olam has with the world, each one of the ten *sefiros* has ten subdivisions which continues onward with another ten subdivisions.

Q13: Must a blind person put the *tzitzis* over his eyes by וּרְאִיתֶם אֹתוֹ when *davening b'yechidus*?

A: He's certainly allowed to put them over his eyes, and I think he should do so as not to be different than the *minhag hamakom*. If someone has the *minhag* not to put on *tefillin* on Chol HaMoed but is *davening* in a place where the *minhag* is to wear *tefillin*, he should put on his *tefillin* in order not to be different than the *minhag hamakom*.[37]

---

[35] Bamidbar (15:39) - וְהָיָה לָכֶם לְצִיצִת וּרְאִיתֶם אֹתוֹ וּזְכַרְתֶּם אֶת־כָּל־ מִצְוֹת יְהוָה וַעֲשִׂיתֶם אֹתָם וְלֹא־תָתֻרוּ אַחֲרֵי לְבַבְכֶם וְאַחֲרֵי עֵינֵיכֶם אֲשֶׁר־אַתֶּם זֹנִים אַחֲרֵיהֶם

[36] Shulchan Aruch OC (24:5) - כשמסתכל בציציות מסתכל בב' ציציות שלפניו שיש בהם עשרה קשרים רמז להויות וגם יש בהם ט"ז חוטים ועשרה קשרים עולות כ"ו כשם ההויה and Mishna Berura (24:8) - להויות - פי' לספירות שהם קשורים ואחודים זה בזה

[37] Mishna Berura (31:8) - דאין נכון שבהכ"נ אחת קצתם יניחו תפילין וקצתם לא יניחו משום לא תתגודדו. ומי שאין מניח תפילין בחוה"מ שמתפלל בבה"מ שמניחין תפילין יש לו ג"כ להניחן ובלי ברכה וצבור שנהגו להניח תפילין אין להם לשנות מנהגם

Q14: Why may one not engrave[38] *pesukim* on his *tallis*?

A: What happens after the *tallis* is worn out? You cannot double wrap the *tallis* and put it in the garbage. According to the letter of the law, you're allowed to enter into a bathroom with a *tallis*,[39] as we go into the bathroom with the *tallis kattan*. We just don't enter the bathroom with a *tallis* because it's a *beged* designated for *davening* just like a *kittel*.[40] However, if you have *pesukim* written on your *tallis* then *min hadin* you may not enter a bathroom.[41]

Q15: Why must one tuck in his *tzitzis* when passing by the *kever* of a child?

A: The Gemara[42] says "A child who knows how to be *misatef* wears *tzitzis*" which means he knows how to put two *tzitzis* in the front and two in the back. At that point, his father is *mechanech* him with *tzitzis*.[43] Even though the child was only obligated *mid'rabanan*, there's still an issue of לעג לרש – making fun of someone for not being able to fulfill a *mitzva* which you can.[44] If he's a child who was too young

---

[38] Shulchan Aruch YD (283:4) - אָסוּר לְרַקֵּם פְּסוּקִים בְּטַלִּית

[39] Shulchan Aruch OC (21:3) - מותר ליכנס בציצית לבית הכסא

[40] Mishna Berura (21:14) - ודוקא בד' כנפות הקטן שלובשו כל היום אבל אלו טליתות של מצוה שמיוחדין רק להתפלל בהן אין נכון שיכנס בהן לבהכ"ס אך להשתין בהן מותר גם ההולכים ביוה"כ לפנות ומלובשים בקיט"ל צריך שיפשוט הקיט"ל כיון שבגד זה מיוחד רק להתפלל

[41] Mishna Berura (43:25) - ושאר ספרים וכתבים שיש בהן שמות אם הם בכיס שרי להכניסן ויש אומרים דבעינן דוקא תיק בתוך תיק אם צריך ליכנס לבה"כ וכדלעיל לענין תפילין וס"ת אסור בכל גווני

[42] Sukkah (42a) - ת"ר קטן היודע לנענע חייב בלולב להתעטף חייב בציצית לשמור תפילין אביו לוקח לו תפילין

[43] Shulchan Aruch OC (17:3) - קטן היודע להתעטף אביו צריך ליקח לו ציצי' לחנכו

[44] Shulchan Aruch YD (367:4) - מתר לכנס לבית הקברות או לתוך ד 'אמות של מת או של קבר והוא לבוש ציצית והוא שלא יהא נגרר על הקבר אבל אם נגרר אסור משום לעג לרש במה דברים אמורים בימיהם

to be obligated in *tzitzis*, then there's no issue of לעג לרש for you to have your *tzitzis* out.

Q16: Should one wear his *tallis kattan* over his shirt?

A: The Mechaber[45] seems to say that you wear it on top of your clothing while the Arizal says you should wear it under your clothing, so whatever you do, you have whom to rely on.[46] The *minhag* in most places is to wear the *beged* under your shirt. The Rosh Yeshiva and my Rosh Yeshiva wore the *beged* on top of the shirt, but under a vest.

Q16: Should the Chazzan say ה' שפתי תפתח out loud before Chazaras HaShatz?

A: It's not the *minhag* to do so. In general, since the Chazaras HaShatz is the *tefillah* of the *rabbim* as we say "*chanenu me'itcha de'ah*" not "*chaneni*", "*slach lanu*" not "*slach li.*" On the other hand, Elokai Neshama is *b'lashon yachid* "*netzor l'shoni*", so the Chazzan doesn't say it outloud. Therefore, the Chazzan doesn't say ה' שפתי תפתח outloud either. However, on Rosh Hashana and Yom Kippur when he says "*hineni*", the Chazzan is *davening* for himself while saying it outloud to be *me'orer* the *tzibur* to how we must be מכניע ourselves before Shemoneh Esrei.

שהיו מטילים ציצית במלבוש שלובשים לצרך עצמן אבל האידנא שאין אנו לובשין אותו אלא לשם מצוה אסור אפלו אינם נגררים והני מלי כשהציציות מגלים ,אבל אם הם מכוסים מותר

[45] Shulchan Aruch OC (8:26) - עיקר מצות טלית קטן ללבשו על בגדיו כדי שתמיד יראהו ויזכור המצות

[46] Mishna Berura (8:25) - ובכתבים איתא דטלית קטן תחת בגדיו וכתב המגן אברהם דעל כל פנים צריך שיהיו הציצית מבחוץ ולא כאינך שתוחבין אותן בהכנפות אך האנשים שהולכים בין העכו"ם יוצאין בזה ומכל מקום בשעת הברכה יהיו מגולין [כדי הילוך] ארבע אמות

Chapter 2: Shonim 5769

Q1: Is there an *inyan* to eat the *esrog peiri shevi'is* rather than let it dry by itself and throw it out?

A: It's my humble opinion that if you let the *esrog* dry by itself, then you're not allowed to throw it out. Although once the *esrog* is no longer edible you're allowed to throw it out, that doesn't mean a dried *esrog* is no long edible. I took a normal sized *esrog* which dried to the size of a walnut – and looked hard and brown like a walnut also – put it into a glass of regular Baltimore city water, and it slowly regenerated back into its original size. The color of the *esrog* was still tan, but it reached its previous shape. The color isn't an issue in this case for the *kashrus* of the *esrog* because you're not trying to be *yotzei* with the *esrog*. In fact, you wouldn't be able to be *yotzei* with this *esrog* because it's *kavush*.[1] Nonetheless, the question is whether the *esrog* is ruined as a fruit when it dries out. If you put raisins or dried apricots into water, then they will also return to their former state as well. The Gemara Beitza (26b)[2] says that when גרוגרות וצימוקים are left out on the roof to dry and it rains, then they get bigger again. Nevertheless, if the *esrog* gets moldy then you may certainly throw it out.

Q2: If someone pickles an *esrog shevi'is*, what should be done with the juice?

A: I didn't know you could pickle an *esrog shevi'is* since that might be considered that you're destroying it. If the juice has no use, then you may throw it out. The issue of throwing out *peiros shevi'is* only applies to food which is edible,

---

[1] Rambam Sukkah and Lulav (8:8) - אֶתְרוֹג שֶׁהוּא תָּפוּחַ סָרוּחַ כָּבוּשׁ שָׁלוּק שָׁחֹר לָבָן מְנֻמָּר יָרֹק כְּכַרְתִּי פָּסוּל

[2] Beitza (26b) - ת"ש היה אוכל בענבים והותיר והעלן לגג לעשות מהן צמוקין בתאנים והותיר והעלן לגג לעשות מהן גרוגרות לא יאכל מהן עד שיזמין מבעוד יום וכן אתה מוצא באפרסקין ובחבושין ובשאר כל מיני פירות

however the juice isn't necessarily edible so you would be able to throw it out.[3] The Chazon Ish[4] goes so far as to say that if you eat a *peiros shevi'is* apple, you only need to eat as much as it is the *derech* to eat it. When you eat an apple close to the core, there will still be edible pieces of the apple which you can eat. You don't need to get into all the חורין וסדקים to find every *mashehu* – just eat the apple the way people normally eat it. Similarly, if it's not the *derech* to eat the pickle juice, you are allowed to throw it out.

Q3: If one could find a beautiful set of *esrogim* from NY for a very cheap price, must one suspect they might be lemons?

A: The question is really whether you should suspect the seller stole these *esrogim* and is trying to get rid of them as fast as he can. The Kitzur Shulchan Aruch[5] says that if

---

[3] Rambam Shemitta (5:19) - אֵין שׂוֹרְפִין תֶּבֶן וְקַשׁ שֶׁל שְׁבִיעִית מִפְּנֵי שֶׁהוּא רָאוּי לְמַאֲכַל בְּהֵמָה

[4] Chazon Ish Shevi'is (14:10) - נראה דמותר לקלוף פירות שביעית אף בפירי שאפשר לאכול עם הקליפה כמו תפוחים וכיו״ב וכדאמר בירו׳ בתרומה פי״א דתרומות ה״ד ומקנב בירק כל שהוא רוצה ונראה דה״ה בשביעית וכמש״כ הר"מם פ״ה ה״ב ג׳ דדין שביעית כתרומה מיהו הקליפה שקלף קדוש עדיין בקדושת שביעית שהרי יש בה אוכל וכמש״כ הר״מם פי״א דתרומות ה״י [ואף בלא אוכל פעמים שהקליפה אוכל כמש״כ הר״מם שם] ומניח הקליפה בכלי עד שיתעפש ויפסל מאכילת אדם ואז מותר להשליכה ואם עדיין ראוי׳ לבהמה נראה שאם רוב בני אדם אין מיחדין אותן לבהמה עדיין קדשי בק״ש ואם רוב בני אדם מיחדין אותן לבהמה פקעה קדושתה

[5] Kitzur Shulchan Aruch (182:10) - וְכֵן אִם אֶחָד רוֹצֶה לִמְכֹּר אֵיזֶה חֵפֶץ שֶׁנִּרְאֶה שֶׁהוּא גָנוּב כְּגוֹן שׁוֹמְרֵי פֵּרוֹת שֶׁמּוֹכְרִים פֵּרוֹת בְּמָקוֹם צָנוּעַ אוֹ מוֹכֵר אַחֵר שֶׁנּוֹשֵׂא אֵיזֶה דָבָר בְּהַצְנֵעַ לְמָכְרוֹ אוֹ שֶׁאוֹמֵר לְהַקּוֹנֶה הַטְמֵן אָסוּר לִקְנוֹת וַאֲפִלּוּ לִקְנוֹת מֵאִשָּׁה אֵיזֶה דָבָר שֶׁיֵּשׁ לָחוּשׁ שֶׁהִיא מוֹכֶרֶת שֶׁלֹּא מִדַּעַת בַּעְלָהּ אוֹ לִקְנוֹת מֵאִישׁ דָּבָר מִתַּכְשִׁיטֵי הָאִשָּׁה וּמַלְבּוּשֶׁיהָ שֶׁיֵּשׁ לָחוּשׁ שֶׁהוּא מוֹכְרוֹ שֶׁלֹּא מִדַּעַת אִשְׁתּוֹ אָסוּר. See Shulchan Aruch CM (358:1) - כל דבר שחזקתו שהוא גנוב אסור ליקח אותו וכן אם רוב אותו דבר שהוא גנוב אין לוקחין אותו לפיכך אין לוקחים מהרועים צמר או חלב או גדיים

someone sells you a cheap item, like a washing machine for $10, then you should be suspicious that it was stolen. Why else would he be selling it so cheap? The same suspicion would apply to these cheap *esrogim*. About 60 years ago it was very difficult to find an *esrog* in America which wasn't grafted. Once Reb Leib Puretz came along and planted an orchard himself, then it became easier to find non-grafted *esrogim*. Rav Moshe Feinstein and my Rosh Yeshiva *zecher tzaddik l'vracha* both said there was no way you could tell an *esrog* isn't grafted. You need to buy it from a couple of honest salesmen with the hope that one of the *esrogim* isn't grafted. They would make a *beracha* on all six together by picking each *esrog* up one at a time with the other minim.

Q4: For one who finds it uncomfortable to sleep on his side, is there any way for him to sleep on his back?

A: You can get used to anything including sleeping on your side. If it's really too uncomfortable for him to sleep on his side, then he should try sleeping while sitting in an armchair. As long as it's noticeable that you're on your side, that's good enough.[6]

אבל לוקחים מהם חלב וגבינה במדבר אבל לא ביישוב ומותר ליקח מהרועים ד' צאן או ד' גיזות של צמר מעדר קטן או חמשה מעדר גדול שאין חזקתו שהוא גנוב כללו של דבר כל שהרועה מוכרו אם היה ב"ה מרגיש בו מותר ללוקחו ואם לאו אסור

[6] Shulchan Aruch OC (63:1) - קורא אותה מהלך או עומד או שוכב או רוכב על גבי בהמה או יושב אבל לא פרקדן דהיינו שפניו טוחות בקרקע או מושלך על גבו ופניו למעלה אבל קורא והוא שוכב על צדו: הגה מאחר שכבר שוכב ואיכא טרחא לעמוד ואם היה בעל בשר הרב ואינו יכול להתהפך על צדו או שהיה חולה נוטה מעט לצדו וקורא and see Shulchan Aruch EH (23:3) - אסור לאדם שיקשה עצמו לדעת או יביא עצמו לידי הרהור אלא אם יבא לו הרהור יסיע לבו מדברי הבאי לדברי תורה שהיא אילת אהבים ויעלת חן לפיכך אסור לאדם לישן על ערפו ופניו למעלה עד שיטה מעט כדי שלא יבא לידי קישוי

Q5: Must one give special care to *lulav*, *hadasim*, or *aravos* from *shemitta* after sukkos?

A: The *lulav* does not have any more use nowadays as in former times it was used as a broom to sweep.[7] Therefore, there is no *din* of *shemitta* on it. *Aravos* certainly don't have a *din* in *shemitta* if they come from Eretz Yisroel, and I don't think *hadasim* are really used for smelling. People only use them for smelling because they have nothing else to do with them. I don't think the *hadasim* are actually sold anywhere for their fragrance since there are more powerful scents nowadays.

Q6: What does one do with *lulav* rings after succos in a non-*shemitta* year?

A: We have a general rule that *tashmishei kedusha* are *nignazim* and *tashmishei mitzva* are *nizrakin*.[8] The *lulav* and *tzitzis* are considered *tashmishei mitzva*, so you're not obligated to bury them or put them in *shaimos*.[9] You may burn them if you want, but you should not put them directly into the garbage. We're accustomed to be lenient and wrap the *lulav* and *esrog* in a bag and throw them out.[10]

---

[7] Sukkah (32a) - אמר רב פפא נפרצו דעביד כי חופיא נפרדו דאיפרוד אפרודי

[8] Megilla (26b) - תנו רבנן תשמישי מצוה נזרקין תשמישי קדושה נגנזין

[9] Shulchan Aruch OC (21:1) - חוטי ציציות שנפסקו יכול לזורקן לאשפה מפני שהוא מצוה שאין בגופה קדושה אבל כל זמן שהם קבועים בטלית אסור להשתמש בהם כגון לקשור בהם שום דבר וכיוצא בזה משום ביזוי מצוה וי"א דאף לאחר שנפסקו אין לנהוג בהם מנהג בזיון לזורקן במקום מגונה אלא שאינן צריכין גניזה ויש מדקדקין לגונזן והמחמיר ומדקדק במצות תע"ב

[10] Shulchan Aruch OC (664:8) - יש מי שאומר שהושענא שבלולב אע"פ שנזרקת אין לפסוע עליה

Q7: Are you *yotzei nichum aveilim* by phone?

A: The *mitzva* of *nichum aveilim* is a *mitzva* of *chesed*.[11] This person had a big loss and feels bad, so you're coming to comfort him. Just by telling him that someone is thinking of him is a comfort – עִמּוֹ־אָנֹכִי בְצָרָה – I am with you and feel bad for you (Tehillim 91:15). That is a comfort for people. It says in the *posuk* (Eicha 2:13) מָה־אֲעִידֵךְ מָה אֲדַמֶּה־לָּךְ הַבַּת יְרוּשָׁלַםִ מָה אַשְׁוֶה־לָּךְ וַאֲנַחֲמֵךְ בְּתוּלַת בַּת־צִיּוֹן כִּי־גָדוֹל כַּיָּם שִׁבְרֵךְ מִי יִרְפָּא־לָךְ – What is there that I can compare you to in order to make you feel your loss isn't the biggest loss in the world since other people felt this loss too. Although it's better to comfort mourners in person if possible, if it's not practical then you can be *yotzei* by phone as you're still providing some comfort. It's not a *halacha* that you must say the words "*HaMakom yenachem*" as a magical phrase. The fact that you came, and he knows you're thinking about him is a comfort.[12] The words *HaMakom yenachem* is telling him

---

[11] Rambam Aveilus (14:1) - מִצְוַת עֲשֵׂה שֶׁל דִּבְרֵיהֶם לְבַקֵּר חוֹלִים וּלְנַחֵם אֲבֵלִים וּלְהוֹצִיא הַמֵּת וּלְהַכְנִיס הַכַּלָּה וּלְלַוּוֹת הָאוֹרְחִים וּלְהִתְעַסֵּק בְּכָל צָרְכֵי הַקְּבוּרָה לָשֵׂאת עַל הַכָּתֵף וְלֵילֵךְ לְפָנָיו וְלִסְפֹּד וְלַחְפֹּר וְלִקְבֹּר וְכֵן לְשַׂמֵּחַ הַכַּלָּה וְהֶחָתָן וּלְסַעֲדָם בְּכָל צָרְכֵיהֶם וְאֵלּוּ הֵן גְּמִילוּת חֲסָדִים שֶׁבְּגוּפוֹ שֶׁאֵין לָהֶם שִׁעוּר אַף עַל פִּי שֶׁכָּל מִצְוֹת אֵלּוּ מִדִּבְרֵיהֶם הֲרֵי הֵן בִּכְלַל "וְאָהַבְתָּ לְרֵעֲךָ כָּמוֹךָ" כָּל הַדְּבָרִים שֶׁאַתָּה רוֹצֶה שֶׁיַּעֲשׂוּ אוֹתָם לְךָ אֲחֵרִים עֲשֵׂה אַתָּה אוֹתָן לְאָחִיךָ בְּתוֹרָה וּבְמִצְוֹת

[12] Igros Moshe OC (4:40:11) – ניחום אבלים ע"י הטעלעפאן ובדבר אם מקיים מצות נחום אבלים ע"י הטעלעפאן הנה בנחום אבלים איכא תרתי ענינים חדא לטובת אבלים החיים שהם טרודים מאד בצערם מחוייבין לדבר על לבו ולנחמו שבשביל זה הרי ג"כ מחוייבין לילך לביתו למקום שהוא נמצא ושנית לטובת המת כדאיתא בשבת דף קנ"ב א"ר יהודה מת שאין לו מנחמין הולכין עשרה בנ"א ויושבין במקומו ומסיק עובדא דמת שאין לו מנחמין שבכל יומא הוה דבר ר' יהודה בי עשרה ותיתבי בדוכתיה ואיתחזי ליה בחלמו דר' יהודה וא"ל תנוח דעתך שהנחת את דעתי הרי ממילא ידעינן דכשיש מנחמין איכא בזה גם טובת המת ומטעם זה כתב הרמב"ם בפי"ד מאבל ה"ז יראה לי שנחמת אבלים קודם לבק"ח שנחום אבלים גמ"ח עם החיים ועם המתים ומשמע לי שמצד האבל החי שייך לקיים גם ע"י הטעלעפאן אבל המצוה שמצד טובת המת לא שייך אלא דוקא כשיבא לשם

that he's not the only one in this *tzara* since we're all *aveilei Tzion*, which you can accomplish over the phone too.

Q8: If one is comforting a mourner by phone should he say *HaMakom yenachem es'chem* in the plural?

A: There's a lot of talk about this.[13] Even if there's only one person sitting shiva who you are comforting in person, perhaps you say *HaMakom yenachem es'chem* instead of *HaMakom yenachem* אותךְ or אוֹתָךְ. Some say that *es'chem* refers to the Ribbono Shel Olam and the mourner together since there's an element of עִמּוֹ־אָנֹכִי בְצָרָה (Tehillim 91:15) as Hashem is in pain with the mourner. We're saying *HaMakom*, Hashem should comfort Himself along with the mourner. Therefore, there's no *issur* of saying *es'chem* everytime you comfort a mourner. If I comfort an *aveil* by himself, I usually say אוֹתָךְ, but doing it the other way isn't wrong.

Q9: Should one initiate discussing the *niftar* when being *menachem aveil* over the phone?

A: I just saw a chiddush recently from Rav Shlomo Zalman that the *halacha* of the *aveil* starting the discussion[14] is not

---

במקום שמתנחמין או במקום שמת ואף מצד האבל החי נמי ודאי עדיף כשבא לשם שהוא גם מכבדו שזה עצמו הוא ג"כ ענין תנחומין כלשון ר"ע במו"ק דף כ"א כשמתו בניו והספידום כל ישראל עמד ר"ע ואמר אחבנ"י שמעו אפילו שני בנים חתנים מנוחם הוא בשביל כבוד שעשיתם וענין הכבוד לא שייך ע"י הטעלעפאן...דלכן למעשה אם אפשר לו לילך לבית האבלים שהוא קיום מצוה שלמה לא שייך שיפטר בטעלעפאן אך קצת מצוה יש גם ע"י הטעלעפאן שלכן אם א"א לו ללכת לבית האבלים כגון מחמת חולי או שהוא טרוד בטירדא דמצוה יש עליו חיוב לקיים מה שאפשר לו יש לו לנחם ע"י הטעלעפאן דג"כ איכא בזה מצוה ולא יאמר כי מאחר שאינו יכול לילך לבית האבלים אין עליו שוב שום חיוב כלל

[13] See Gesher Hachaim (20:5:8) and Nitei Gavriel Aveilus (90:1)

[14] Shulchan Aruch YD (376:1) - אין המנחמים רשאים לפתוח עד שיפתח האבל תחלה

noheg nowadays because the mere fact that he opened his door to allow others to enter his house is already enough of a *siman* that he wants to be comforted. The reason why the mourner has to start the conversation is because maybe he's not in the mood for *nechama*. However, why else would he have opened his door to let others in? Therefore, you don't need to wait for the *aveil* to begin speaking anymore. Similarly, you may initiate the conversation about the *niftar* over the phone with the *aveil* because he knew why you were calling and could've ignored the call – he knows it wasn't the electric company calling that he didn't pay his bill, otherwise they wouldn't have given him the phone. Therefore, you may start the conversation when comforting a mourner over the phone.

Q10: May one change the topic of conversation when comforting a mourner in person?

A: The gist of the conversation should be about the *niftar*, about mourning in general, or the connection between the *aveil* and the *niftar*. It's not appropriate to discuss the stock market in the mourner's home since you're coming to comfort him.

Q11: Are you *yotzei bikur cholim* over the phone?

A: There are three aspects to *bikur cholim*. One is similar to *nichum aveilim* that the person knows you're thinking about him. The second *inyan* is as the Kitzur Shulchan Aruch (193:3) says עִקַּר מִצְוַת בִּקּוּר חוֹלִים הוּא לְעַיֵּן בְּצָרְכֵי הַחוֹלֶה מַה הוּא צָרִיךְ לַעֲשׂוֹת לוֹ וְשֶׁיִּמְצָא נַחַת רוּחַ עִם חֲבֵרָיו וְגַם שֶׁיִּתֵּן דַּעְתּוֹ עָלָיו וִיבַקֵּשׁ רַחֲמִים עָלָיו - you come to see if the *choleh* needs anything like calling a nurse or getting something else at the hospital. The second aspect you can't be *yotzei* over the phone, but it's still a *chesed* to call in order for him to feel you're thinking of him.[15] The third is to *daven* for him.[16] While it's better to *daven* in the place where the *choleh* is lying because the Shechina is above the *choleh*,[17] so you are *daven*ing straight to he Ribbono Shel Olam, but even if you are not there one can be mispalel for the *choleh*. In general, there's a rule that you're not obligated to travel out of town to fulfill a *mitzvas aseh*. For instance, you have a *mitzva* to get married – פריה ורביה.[18] You're not obligated to go out of town to find a *shidduch* because it's no different than any other *mitzva*. I'm

---

[15] Igros Moshe YD (1:223) - הנה פשוט לע"ד שאף שמקיים מצוה דבק"ח אבל אינו שייך לומר שיצא י"ח כיון שחסר בבקור זה ענינים האחרים שיש בבק"ח. ורק יצא מזה שאם א"א לו לקיים בהליכה לשם לא נפטר לגמרי אלא צריך לבקרו במה שאפשר לו לכל הפחות ענין אחד או שנים שהוא גם ע"י הטעלעפאן. וזהו הדין דחלה בנו שואלו בשוק בנדרים דף ל"ט לא שיצא בזה כל ענין בק"ח אלא שאף שלא יצא בזה הא פטור משום שאינו יכול לקיים כיון דאדריה גם מן חיותיה דבנו אך השמיענו דמ"מ מחוייב לקיים במה שאפשר לו דהוא לשאול עליו בשוק ובחלה הוא שלא אדריה מן חיותיה מחוייב ליכנס ולראות ובעצמו כדי שיקיים בק"ח בכל הענינים ולא יצא בשאלה בשוק. וכן אינו כלום הראיה שהביא כתר"ה מסעי' ח' דבחולה שקשה לו הדבור אין מבקרין אותו בפניו אלא נכנסין בבית החיצון ושואלין אם צריכין לכבד ולרבץ ושומעין צערו ומבקשין רחמים אלמא שא"צ להיות נוכח החולה בכדי לקיים המצוה דשם הא הוא חולה שא"א בפניו דיש לחוש שידבר שקשה לו זה אך עכ"פ לא נפטר לגמרי אלא צריך לבקרו ולשאול עליו בבית החיצון כדי לקיים מה שאפשר וזהו עיקר החדוש דשם אבל בחולה שאפשר לבקרו בפניו מחוייבין לבקרו בפניו בשביל הטעם שימצא נחת רוח בזה שאין שייך זה שלא בפניו וגם מחמת שמהראיה מתרגש המבקר יותר ומבקש ביותר תחנונים וכדכתב גם כתר"ה וגם אולי מתקבלת שם התפלה ביותר משום דהשכינה מצויה שם עם החולה. ומש"כ כתר"ה דנראה דעיקר בק"ח היא התפלה שלזה גם בטעלעפאן הוא כראה יקשה א"ך למה צריך בכלל ליל לשם יסגי בשאלה מאחרים ויתפלל אלא צריך לומר שאם לתפלה יותר טוב כשיראה בעצמו מטעם שיותר מתרגש ומטעם שהתפלה יותר מקובלת כדלעיל

[16] Rema YD (335:4) – וכל שביקר ולא ביקש עליו רחמים לא קיים המצוה

[17] Shulchan Aruch YD (335:3) – המבקר את החולה לא ישב ע"ג מטה ולא ע"ג כסא ולא ע"ג ספסל אלא מתעטף ויושב לפניו שהשכינה למעלה מראשותיו

[18] Rambam Ishus (15:2) - האיש מצווה על פריה ורביה

not saying you shouldn't go out of town, but you're not obligated to leave even after you've exhausted all the possibilities in town. I would think such a person would be exempt from פריה ורביה after exhausting all the possible *shidduchim* in his city. That doesn't mean I wouldn't be advise him not to go out of town, but he's just not obligated to leave town.

Q12: May the same *amen* be used for two things – like hearing two *berachos* end at the same time?

A: If you have *kavana* that the *amen* should work for both *berachos* – that they are both true – then it will work for both.[19] For instance, if two people wish you a *mazal tov*, then you can say one *amen* to both of them together. You could say *baruch tihyeh* to *mazal tov* if you want. If you're saying *amen* in your own *tefilla*, and want it to work for saying *amen* to another person's *beracha* as well, you may do so as long as you had intention for both.

Q13: Is there a *tzad heter* for someone to be *m'kane'ach* himself after going to the bathroom with his right hand?

A: It says that you should not use the right hand because the right hand is used to put on *tefillin*.[20] Therefore, it's not *lechatchila* to do so. If it's the only way he can be *m'kane'ach* himself then he has no choice. A lefty is the opposite of the righty and would be *m'kane'ach* with his right hand instead of his left.[21]

---

[19] Mishna Berura (124:25) - מי שנזדמן לו לענות אמן על ב' דברים עונה שני אמנים זה אחר זה ויכוין בכל אמן את הענין על מה הוא עונה וטפי עדיף לומר אמן ואמן

[20] Mishna Berura (3:17) - ביד ימין מפני שקושר בה תפילין על זרוע השמאלי ועוד טעמים אחרים עיין בגמרא וטוב ליזהר מלקנח באצבע האמצעי שכורך עליו הרצועה

[21] Mishna Berura (3:17) - וכתבו האחרונים דאיטר יד שכל עניניו עושה בשמאל מקנח בשמאל דידיה שהוא ימין כל אדם ואם כותב בשמאל ושאר מעשיו עושה בימין או להיפך עיין בבה"ל

Q14: May one list multiple חולים מסוכנים in one *meshaberach* or personal *tefillah*?

A: Yes, you may list them in the same *meshaberach* or personal *tefillah*.

Q15: How long should you continue *davening* for *cholim* if you don't hear about them?

A: After a week you may assume the *choleh* got better as the Ribbono Shel Olam listened to your *tefillah*. If you don't hear anything then you can assume he's OK now and you don't need to make sure.

Q16: Is it permitted to pull out hair during *sefira*?

A: Yes, I'm lenient to pull out hair during *sefira*.

Q17: If one holds it's forbidden to open a soda bottle on Shabbos, is he allowed to ask someone who holds it's permitted to open it?

A: If you have a bottle which you are stringent *m'tzad halacha* not to open on Shabbos, then I don't think you may give it to someone else to open since you hold it's really forbidden. Why are you giving the bottle to someone else? However, if it's just a question of *minhag*, then you may give the bottle to someone else to open. If someone else opened the bottle on his own, then you may use it.[22] However, if he opened the bottle for you then you may not use it. I remember my Rosh Yeshiva *zecher tzaddik l'vracha* said you may not open cans on Yom Tov or Shabbos, but would give it to a non-Jew to open if it was necessary. Usually they

---

[22] Igros Moshe OC (4:119:5) - ואם פתח ישראל שסובר ע"פ הוראת חכם להיתר אם מותר לאחד שסובר שאסור לפתוח ע"פ הוראת חכם אחר יש להסתפק דכיון שנעשה בהיתר אין זה בכלל איסור מעשה שבת ובפרט באיסור דרבנן ויש להקל כדי שלא יתדמדה כחולק עליהם

would open the cans before Shabbos or Yom Tov, but if it wasn't done then he would give it to a non-Jew.

Q18: If someone purchased a *sefer* online but never had it delivered, may he put in a claim to Paypal after not receiving any response from the Jewish seller?

A: If it's been a few weeks and you really tried to get a hold of him, then you may put in a claim to Paypal. It's not a dispute being sent to a non-Jewish Beis Din because there's no dispute here.[23] They took your money without giving you what you paid for, so now you want your money back. Your case isn't with this *yid* – it's with Paypal.

---

[23] Shulchan Aruch CM (26:1) - אסור לדון בפני דייני עכו"ם ובערכאות שלהם (פי' מושב קבוע לשרים לדון בו) אפי' בדין שדנים בדיני ישראל ואפי' נתרצו ב' בעלי דינים לדון בפניהם אסור וכל הבא לידון בפניהם הרי זה רשע וכאלו חירף וגידף והרים יד בתורת מרע"ה: הגה ויש ביד ב"ד לנדותו ולהחרימו עד שיסלק יד עכו"ם מעל חבירו

Chapter 3: Shonim 5778

Q1. How long is כדי שתיית רביעית – the time it takes to drink a *revi'is*?

A: About 30 seconds because a *revi'is* is 1 ½ eggs.[1] There are 6 *beitzim* in a *lug*, and a *revi'is* is a quarter of that – which is 1 ½ eggs. *B'pashtus* we should follow the medium sized eggs, but just because we call an egg "medium" nowadays doesn't mean that it is truly a medium egg. For instance, Colgate toothpaste is sold in three sizes: large, giant, and economy. The "large" is really Colgate's small size, "giant" is medium, and "economy" is the large one. There are no small eggs for sale. Rather, the eggs sold as "medium" are the small ones, the eggs sold as "large" are really medium sized, and the truly large eggs are sold as "extra large" and "jumbo." Therefore, the large eggs are what we use to determine the medium *shiur* – which is 1.9 fl oz, and Rav Moshe Feinstein confirmed the same reasoning. Now the question is whether *niskatnu habeim*, that the eggs nowadays are half the size they used to be in the times of Chazal.[2] Consequently, the *shiur revi'is* would be 3 eggs – which is 1.9 x 3 = 5.7 fl oz, as the Chazon Ish holds. However, if you don't hold the eggs became smaller over time, then it would be 2.85 fl oz. I'm sure people can drink the *revi'is* in 3 or 4 seconds easily. It's less than half an eight-ounce cup which you could drink in one second. However, the Gemara[3] says

---

[1] Shulchan Aruch OC (158:10) - אע"פ ששיעורם ברביעית [פירוש רביעית הלוג דהיינו שיעור ביצה וחצי] יוסיף ליטול בשפע דאמר רב חסדא אנא משאי מלא חפני מיא ויהבי לי מלא חפני טיבותא

[2] Mishna Berura (486:1) - ועתה נחזור לענינו דע דמש"כ המחבר כזית כחצי ביצה לאו מלתא פסיקתא היא בזמנינו דיש מאחרונים שהוכיחו דביצים המצויים בזמנינו נתקטנו הרבה עד למחצה מכפי שהיו בימים הקדמונים שבהם שיערו חכמים ולפ"ז בכל מקום שהשיעור הוא כחצי ביצה צריך לשער בכביצה בזמנינו ועיין בשע"ת שהכריע שיש לחלק בזה לענין שיעורין בין דבר שחיובו מן התורה לדבר שחיובו מדרבנן

[3] Beitza (25b) - תנו רבנן השותה כוסו בבת אחת ה"ז גרגרן שנים דרך ארץ שלשה מגסי הרוח

drinking the entire *revi'is* is considered a גרגרן when he drinks it at one time – a drunkard who gulps wine, drinking in two sips is *derech eretz* - these two sips must be socially accepted intervals between the two sips, and three sips is considered arrogant.

Q2. Is it *bittul* Torah to read Gedolim books? May one read them before saying Birchas HaTorah?

A: This is not a yes or no answer. What do the Gedolim books speak about? If they discuss the *gadol's hanhagos*, like Rav Chaim Kanievsky would wash *netilas yadayim* on the side of his bed, but not under his bed in order to ensure the water didn't become *tameh* by him sleeping over it,[4] then there's a *halacha* involved in the story. The book is telling readers how to follow a *middas chassidus*, so you shouldn't read those before Birchas HaTorah.[5] On the other hand, if the book discusses how great the *gadol* is that he knew Shas at such a young age and everyone tried to get him as a son-in-law, then that's not Torah. It's a biography which you can read before Birchas HaTorah. It's not *bittul* Torah since it is a *chizuk* for some people to read, telling you that this *gadol* was a human being and that you can do it too. For other people who could be learning during that time, then it's better to be learning instead. My Rosh Yeshiva was in the hospital after falling out of a car going 60 mph on the highway and broke his collar bone. They thought they found something wrong with his kidney and performed all forms of tests which severely weakened the Rosh Yeshiva to the

---

[4] Shulchan Aruch YD (116:5) - וְלֹא יִתֵּן תַּבְשִׁיל וְלֹא מַשְׁקִים תַּחַת הַמִּטָּה מִפְּנֵי שֶׁרוּחַ רָעָה שׁוֹרָה עֲלֵיהֶם

[5] Mishna Berura (47:2) - שלא ללמוד עד שיברך ויברך אותה בשמחה גדולה דמצינו שאחז"ל על מה אבדה הארץ ויאמר ה' על עזבם תורתי ואחז"ל שדבר זה נשאל לנביאים על מה אבדה הארץ שישראל היו עוסקים בתורה ומצינו שכל זמן שהיו עוסקים בתורה ויתר הקב"ה על עונותיהם ולכן לא ידעו על מה אבדה והקב"ה הבוחן לבבות ידע כי אע"פ שהיו עוסקין בתורה לא היו עוסקין לשם לימוד התורה אלא כמו שלומדין שאר חכמות ולכן לא ברכו בה"ת שלא היתה התורה חשובה בעיניהם ולכן לא הגינה

extent that he couldn't learn. Consequently, he asked us to bring him stories of Gedolim. We brought a story of the Chiddushei HaRim and asked the Rosh Yeshiva what he thought of the *Chassidish* stories. The Rosh Yeshiva – Rav Aharon *zecher tzaddik l'vracha* – told us he read that the Chiddushei HaRim was once invited to a *bris* and didn't eat the meat. They investigated where the meat came from and found it was a firstborn animal which wasn't redeemed properly according to *halacha*. The story even included witnesses who testified they saw the Chiddushei HaRim didn't eat the meat. After telling us the story, the Rosh Yeshiva began laughing, but we didn't understand what the joke was. He told us, "There are only two types of a *bechor* which need *pidyon*: 1) פטר חמור – redeeming a donkey,[6] and 2) בכור אדם – a person's firstborn.[7] A firstborn bechor of a *beheima tehora* must be given to a kohen and brought as a korban – it doesn't have pidyon. Either the story is telling you that they tried serving *basar chamor* or *basar adam* at this *bris*, or the Chiddushei HaRim just didn't like meat. You don't need to make a *mofeis* out of it." If you can't learn for whatever reason, then such biographies are good to read for inspiration. Otherwise, it's better to just learn.

Q3. Is הרהור כדיבור דמי – thinking tantamount to speaking?

---

[6] Shulchan Aruch YD (321:1) - בכור בהמה טמאה נוהג בכל מקום ובכל זמן ואינו נוהג אלא בחמורים וזה מצותו שכל ישראל שיש לו חמורה שבכרה פודהו בשה מן הכשבים או מן העזים בין זכר בין נקבה בין תם בין בעל מום בין גדול בין קטן ויתננו לכהן

[7] Shulchan Aruch YD (305:1) - מִצְוַת עֲשֵׂה לִפְדּוֹת כָּל אִישׁ מִיִּשְׂרָאֵל בְּנוֹ שֶׁהוּא בְּכוֹר לְאִמּוֹ הַיִּשְׂרְאֵלִית בְּה' סְלָעִים שֶׁהֵם ק"כ מָעִים שֶׁהֵם שְׁלֹשִׁים דַּרְהֲמִים כֶּסֶף מְזֻקָּק

A: Most *Poskim* hold you may think in learning before you say Birchas HaTorah[8] because thinking Torah is not like speaking it.[9]

Q4. Must one sell his shirt to buy candles for Shabbos?

A: You only need to sell your shirt for the lights of the Menorah on Chanuka[10] and four cups for the Seder.[11] Both have an *inyan* of *pirsumei nisah*, which is why you must sell your shirt. On the other hand, Neiros Shabbos aren't *pirsumei nisah* and you don't need to sell your shirt. As a matter of fact, the Gemara[12] writes if you only have enough money for Ner Shabbos or Chanuka, Neiros Shabbos is more important for *shalom bayis*. The reason for lighting Neiros Shabbos is to ensure you don't trip in the dark.[13] I would think not having a shirt would detract from your oneg Shabbos, so you shouldn't sell your shirt to buy Neiros Shabbos.

Q5. If someone is late for Maariv, is it better to skip Shema to *daven* Shemoneh Esrei with the *minyan* or say Shema now to be *somech geula l'tefilla*?

---

[8] Shulchan Aruch OC (47:4) - המהרהר בדברי תורה א"צ לברך

[9] Mishna Berura (47:5) - דהרהור לאו כדיבור דמי ולפ"ז יש ליזהר לאותן הלומדים בעיון מתוך הספר שיזהרו להוציא קצת ד"ת בפה אחר הברכה אם אינו אומר פסוקי ברכת כהנים או שאר ד"ת אחר הברכה כמו שנוהגין

[10] Shulchan Aruch OC (671:1) - צריך ליזהר מאוד בהדלקת נרות חנוכה ואפילו עני המתפרנס מן הצדקה שואל או מוכר כסותו ולוקח שמן להדליק

[11] Shulchan Aruch OC (472:13) - אפילו עני המתפרנס מן הצדקה ימכור מלבושו או ילוה או ישכיר עצמו לד' כוסות

[12] Shabbos (23b) - אמר רבא פשיטא לי נר ביתו ונר חנוכה נר ביתו עדיף משום שלום ביתו נר ביתו וקידוש היום נר ביתו עדיף משום שלום ביתו

[13] Rashi Shabbos (25b) - הדלקת נר בשבת. שלא היה לו ממה להדליק ובמקום שאין נר אין שלום שהולך ונכשל והולך באפילה

A: Tosafos says there is no *din* of being *somech geula l'tefillah* by Maariv, hence we say Kadesh after the *beracha* על כל מעשיו by Maariv.[14] Therefore, you should skip Shema and instead say Shemoneh Esrei with the *tzibur*, then return to the rest of Maariv. However, when you return to say Baruch Hashem L'Olam, you should not say the *beracha* if you already *davened* Shemoneh Esrei.[15]

Q6. How long is *toch k'dei dibur*?

A: 2 ½ seconds. The *shiur* is saying "Shalom Alecha Rebbi u'Mori" with *derech eretz*.[16] You don't speak to a Rebbi with quick words.

Q7. Must one wash his hands three times after cutting his nails or hair[17]?

A: *B'dieved* if you just wash your hands once, that is enough.[18]

---

[14] Aruch HasShulchan OC (111:3) - ואם עד שלא קרא קריאת שמע מצא ציבור מתפללין לא יתפלל עמהם אלא מתפלל על הסדר כדי שיסמוך גאולה לתפילה דעדיף מתפילת ציבור וזהו בשחרית אבל בערבית אינו כן

[15] Mishna Berura (236:11) - [והנה בדברי הט"ז וא"ר מבואר בהדיא דברוך ה' לעולם וכו' וגם יראו עינינו יאמר אחר התפלה וכן העתיק הח"א וכן משמע קצת במ"א סק"ב אכן במעשה רב כתב דאחר התפלה לא יאמר הפסוקים דברוך ה' לעולם וכו' ומשמע דטעמיה דלא נתקן אלא לאומרו במקומו ולא אחר שכבר התפלל ערבית וע"כ נראה דטוב שלא יחתום ברכת יראו עינינו אלא יאמר עד כי אין לנו מלך אלא אתה ואע"ג דברכה בלא חתימה בעלמא אינה חשובה ברכה כלל מ"מ כיון דאפילו קודם י"ח הוא רק מנהגא בעלמא הבו דלא להוסיף עלה]

[16] Bava Kamma (72b) - אמרי תרי תוך כדי דיבור הוי חד כדי שאילת תלמיד לרב וחד כדי שאילת הרב לתלמיד כי לית ליה לרבי יוסי כדי שאילת תלמיד לרב שלום עליך רבי ומורי דנפיש כדי שאילת הרב לתלמיד שלום עליך אית ליה

[17] Shulchan Aruch OC (4:19) - המגלח ולא נטל ידיו מפחד ג' ימים. הנוטל צפרניו ולא נטל ידיו מפחד יום א' ואינו יודע ממה מפחד

[18] See Kaf Hachaim OC (4:61:2) "והרב סולת בלולה"

Q8. What is the *beracha* on granola bars?

A: That's the same as asking, "What's the *beracha* on cholent?" It depends on what the granola bar is made out of. If the main ingredient is oats or grain, then you make a *mezonos*. If another ingredient is the majority, then make a *beracha* on the *ikkar*.[19] The *ikkar* doesn't necessarily mean it's the majority of all the ingredients, rather it's the ingredient with the largest proportion to the rest of the food. For instance, a granola bar might have less than 50% oats, but still be *mezonos* because the oats are the largest portion of the ingredients.[20] You can look at the ingredient list to see the order of predominance of the food. Let's say granola is the first ingredient listed as 40% of the bar, then almonds are the second ingredient on the list at 29%, then the next ingredient is 28%. Still, the granola is the *ikkar* of the bar. Although חמשת מיני דגן has its limitations[21], we say the *beracha* follows the reason why people eat the food. Soup is commonly thickened with flour, but it's still *shehakol* despite the flour since the *mezonos* isn't the reason why people are having the soup.[22] Peanut chews are chocolate covered peanuts. Are people eating the peanut chew for the *shehakol* chocolate or the *hoadama* peanuts? We follow the

---

[19] Shulchan Aruch OC (208:7) - הכוסס [פירוש האוכל] את האורז מברך עליו בורא פרי האדמה ואחריו בורא נפשות ואם בשלו הגה עד שנתמעך או שטחנו ועשה ממנו פת מברך עליו בורא מיני מזונות ואחריו בורא נפשות והוא שלא יהא מעורב עם דבר אחר אלא אורז לבדו ואם עירב ממנו בתבשיל אחר והתבשיל האחר הוא הרוב מברך עליו כברכת אותו תבשיל

[20] Shulchan Aruch OC (208:2) - חמשת מיני דגן ששלקן או כתשן ועשה מהם תבשיל כגון מעשה קדירה הריפות וגרש כרמל ודייסא אפילו עירב עמהם דבש הרבה יות' מהם או מינים אחרי' הרבה יות' מהם מברך עליו בורא מיני מזונות ולבסוף על המחיה

[21] Berachos (37b) - דרב ושמואל דאמרי תרוייהו כל שיש בו מחמשת המינים מברכין עליו בורא מיני מזונות

[22] Shulchan Aruch OC (208:2) - אבל אם לא נתן הדגן בתבשיל אלא לדבקו ולהקפותו בטל בתבשיל

main ingredient purpose for the *beracha*. The Be'er Heitev[23] asks a similar question about drinking whiskey in the morning to get your day started. However, the person feels he must eat bread in order to drink the whiskey. Do we say the bread is *shehakol* since it's only being eaten to successfully drink the whiskey, or do we say *ikkar* and *tofel* only applies when the foods are eaten together – while this case you're eating the bread separately and would require *hamotzi*? Therefore, the *beracha* on a granola bar is whatever the main purpose of eating the bar is.

Q9. Should one make an effort to live in Eretz Yisroel?

A: The Gemara[24] says, "Anyone who doesn't live in Israel is as if he doesn't have a Ribbono Shel Olam." Rashi in Nach quotes this Gemara and says it only refers to *zman haMikdash*. When we had the Beis HaMikdash, Hakadosh Baruch Hu's presence was in Yerushalayim and this person didn't want to live in Israel – that is tantamount to rejecting Hakadosh Baruch Hu. But if there's no Mikdash then it's not necessarily considered to be that you're doing something wrong by living in *chutz la'aretz*. Moreover, Tosafos[25] asks the question on the Gemara how are we all in *chutz la'aretz* today? Tosafos answers that you're not obligated to put

---

[23] Be'er Heitev OC (212:2) - מי שאוכל פת למתק השתיה מברך על המשקה ופוטר את הפת אם היה דעתו עליו בבירור או שדרכו בכך ברוב הפעמים לאכול פת באמצע השתיה והוי כאלו דעתו עליו ובלא"ה צריך לברך מ"א של"ה וכ"כ הט"ז סק"א. ויש למנוע מלאכול פת בשעת השתיה כי מי יוכל להבחין אם אוכלו משום מילוי כרסו דאז צריך לברך המוציא או שאוכלו למיתוק השתיה

[24] Kesubos (110b) - ת"ר לעולם ידור אדם בא"י אפי' בעיר שרובה עובדי כוכבים ואל ידור בחו"ל ואפילו בעיר שרובה ישראל שכל הדר בארץ ישראל דומה כמי שיש לו אלוה וכל הדר בחוצה לארץ דומה כמי שאין לו אלוה

[25] Tosafos Kesubos (110b) - הוא אומר לעלות כו' - אינו נוהג בזמן הזה דאיכא סכנת דרכים והיה אומר רבינו חיים דעכשיו אינו מצוה לדור בא"י כי יש כמה מצות התלויות בארץ וכמה עונשין דאין אנו יכולין ליזהר בהם ולעמוד עליהם

yourself in danger by traveling for this *mitzvah*, and also it's difficult to be careful in all the *mitzvos* of Eretz Yisroel like *teruma*, *orlah*, etc. Rav Moshe[26] says it's a *mitzva kiyumes*, not a *mitzva chiyuves*. Meaning, you are not required to buy a house in order to fulfill the *mitzvas mezuza*. The Torah doesn't require you to have a house. On the other hand, you're obligated to buy a *lulav* and *esrog*. Living in Israel is a *mitzva*, but not one which you are obligated to do. Rav Moshe continues saying there is no real danger in traveling any more, however it's still not so easy to keep all the added *halachos* in Eretz Yisroel. Nowadays, the kosher *hechsherim* in Eretz Yisroel make even that easier since *terumos* and *maaseros* are removed before you buy it. Nonetheless, living in Israel is a *mitzva kiyumes*. Furthermore, the Chazon Ish writes in a letter to someone before WWII that living in Poland - where there were a lot of Yeshivos at the time - is the equivalent of living in Eretz Yisroel. Living in a *makom* Torah is equal to living in Eretz Yisroel today.

Q10. If something is left in a place left for *hefker* objects, may one assume it is *hefker*?

A: The Gemara[27] says, "If you find a lost object in a place of a majority of non-Jews, then you can assume the owner was

---

[26] Igros Moshe EH (1:102) - הנה רוב הפוסקים סברי דהוא מצוה. אבל פשוט שאין זה בזה"ז מצוה חיובית שעל הגוף דא"כ היה ממילא נמצא שאסור לדור בחו"ל משום שעובר על עשה כמו מי שילבש בגד של ד' כנפות בלא ציצית שיש איסור ללבוש כדי שלא יעבור על עשה דציצית ולא הוזכר איסור אלא על הדר בא"י שאסור לצאת ע"מ לשכון בחו"ל ברמב"ם פ"ה ממלכים ה"ט וג"כ הא ודאי אינו איסור לאו ואם היה איסור גם לאנשי חו"ל הי"ל לרמב"ם לומר סתם אסור לשכון בחו"ל אא"כ חזק בא"י הרעב משמע דרק ליושבי א"י יש איסור שאסרו חכמים אבל מצד העשה אינה חיובית אלא כשדר שם מקיים מצוה ובחדושי הארכתי הרבה בדברי ר"ח שבתוס' כתובות וכיון שאינה מצוה חיובית יש ודאי להתחשב בהחשש של הר"ח בתוס' אם יוכל ליזהר במצות התלויות בארץ

[27] Bava Metzia (24a) - ת"ש מצא בה אבידה אם רוב ישראל חייב להכריז אם רוב כנענים אינו חייב להכריז מאן שמעת ליה דאמר אזלינן

meya'eish – gave up hope of finding it. If the area was inhabited by a majority of Jews and there was a *siman* on the object, then you say the owner wasn't *meya'eish* and you may not keep it."[28] That Gemara applies only if the item was lost. However, if the object looks like it was placed in the spot intentionally, then it's not an *aveida* since the owner plans to return and retrieve it – and you may not take it. If you took it accidentally, you cannot return the object there either since the owner may have already returned, saw the object was taken, and was *meya'eish* finding it again.[29] The Gemara is telling us that if you find an object in an area where it appears it was left intentionally, you may assume it is an *aveidah*. If you find a *sefer* on one of the tables in the Beis Midrash during lunch time, that's a *makom hinuach* and you may not take it. Therefore, if this object looks like it was placed in the *hefker* area then you cannot take it because the owner still plans to return. However, if the object seems like it was lost – like it was thrown there or it fell there – in the *hefker* area, then you may take it.

בתר רובא רשב"א שמעת מינה כי קאמר רשב"א ברוב כנענים אבל ברוב ישראל לא

[28] Shulchan Aruch CM (259:3) - כיצד המוציא מציאה במקום שישראל מצוים שם חייב להכריז שלא נתייאשו הבעלים ואפי' העיר מחצה עכו"ם ומחצה ישראל או אפי' רובה עכו"ם והוא מצאה במקום שרוב העוברים שם ישראל חייב להחזיר אבל אם רוב העיר עכו"ם או אפי' רובה ישראל ומצאה במקום שרוב העוברים שם עכו"ם אינו חייב אפי' אם ידע שמישראל נפלה

[29] Shulchan Aruch CM (260:9) - כל המוצא אבידה בין שיש בה סימן בין שאין בה סימן אם מצאה דרך הנחה אסור ליגע בה שמא בעלי' הניחוה שם עד שיחזרו לה ואם יבא ליטלה והוי דבר שאין בו סימן הרי איבד ממון חבירו שהרי אין לו בה סימן להחזיר בו ואם היה דבר שיש בו סימן ה"ז הטריחן לרדוף אחריה ולתת סימניה לפיכך אסור לו שיגע בה עד שימצאנה דרך נפילה אפי' נסתפק לו הדבר ולא ידע אם דבר זה אבוד או מונח ה"ז לא יגע בו ואם עבר ונטלו אסור לו להחזירו לשם ואם היה דבר שאין בו סימן זכה בו ואינו חייב להחזירו וכל דבר שיש בו סימן בין ספק הנחה בין בדרך נפילה בין ברה"י בין בר"ה חייב להכריז

Q11. If one loses an object without a *siman*, and later finds an identical object, can he assume it is his own?

A: If this object didn't have a *siman*, then there's no *mitzvas hashavas aveidah*.[30] Either way you may take it: either this object is yours or this identical object lacks a *siman*, which allows you to take the object as well. When I was in Yeshiva in Lakewood around 1955, someone found a five-dollar bill. In those days, a five-dollar bill was worth about $50 or more. We asked the Rosh Yeshiva if we need to return to money since a *talmid chacham* is believed *b'teviyas ayin*.[31] Most people don't remember the serial number of the dollar bill,[32] but the Rosh Yeshiva said, "If he's saying he lost it, and you're saying you found it, then you should return the money."

Q12. How *makpid* must one be in saying something in the name of the one who said it[33]?

---

[30] Shulchan Aruch CM (262:3) - אין המוצא מציאה חייב להכריז אלא בדבר שיש בו סימן בגופו או שראוי ליתן סימן במקומו או בקשריו או במנינו או במדתו או במשקלו אבל אם אין בו שום סימן אפי' במקומו כגון שניכר שלא הונח שם בכוונה אלא דרך נפילה בא שם אם הוא דבר שיש לתלות שבעליו הרגישו בו מיד כשנפל ממנו או מחמת כובדו או מחמת חשיבותו ותמיד היה ממשמש בו ומרגיש כשנופל הרי הוא של מוצאו שהרי נתייאש מיד כשידע שנפל כיון שאין בו סימן ובא לידו בהיתר כיון שנתייאשו בעליו ואם לא צריך להחזיר אע"פ שנתייאש אח"כ כיון שבא לידו קודם יאוש

[31] Bava Metzia (23b) - נפקא מינה לאהדורי לצורבא מרבנן בטביעות עינא שבעתן העין קים ליה בגוייהו ומהדרינן ליה כי לא שבעתן העין לא קים ליה בגוייהו ולא מהדרינן ליה

[32] Shulchan Aruch CM (262:13) - בד"א שמחזירים מטבע בסימנים שאמרנו אבל אם אין בו סימנים הללו אפי' אמר רשומה היא בחותם מלך פלוני או אפי' אמר שמי כתוב עליה אין מחזירין לו מפני שמטבע ניתן להוצאה ושמא הוציאה ומאחר נפלו

[33] Avos (6:6) - וְהָאוֹמֵר דָּבָר בְּשֵׁם אוֹמְרוֹ הָא לָמַדְתָּ שֶׁכָּל הָאוֹמֵר דָּבָר בְּשֵׁם אוֹמְרוֹ מֵבִיא גְאֻלָּה לָעוֹלָם שֶׁנֶּאֱמַר וַתֹּאמֶר אֶסְתֵּר לַמֶּלֶךְ בְּשֵׁם מָרְדֳּכָי

A: We learn this *din* from Mordechai as the Megillah[34] says, "The story of Bigsan and Teresh was told to Achashverosh by Esther *b'shem* Mordechai." Due to this recognition, not only was Mordechai saved from the clutches of Haman, but Mordechai was given Haman's prestigious job in the government. Although the Chachamim felt Mordechai lowered his *madreiga* to take the position,[35] Mordechai felt he was obligated to take the royal position to ensure another future Haman wouldn't rise again during that time. This story doesn't have anything to do with quoting Torah insights from the source, rather it applies to saying anything in the name of the person who said the statement. One *sefer* explains the reason behind this idea is that Hashem doesn't want to bring *geulah* through someone who will arrogantly say they brought the *geulah*.[36] Someone who doesn't say in the name of the person who said the original statement means they want to take the honor for themselves. On the other hand, someone willing to admit he heard the insight from someone else is fit to be *mashiach*. As long as you say, "I saw this idea in a *sefer*," then that's good enough for bring *geulah l'olam* since you're humbly admitting the insight isn't your own.

---

[34] Esther (2:22) - וַיִּוָּדַע הַדָּבָר לְמָרְדֳּכַי וַיַּגֵּד לְאֶסְתֵּר הַמַּלְכָּה וַתֹּאמֶר אֶסְתֵּר לַמֶּלֶךְ בְּשֵׁם מָרְדֳּכָי

[35] Megilla (16b) - כי מרדכי היהודי משנה למלך אחשורוש וגדול ליהודים ורצוי לרוב אחיו ולא לכל אחיו מלמד שפירשו ממנו מקצת סנהדרין

[36] Ben Yehoyada Megilla (15a) - נמצא למדנו מכאן שהאומר דבר תורה בשם אומרו מביא גאולה וצריך להבין מה טעם יש בזה על דברי תורה ונראה לי בס"ד דאם אומר דבר תורה ואינו אומרו בשם אומרו זה יהיה מחמת גאוה שרוצה להתגאות בטלית אחרים שיחשבו העולם שדבר זה הוא המחדש אותו מדעתו ולפי זה המדקדק לומר דבר בשם אומרו הרי זה מואס בגאוה ולומד תורה לשמה לכן מדה כנגד מדה בזכות זה שלומד לשמה יטיל הקב"ה אות למ"ד שבו רמוז לימוד התורה בתוך אותיות גאוה אשר מאס זה האדם ויהיה כאן צירוף גאולה ולזה אמר מביא גאולה לעולם

Q13. When one writes a *sefer*, should he be *meramez* to his name in the title?

A: The Roke'ach says you should do so. Nonetheless, you should be careful to not put too much grandeur into the title of your *sefer*. There were three people who wrote *seforim* and made it sound like it was the world's greatest gift to mankind, and none of their titles were *mekuyam*. The Chasam Sofer named his *sefer* 'Toras Moshe', but everyone calls it "Chasam Sofer on Chumash." Another *sefer* is the Rambam's Mishna Torah[37] which everyone simply calls "The Rambam." The Ra'avad argued with the Rambam saying it's not correct to say the way you learned the Gemara is correct and the only way to learn it. The 3rd *sefer* is the Shelah who wrote Shnei Luchos HaBris which everyone calls "The Shelah."

Q14. Is it permitted to copy music from another's CD?

A: If the publisher of the CD is *makpid* not have copies made, then you may not do so under the copyright laws.[38] However, the copyright laws don't necessarily cover

---

[37] Hakdamas HaRambam L'Yad Hachazaka - עַד שֶׁיִּהְיוּ כָּל הַדִּינִין גְּלוּיִין לַקָּטָן וְלַגָּדוֹל בְּדִין כָּל מִצְוָה וּמִצְוָה, וּבְדִין כָּל הַדְּבָרִים שֶׁתִּקְּנוּ חֲכָמִים וּנְבִיאִים: כְּלָלוֹ שֶׁל דָּבָר, כְּדֵי שֶׁלֹּא יְהֵא אָדָם צָרִיךְ לְחִבּוּר אַחֵר בָּעוֹלָם בְּדִין מִדִּינֵי יִשְׂרָאֵל; אֶלָּא יִהְיֶה חִבּוּר זֶה מְקַבֵּץ לְתוֹרָה שֶׁבְּעַל פֶּה כֻּלָּהּ, עִם הַתַּקָּנוֹת וְהַמִּנְהָגוֹת וְהַגְּזֵרוֹת שֶׁנַּעֲשׂוּ מִימוֹת מֹשֶׁה רַבֵּנוּ וְעַד חִבּוּר הַתַּלְמוּד, וּכְמוֹ שֶׁפֵּרְשׁוּ לָנוּ הַגְּאוֹנִים בְּכָל חִבּוּרֵיהֶן, שֶׁחִבְּרוּ אַחַר הַתַּלְמוּד. לְפִיכָךְ קָרָאתִי שֵׁם חִבּוּר זֶה מִשְׁנֵה תוֹרָה לְפִי שֶׁאָדָם קוֹרֵא תּוֹרָה שֶׁבִּכְתָב תְּחִלָּה, וְאַחַר כָּךְ קוֹרֵא בְּזֶה, וְיוֹדֵעַ מִמֶּנּוּ תּוֹרָה שֶׁבְּעַל פֶּה כֻּלָּהּ, וְאֵינוֹ צָרִיךְ לִקְרוֹת סֵפֶר אַחֵר בֵּינֵיהֶם

[38] Igros Moshe OC (4:40:19) - בדבר אחד שעשה טייפ מדברי תורה וכותב שאסור לעשות מטייפ שלו עוד טייפס ודאי אסור כי הוא ענין שוה כסף ועשה הטייפ להרויח מזה שאחרים שירצו יצטרכו לשלם לו שאם כן ליכא משום מידת סדום וממילא כיון שהוא חפצו אין רשאין ליקח אותו להשתמש בו שלא ברשות ואף כשלא שמעו ממנו שאינו נותן רשות אסור להעתיק ממנו בסתמא כל זמן שלא הרשה בו בפירוש וכו' וטייפ אחר מטייפ אחד שלא ברשות הוא איסור גזל

everything. For instance, copyright law allows you to copy articles from a book for educational purposes. The main idea of a copyright is that a person invested a lot of effort into a work and wants to make it worthwhile for himself by copyrighting the work. If something is not copyrighted, then today you have the right to assume the publisher gives you the right to make copies of it.

Q15. May one download YouTube content?

A: If a singer puts up the music or video himself, then he's giving permission for people to download it. I have a right to prevent others from selling my content which I worked to create. Therefore, if I sell you my work on condition that you don't copy it for others, you are a *gazlan* if you copy the work illegally.[39] It all depends on the person who was *mechadesh* the work.

Q16. What *beracha* should one say on a rice dessert? What about ice cream?

A: If the rice dessert is part of the meal, then there is no *beracha*. If it's not being eaten as part of the meal, then you say *mezonos* and *borei nefashos*.[40] If we're discussing a bread meal, then everything eaten with the bread during a *seuda* is covered as part of the *hamotzi* – soup, vegetables, meat, etc.[41] You could ask the question that nowadays since

---

[39] Shulchan Aruch CM (212:3) - אבל אם מכר לא' בית ואילן והורבה וחצר ושייר לעצמו דירת הבית ואכילת הפירות ואויר החורבה ואויר החצר מהני דהוי כאילו פירש ששייר לעצמו מקום ואפי' לא הזכיר שיור בחצר כלל אלא מכר לו בית ואמר לו על מנת שדיוטא העליונה שלי אמרינן ששייר לו מקום בחצר להוציא זיזין מהדיוטא לחצר

[40] Mishna Berura (208:25) - ובלחם חמודות כתב דסוגיין דעלמא אורז ריי"ז דוחן היר"ז וכן מוכח בברכי יוסף ומטה יהודה וכן מצאתי במעשה רב מהנהגות הגר"א דאורז הוא ריי"ז ומברך עליהם במ"מ

[41] Shulchan Aruch (117:1) - דברים הבאים בתוך הסעודה אם הם דברים הבאים מחמת הסעודה דהיינו דברים שדרך לקבוע סעודה עליהם

people think meat is the main part of the meal because it's the most expensive part of the *seuda*. However, Chazal say bread is the main part of the meal, so we don't change based on what people think today. Moreover, you still see many Europeans eat much of their meal with bread. The reason people eat desserts is to remove the rest of dinner's taste from your mouth to replace it with something which tastes good. Therefore, dessert is not secondary to the bread, and you should make a *beracha* on every dessert.[42] Still, if you're eating cake as dessert then there's no *beracha* since the Shulchan Aruch has different opinions of *pas haba'ah b'kisnin* – either bread you put in your pocket as a snack which is *mezonos* since it's not a *kevias seuda*, or bread which is itself a pocket like pita filled with fruit.[43] The third opinion regarding *pas haba b'kisnin* is something which is baked with sweet ingredients. That is the cake or cracker we're talking about which isn't eaten as a *seuda*. Each opinion holds the other breads are *hamotzi*. Therefore, since we're lenient for *safek berachos* regarding the *machlokes* on

---

ללפת בהם את הפת כגון בשר ודגים וביצים וירקות וגבינה ודייסא ומיני מלוחים אפי' אוכלם בלא פת אין טעונין ברכה לפניהם דברכת המוציא פוטרתן ולא לאחריהם דבהמ"ז פוטרתן

[42] Shulchan Aruch (117:1) - ואם הם דברים הבאים שלא מחמת הסעודה דהיינו שאין דרך לקבוע סעודה עליהם ללפת בהם את הפת כגון תאנים וענבים וכל מיני פירות אם אוכל אותם בלא פת טעונין ברכה לפניהם דברכת המוציא אינה פוטרתן דלאו מעיקר סעודה הם ואינם טעונים ברכה לאחריהם דכיון שבאו בתוך הסעודה ברכת המזון פוטרתם

[43] Shulchan Aruch (168:7) - פת הבא בכיסנין יש מפרשים פת שעשוי כמין כיסים שממלאים אותם דבש או סוקר ואגוזים ושקדים ותבלין והם הנקראי' רושקלאיי"ש דיאלחש"ו וי"א שהיא עיסה שעירב בה דבש או שמן או חלב או מיני תבלין ואפאה והוא שיהי' טעם תערובת המי פירות או התבלין ניכר בעיסה: [וי"א שזה נקרא פת גמור אא"כ יש בהם הרבה תבלין או דבש כמיני מתוקה שקורין לעקו"ך שכמעט הדבש והתבלין הם עיקר וכן נוהגים]: וי"מ שהוא פת בין מתובלת בין שאינה מתובלת שעושים אותם כעבים יבשים וכוססין אותם והם הנקראים בישקוני"ש והלכה כדברי כלם שלכל אלו הדברים נותנים להם דינים שאמרנו בפת הבאה בכסנין

cake, we don't say *mezonos* if it's eaten as a dessert.[44] A rice dessert is a question regarding what its identity is. The *minhag* is to consider *orez* as rice, but the question is whether you are *yotzei b'dieved* on a rice dessert by saying *hamotzi*. Consequently, it's better to not eat a rice dessert. However, other desserts – like ice cream – which certainly aren't a part of the meal receive a *beracha rishona* even in the middle of the meal.

Q17. Must one write B"SD – *b'siyata dishmaya* on a paper he writes *chiddushei* Torah on?

A: I don't think writing B"SD will make much of a difference whether you'll be able to write a *chiddush* or not. You don't have to write it on the paper – if you really mean it, then perhaps it's a *middas chassidus*,[45] but it's not necessary to write that. Most *seforim* don't have B"SD on

---

[44] Biur Halacha (168:8) - ספק דרבנן להקל ושמא מין זה פת גמור הוא ונפטר בברכת המוציא ע"כ אין לברך על פת כיסנין בתוך הסעודה אא"כ הוא פת כיסנין לכו"ע [דהיינו שממולא וגם נילוש בדבש וכה"ג והוא דק ויבש] כ"כ דגמ"ר והגר"ז וכעין זה כתב ג"כ בחידושי רע"א וח"א ולפי מה שכתבנו לעיל בשם המאמר מרדכי דאפשר דמודו זה לזה אין קושיא כ"כ ולדינא נראה דבאוכל דבר הנילוש בדבש ומי ביצים וכה"ג בתוך הסעודה כגון לעק"ך וקיכלי"ך או שאוכל כעבי"ן יבשים לא יברך בתוך הסעודה אפילו אם אוכלן לקינוח ואם אוכל מדברים הממולאים בפירות [וכמה שצייר המחבר באופן הראשון] המברך עלייהו בתוך הסעודה לא הפסיד דמשמע דרוב הפוסקים סוברין כן דזהו פת כיסנין ובח"א משמע דאף על לעק"ך וקיכלי"ך לכתחלה ראוי שיכוין בשעת ברכת המוציא לפטור אותן

[45] Sefer Chassidim (884) - כתיב (בראשית ד:כו) אז הוחל לקרא בשם ה' ומיד סמך לו זה ספר. כשמתחיל הסופר יתפלל להקב"ה להצליחו לגמור הספר החכם ראה סופר שכתב בתחלת הספר בשם ה' בגליון למעלה. אמר למה עשית כן אמר ע"ש שסמך אצל בשם ה' זה ספר א"ל החכם כתוב לקרא בשם ה' זה ספר שצריך הסופר להתפלל להקב"ה שיצליחנו לכתוב ושיסיים הספר ולא לכתוב בשם ה' דכתיב (דברים יג:א) לא תוסיף עליו ולא תגרע ממנו

the top of every page, so I see no need to have them on pages you write on either.

Q18. Should one write B"SD on an English test or essay?

A: If you need *siyata dishmaya*, then maybe you should, but I don't think it's going to help.

Q19. May one make his bed on Shabbos if he won't sleep in it until after Shabbos?

A: You don't make your bed in order to sleep in it. Rather, the reason you make your bed is in order for the room to look more presentable. It's an honor for Shabbos to make your bed after waking up. However, if no one is planning on being in the room the entire Shabbos and will only return on Motza'ei Shabbos, then it would be an issue of *hachana*.[46] Nonetheless, if anyone might enter the room then it's permitted to make the bed on Shabbos.[47]

Q20. When beginning to learn *halacha*, should one learn Mishna Berura, Chayei Adam, or Kitzur Shulchan Aruch?

A: I am a big *chassid* of the Kitzur Shulchan Aruch. I started out learning the Kitzur Shulchan Aruch and still learn it today. The Kitzur Shulchan Aruch wrote three classic *seforim* – Lechem V'Simla on *hilchos nidda*, Kesses HaSofer on *hilchos safrus* – which the Chasam Sofer was so *nispoel* from the *sefer* that he said, "From now on I will not give *safrus kabbala* to anyone who didn't learn the Kesses HaSofer," and the Pnei Shlomo on Bava Basra. The Kitzur Shulchan Aruch is not merely a *kitzur* of the Shulchan Aruch. The Kitzur Shulchan Aruch was such a beloved *sefer*

---

[46] Shulchan Aruch OC (302:3) - מקפלים כלים בשבת לצורך שבת ללבשם בו ביום

[47] Mishna Berura (302:13) - ולכן אסור לקפל הטלית אע"פ שמצות ציצית כל היום ויכול להתעטף בו מ"מ כיון שאין בדעתו להתעטף בו אסור אם לא במקום שנהגו להתעטף בטליתות במנחה

that it was republished 18 times during his lifetime. It was made for regular people to learn *halacha* – never becoming involved in difficult *shailos*. When the matter became too complex, the Kitzur Shulchan Aruch said 'ask a chacham' as opposed to the Chayei Adam who goes through the intricacies. The Kitzur Shulchan Aruch[48] only entered discussions in *sugyos* which were practical in those times. Although making cheese and salting meat on Yom Tov[49] has become outdated, all of the *inyanim* covered were practical during those times. In the full Shulchan Aruch, *hilchos tefillin* is a full 20 *simanim*, while the Kitzur Shulchan Aruch only includes all the *halachos* in one *siman*. You don't need to know all the *halachos* of how to write the *yud* with three projections. That's not necessary for a regular person. The Chofetz Chaim said it took him many weeks to write the Mishna Berura[50] on Siman **לב** which discusses the aleph-beis in depth. Someone came to me from Salisbury, Maryland asking to become a convert. I told him there were certain laws he needed to learn to know how to be a Jew before converting. When he asked me where to find these laws, I told him to purchase an English Kitzur Shulchan Aruch from a Jewish bookstore and return to me after learning through the *halachos* if he's still interested. I never heard from him again. A convert must accept all the *mitzvos* on himself in order to be a valid convert – they don't need to know all of the *halachos*, but must be willing to fully commit to even the

---

[48] Kitzur Shulchan Aruch (98:2) - אין עושין גבינה ביום טוב ואין עושין חמאה ביום טוב. וכן אין מעידין חלב על ידי קיבה או שאר דברים שיתקבץ החלב ויקפה

[49] Kitzur Shulchan Aruch (98:23) - מותר למלוח בשר להכשירו מדמו אפילו היה אפשר למלחו מאתמול

[50] Mishna Berura Hakdama - וללמוד כל דין ודין שבשו"ע במקורו וטעמי מן הטור וב"י וכבד זה בזמננו מאד על האדם כי בעו"ה נתמעטו הלבבות וגם הטרדות נתגברו מאד אשר אם ירצה האדם בלימוד כזה לידע על נכון סי' אחד בינוני למעשה יצטרך לעמול בו כמה ימים ולפעמים כמה שבועית כמו סי' ל"ב וכדומה

most difficult *mitzvos*.[51] Being *mekarev* someone who is Jewish but not yet religious is a different story since you can guide them step-by-step, slowly accepting *kashrus*, then Shabbos, etc.

Q21. Is it *lashon hara* to write an online review about a store?

A: *Lashon hara* only applies if you write about a Yid. Also, there is no *issur lashon hara* on a *yid* who isn't *frum*[52] – "לֹא־תֵלֵךְ רָכִיל **בְּעַמֶּיךָ**" (Vayikra 19:16).[53] If the storeowner is a *frum yid,* then it's permitted if he sells inferior products. In such a case, you can tell others *l'toeles* that this storeowner sells watches which break after a couple weeks since people

---

[51] Shulchan Aruch YD (268:2) - כשבא להתגייר אומרים לו מה ראית שבאת להתגייר אי אתה יודע שישראל בזמן הזה דחופים סחופים (פי' אבודים וסחופים מן מדוע נסחף אביריך) ומטורפים ויסורים באים עליהם אם אמר יודע אני ואיני כדאי להתחבר עמהם מקבלין אותו מיד ומודיעים אותו עיקרי הדת שהוא יחוד ה' ואיסור עבודת כוכבים ומאריכין עמו בדבר זה ומודיעים אותו מקצת מצות קלות ומקצת מצות חמורות ומודיעים אותו מקצת עונשין של מצות שאומרים לו קודם שבאת למדה זו אכלת חלב אי אתה ענוש כרת חללת שבת אי אתה חייב סקילה ועכשיו אכלת חלב אתה ענוש כרת חללת שבת אתה חייב סקילה ואין מרבין עליו ואין מדקדקין עליו וכשם שמודיעים אותו ענשן של מצות כך מודיעים אותו שכרן של מצות ומודיעים אותו שבעשיית מצות אלו יזכה לחיי העוה"ב ושאין שום צדיק גמור אלא בעל החכמה שעושה מצות אלו ויודעם ואומרים לו הוי' יודע שהעולם הבא אינו צפון אלא לצדיקים והם ישראל וזה שתראה ישראל בצער בעולם הזה טובה היא צפונה להם שאינם יכולים לקבל רוב טובה בעוה"ז כעובדי כוכבים שמא ירום לבם ויתעו ויפסידו שכר עולם הבא ואין הקב"ה מביא עליהם רוב פורענות כדי שלא יאבדו אלא כל העובדי כוכבים כלים והם עומדים ומאריכין בדבר זה כדי לחבבן אם קבל מלין אותו מיד וממתינים לו עד שיתרפא רפואה שלימה ואח"ך מטבילין אותו טבילה הוגנת בלא חציצה

[52] Chofetz Chaim Lashon Hara (8:13) - כָּל אִישׁ יִשְׂרָאֵל מְצֻוֶּה שֶׁלֹּא לְקַבֵּל לָשׁוֹן הָרָע עַל שׁוּם אָדָם מִיִּשְׂרָאֵל חוּץ מֵעַל אֶפִּיקוֹרְסִים וּמַלְשִׁינִים וְכַיּוֹצֵא בְּאֵלּוּ אוֹתָם שֶׁיָּצְאוּ מִכְּלַל עֲמִיתְךָ

[53] Vayikra (19:16) - לֹא־תֵלֵךְ רָכִיל בְּעַמֶּיךָ לֹא תַעֲמֹד עַל־דַּם רֵעֶךָ אֲנִי ה

expect their watches to last longer.[54] On the other hand, if the storeowner sells something which most people don't buy, like he's an elephant salesman, then you may not write poor reviews about the store since it's not a *to'eles* for anyone.

Q22. Does pasteurizing wine make it *mevushal*?

A: That's a good question. For Hilchos Shabbos, it is *mevushal*.[55] However, for *stam yeinam shailos*, the Shulchan Aruch[56] says it must be *mevushal*, which the Shach writes, "It must be *mevushal* so much that some wine left via steam."[57] Rav Moshe[58] has a different understanding and explains that even though it's not cooked so much, once you

---

[54] Chofetz Chaim Rechilus (9:10) - אִם הוּא רוֹאֶה שֶׁאֶחָד רוֹצֶה לְהִכָּנֵס לַחֲנוּת לִקְנוֹת סְחוֹרָה אֵצֶל אֶחָד וְהוּא מִתְבּוֹנֵן בְּטֶבַע הָאִישׁ הַהוּא כִּי הוּא אִישׁ תָּם (הַיְנוּ שֶׁאֵינֶנּוּ חָרִיף כָּל כָּךְ לְהָבִין עַרְמוּמִיּוּת בְּנֵי אָדָם) וְהוּא מַכִּיר אֶת טֶבַע בַּעַל הַחֲנוּת הַהִיא שֶׁכָּל תְּשׁוּקָתוֹ וְחֶפְצוֹ הוּא לְהַשִּׂיג אִישׁ כָּזֶה לְרַמּוֹתוֹ אִם בִּסְחוֹרָה אוֹ בְּמִדּוֹת וּבְמִשְׁקָלוֹת אוֹ בְּמִקָּח צָרִיךְ לְסַפֵּר לוֹ אֶת עִנְיַן הַחֲנוּת הַהִיא וּלְהַזְהִירוֹ שֶׁלֹּא יִכָּנֵס בָּהּ אֲפִלּוּ אִם כְּבָר פָּסַק עִם בַּעַל הַחֲנוּת הַהִיא שֶׁיִּקְנֶה אֶצְלוֹ וְכָל שֶׁכֵּן אִם הוּא רוֹאֶה בְּפֵרוּשׁ שֶׁאֶחָד רוֹצֶה לְרַמּוֹת לַחֲבֵרוֹ בִּסְחוֹרָה (הַיְנוּ שֶׁמְּפַתֵּהוּ כִּי הִיא מִין סְחוֹרָה פְּלוֹנִית שֶׁמְּפֻרְסֶמֶת בָּעוֹלָם לְמִין חָשׁוּב וְהוּא יוֹדֵעַ שֶׁהוּא שֶׁקֶר) אוֹ בְּמִדּוֹת וּבְמִשְׁקָלוֹת אוֹ בְּשִׁוּוּי הַמִּקָּח בְּוַדַּאי צָרִיךְ לוֹמַר לוֹ כְּדֵי שֶׁלֹּא יָבוֹא לָזֶה אַךְ מְאֹד צָרִיךְ לִזָּהֵר שֶׁלֹּא יֶחְסְרוּ בָּזֶה הַפְּרָטִים הַנַּ"ל בְּסָעִיף ב

[55] Mishna Berura (318:19) - כתבו האחרונים עצה המובחרת מזה דהיינו שיתקן העסענס מע"ש לגמרי שלא יצטרך לערות לתוכו עוד רותחין למחר בשבת ולמחר כשיצטרך לשתות יתן העסענס הצונן לתוך הכוס ששותה בו אחר שעירו המים חמין לתוכו ונעשה כ"ש וה"ה שמותר לתת לתוך הכוס הזה שהוא כ"ש חלב שנצטנן אבל אסור לערות עליהם מכ"ר

[56] Shulchan Aruch YD (123:3) - יין מבושל שלנו שנגע בו העובד כוכבים מותר ומאימתי נקרא מבושל משהרתיחו על גבי האש

[57] Shach YD (123:7) - דהיינו שיתמעט ממדתו על ידי רתיחה

[58] Igros Moshe YD (2:52) - ומדת החום לענין להתחשב יין מבושל פשוט שהוא ביד סולדת אף שלא מעלה רתיחות דיד סולדת הוא בחשיבות בשול לכל הדינים בדבר לחה ומה שכתב הש"ך סימן קכ"ג סק"ז דהיינו שיתמעט ממדתו ע"י רתיחה פשוט שביד סולדת כבר נתמעט משהו והוא בערך קע"ה מעלות לחומרא

see steam leaving the wine then evidently some wine has left and it is considered *bishul*. It doesn't even need to be *yad soledes bo* – only hot enough that steam emerges from the wine. On the other hand, the Tzelemer Rav required the wine to appear to lose some wine from the boiling process. Nonetheless, everyone holds you must have steam emerge from the wine in order to make it *mevushal*. However, pasteurizing is in an enclosed system and doesn't allow for steam to emerge unless there is a valve installed to allow steam to leave.

Q23. Should one have beer and chickpeas at a Shalom Zachor?

A: It doesn't say to have beer, but it does say to have chickpeas.[59] Nonetheless, it seems regular peas would be more mehudar than chickpeas. Why? There are two reasons for a Shalom Zachor mentioned in the Shulchan Aruch. One is that the Ribbono Shel Olam says, "Before we make a bris, I want to first introduce you to the Shabbos Malchusa.[60]

---

[59] Zichron Yaakov (1:22) by Rav Yaakov Lifshitz - ליל שב"ק של לפני הברית מילה היה נקרא "שלום זכר" ושמש בית התפלה של הבעל ברית היה מכריז "פלוני מזמין את הצבור על שלום זכר" ומקורבי הבעל ברית היו נאספים אחר סעודת ליל שב"ק וכבדו אותם בגריסין פולים וקטניות מבושלים ובמשקה שכר אצל העשירים והאמידים והעניים במשקה עליו גם מפל-שכר הנקרא קוואס שהיה ג"כ כחמר מדינה אצל העניים עד שעשו הבדלה וקראו קריאת שמע לפני היולדת ומחר בבקר היה נקרא "בן זכר" ועשו מז"ט אצל הבעל ברית ביי"ש ומגדנות ורק בימים האחרונים שהתגברה ר"ל העניות והתגדל המכס שהוטל על יי"ש עשו הרה"ג תקנות בכמה ערים שעל הבן זכר אסור לטעום מאומה כ"א רק להקרובים עד שני בשני והיו כל המקורבים באים בשב"ק אחר התפלה לברך "ברכת מז"ט" מבלי טעום מאומה ולאט לאט נתפשט המנהג הזה ברוב גלילות ארצנו

[60] Taz YD (265:13) - וראיתי סמך אחד לזה ממדרש רבות פרשת אמור פרשה כ"ז ר' לוי אמר משל למלך שגזר ואמר כל אכסנאין שיש כאן לא יראו פני עד שיראו פני המטרונא תחילה כך אמר הקב"ה לא תביאו לפני קרבן עד שתעבור עליו שבת שאין ז' ימים בלא שבת ואין מילה בלא שבת עכ"ל

Once you understand the beauty of a *ruchniyus* Shabbos, then you can begin to appreciate the *bris* you're about to make with Hashem." We make a *seuda* with others so we can all appreciate the Shabbos Queen. According to this opinion, you only need something to make Shabbos nicer. The second opinion is a *din* of comforting a mourner since the baby lost all of his Torah learned in the womb.[61] Therefore, the chickpeas are an *inyan* of *aveilus*, as the first *seuda* given to a mourner *rachmana litzlan* is an egg,[62] which reminds us people don't live forever.[63] The world is a cycle of a generation leaving and generation entering. However, out of all the peas, chickpeas seem to be the least round. A regular green pea would seem to be better, but the *minhag* is to have chickpeas. Beer doesn't seem to be mentioned anywhere. The third reason for a Shalom Zachor, which I believe to be the main reason, is a Tosafos[64] in Bava Kamma[65] mentioning the "Yeshua HaBen" *seuda* for the mother and child for surviving the dangers of childbirth. If the child is not OK, then you don't make a Shalom Zachor until he gets better. Therefore, this *seuda* is a form of a *seudas hoda'ah*, which takes place on Shabbos for the

---

[61] Taz YD (265:13) - ובדרישה הביא מתשובת מהר"ר מנחם מה שנוהגים בשבת לבקר אצל התינוק הנולד שהוא אבל על תורתו ששכח

[62] Shulchan Aruch YD (378:9) - מקום שנהגו להברות בבשר ויין ומיני מטעמים עושים ומברין תחילה בבצים או בתבשיל של עדשים זכר לאבילות ואח"כ אוכלים כל צרכם

[63] Rashi Bereishis (25:30) - וּבִשֵּׁל יַעֲקֹב עֲדָשִׁים לְהַבְרוֹת אֶת הָאָבֵל וְלָמָּה עֲדָשִׁים שֶׁדּוֹמוֹת לְגַלְגַּל שֶׁהָאֲבֵלוּת גַּלְגַּל הַחוֹזֵר בָּעוֹלָם (וְעוֹד מָה עֲדָשִׁים אֵין לָהֶם פֶּה כָּךְ הָאָבֵל אֵין לוֹ פֶּה שֶׁאָסוּר לְדַבֵּר וּלְפִיכָךְ הַמִּנְהָג לְהַבְרוֹת הָאָבֵל בִּתְחִלַּת מַאֲכָלוֹ בֵּיצִים שֶׁהֵם עֲגֻלִּים וְאֵין לָהֶם פֶּה כָּךְ אָבֵל כָּל שְׁלֹשָׁה יָמִים הָרִאשׁוֹנִים אֵינוֹ מֵשִׁיב שָׁלוֹם לְכָל אָדָם וְכָ"שֶׁ שֶׁאֵינוֹ שׁוֹאֵל בַּתְּחִלָּה מִג' וְעַד ז' מֵשִׁיב וְאֵינוֹ שׁוֹאֵל וְכוּ

[64] Tosafos Bava Kamma (80a) - לבי ישוע הבן - פ"ה פדיון הבן וכן הערוך וקשה דאע"ג דמתרגמינן פדיון פורקן מ"מ אין שייך לשון ישועה ור"ת פי' שנולד שם בן ועל שם שהולד נושע ונמלט ממעי אמו כדכתיב והמליטה זכר נקט לשון ישועה והיו רגילין לעשות סעודה

[65] Bava Kamma (80a) - רב ושמואל ורב אסי איקלעו לבי שבוע הבן ואמרי לה לבי ישוע הבן

reasons we discussed by the Shach and Taz. As for beer, Rav Moshe[66] writes that any beverage you can refuse on the grounds that you are not thirsty is not considered a *chamar medina*. When someone offers you a small glass of whiskey, he's offering it as a social drink for you – not to quench your thirst. In Europe, they would be *yotzei* with tea and coffee as a social drink.[67] About a year ago, I visited the Rav of Paris in France. He asked to honor us with tea and coffee, and had small cups brought out for us to drink. Then I realized why tea and coffee were considered *chamar medina*. These cups were too small to quench your thirst. Their small size was solely for social reasons.

Q24. Why do we have the Shalom Zachor on Shabbos night instead of Shabbos day?

A: We want to perform the mitzva as early as possible.[68]

---

[66] Igros Moshe OC (2:75) - וחשיבות משקה הוא שאין השתיה מחמת שצריכים להם לצמאם אלא שותים אותם אף בלא צורך לגופם אלא בשביל כבוד הסעודה וכבוד האורחים, דאין שום אדם שותה יין וײ"ש ושכר לצמאו דע"ז שותין מים שיותר עדיפי אלא רק לכבוד בעלמא שותין אותן ואלו המינים נקראים בשם משקה וחמר מדינה

[67] Aruch HaShulchan OC (272:14) - אבל הבדלה שקשה לשתות אז יי"ש בהכרח לעשות על איזה משקה וחלב הוי משקה וטיי מתוק גם כן שותים הרבה דבאמת כשנדקדק אין אצלינו חמר מדינה כלל זולת יי"ש דרוב בעלי בתים במדינתינו אין שותים בחול לא יין ולא שכר לכל סעודה ומה שייך לקרותם חמר מדינה

[68] Pesachim (4a) - זריזין מקדימין למצות

Chapter 4: Shonim Tammuz 5777

Q1. Why isn't wearing *techeiles* more widespread if there is a *mitzvah* to wear it?[1]

A: If we knew what *techeiles* was nowadays, it would certainly more widespread. However, we don't know what *techeiles* is today. There have been many attempts to figure out what it is, but it doesn't seem that anyone knows with certainty what *techeiles* is. Therefore, it's forbidden to wear *techeiles* when you don't know if it's the real one. We see that in Shema[2] by אֲנִי ה' אֱלֹקיכֶם – Rashi[3] writes "I am the One who knows the difference between people who are a *bechor* and not a *bechor*, and am the One Who will punish those who say they found *techeiles* when it's not truly *techeiles*."

Q2. If someone puts on *techeiles* saying they aren't sure if it's truly *techeiles*, is there a problem with that?

A: Chazal[4] write that if a *talmid chacham* says a curse on condition, then the bad thing will still happen to you because the *chacham's* words are still fulfilled – like if he says, "Give me $200 or something bad will happen to you," and you give him the money, the curse may still happen to you. Therefore, when Chazal say, "Hashem will punish those who say something is *techeiles* when it's not",[5] their words will also

---

[1] Bamidbar (15:38) - דַּבֵּר אֶל־בְּנֵי יִשְׂרָאֵל וְאָמַרְתָּ אֲלֵהֶם וְעָשׂוּ לָהֶם צִיצִת עַל־כַּנְפֵי בִגְדֵיהֶם לְדֹרֹתָם וְנָתְנוּ עַל־צִיצִת הַכָּנָף פְּתִיל תְּכֵלֶת

[2] Bamidbar (15:41) - אֲנִי ה' אֱלֹקיכֶם אֲשֶׁר הוֹצֵאתִי אֶתְכֶם מֵאֶרֶץ מִצְרַיִם לִהְיוֹת לָכֶם לֵאלֹהִים אֲנִי ה' אֱלֹקיכֶם

[3] Rashi Bamidbar (15:41) - אֲנִי הוּא שֶׁהִבְחַנְתִּי בְּמִצְרַיִם בֵּין טִפָּה שֶׁל בְּכוֹר לְשֶׁאֵינָהּ שֶׁל בְּכוֹר, אֲנִי הוּא עָתִיד לְהַבְחִין וְלִפָּרַע מִן הַתּוֹלֶה קָלָא אִילָן בְּבִגְדוֹ וְאוֹמֵר תְּכֵלֶת הִיא

[4] Makkos (11a) - א"ר אבהו קללת חכם אפילו על תנאי היא באה

[5] Bava Metzia (61b) - אמר הקב"ה אני הוא שהבחנתי במצרים בין טפה של בכור לטפה שאינה של בכור אני הוא שעתיד ליפרע ממי שתולה מעותיו בנכרי ומלוה אותם לישראל ברבית וממי שטומן משקלותיו במלח וממי שתולה קלא אילן בבגדו ואומר תכלת הוא

apply even if the individual knows it's not necessarily *techeiles*. On the other hand, if you know with certainty that this particular *techeiles* is the real one, then there's no curse from the *talmid chacham*. There will come a time when we realize what *techeiles* truly is since it wasn't *nignaz* forever. It's not *pashut* that what they found today is *techeiles* since the Gemara[6] says the color from the creature which produces the *techeiles* must be squeezed out in order to obtain the color. The Gemara continues to say the Chachamim allowed squeezing out the color on Shabbos despite the creature dying because you don't want *netilas neshama* from the creature, rather you only wanted the ink.[7] On the other hand, Rav Yehuda says you're obligated on Shabbos for both *netilas neshama* and trapping. What kind of trapping applies to such a snail? The Gemara Beitza[8] says if you can take the animal in one swoop, then it's not trapped.[9] Snails are already ניצודין ועומדין, so they're not *shayach* to tzeida.[10] Therefore, I would think *techeiles* isn't from a snail. There is a snail which propels itself by blowing bubbles and travels along the waves, but I spoke to the individual behind the

---

[6] Shabbos (75a) - תנו רבנן הצד חלזון והפוצעו אינו חייב אלא אחת רבי יהודה אומר חייב שתים שהיה רבי יהודה אומר פציעה בכלל דישה אמרו לו אין פציעה בכלל דישה אמר רבא מאי טעמא דרבנן קסברי אין דישה אלא לגדולי קרקע וליחייב נמי משום נטילת נשמה אמר רבי יוחנן שפצעו מת

[7] Shabbos (75a) - וליחייב נמי משום נטילת נשמה אמר רבי יוחנן שפצעו מת רבא אמר אפילו תימא שפצעו חי מתעסק הוא אצל נטילת נשמה והא אביי ורבא דאמרי תרווייהו מודה רבי שמעון בפסיק רישא ולא ימות שאני הכא דכמה דאית ביה נשמה טפי ניחא ליה כי היכי דליציל ציבעיה

[8] Beitza (24a) - אמר רב אשי כל היכא דרהיט אבתרה ומטי לה בחד שחיא ביבר קטן ואידך ביבר גדול

[9] Mishna Berura (316:7) - דהני דרכן להשמט כשמרגישין יד אדם וע"כ כשצדו הוי צידה ממש משא"כ בחיגר ודכוותיה שאין יכולין להשמט ואפילו אם החיגר יכול להלך קצת עכ"פ הרי יכול להגיעו בשחיה אחת ע"כ חשיבי כניצודין ועומדין

[10] Shulchan Aruch OC (497:5) - אם סכר אמת המים בכניסה וביציאה מערב יום טוב מותר ליקח ממנה דגים ביום טוב דהוה ליה ניצודין ועומדין (מאחר שאמת המים היא צרה ואינן יכולים להשמט)

techeiles movement and he told me this particular snail isn't used since it doesn't have any color in it. Instead, we wear *zecher l'techeiles* along our *talleisim* as the stripes used to be blue[11] but started to be produced black since they couldn't find a blue which didn't fade. Moreover, I don't think Rav Elyashiv, Rav Aryeh Leib Shteinemann, or other Gedolim wore *techeiles*, so why should we think we should be *frummer* than them?

Q3. Should one purchase a *tallis* with blue stripes, instead of black stripes, which were done as a *zecher l'techeiles*?

A: You can buy the blue striped *talleisim* if it makes you happy, but you don't have to be stringent.[12] There are still old *talleisim* around which have blue stripes, but you don't need to be stringent for that.

Q4. Is it permitted to work for money you don't currently need if you could instead be learning during that time?

A: You are allowed to work even if you don't need the money right now. It's not a *middas chassidus* to stop working in order to learn since you never know when you're going to need money. Not only that, but the Shulchan Aruch says in Shabbos that you may not go on a boat which will depart on the ocean three days before Shabbos.[13] However,

---

[11] Mishna Berura (9:16) - אף בבגדים צבועים - מ"מ ראוי למדקדק לעשות דוקא ד' כנפות או ט"ק לבן כדי שיהיה יצא ידי הכל כשיעשה הציצית לבנים גם משום דכתיב ולבושיה כתלג חיור ומה ששפת הבגד כעין תכלת בטליתות שלנו בתר עיקר הבגד אזלינן

[12] Mishna Berura (9:16)

[13] Shulchan Aruch OC (248:2) - הא דאין מפליגין בספינה בפחות משלש ימים קודם השבת הטעם משום עונג שבת שכל שלשה ימים הראשונים יש להם צער ובלבול ודוקא למפליגים במים המלוחים אבל בנהרות אין שום צער למפליגים בהם ולפיכך מותר להפליג בהם אפילו בערב שבת והוא שלא יהא ידוע לנו שאין בעומקם עשרה טפחים אבל

the Rema says leaving for a *dvar mitzvah* is permitted even before Shabbos – which includes *parnasa*.[14] If a person doesn't have money to pay for food, then he'll die and won't be able to thank Hashem or will need to rely on *tzedakah* which isn't good either. Also, the Torah[15] says שֵׁשֶׁת יָמִים תַּעֲבֹד you should work for six days. The Shach[16] writes you should have some money on the side to pay for emergency situations. There's no problem with being rich as Chazal didn't say having a lot of money is a problem.[17] However, if

---

במקום שידוע לנו שמקרקע הספינ' לקרקע הנהר פחות מעשר' טפחים אסור (לצאת חוץ לתחום) משום איסור תחומין. הגה וכן בספינה שיצטרך הישראל לבא לידי מלאכה בשבת אסור ליכנס בה שלשה ימים קודם השבת אפי' הם נהרות הנובעים והוא למעלה מעשרה

[14] Shulchan Aruch OC (248:1) - מותר להפליג בספינה אפילו בערב שבת אם הולך לדבר מצוה ופוסק עמו שישבות ואם אחר כך לא ישבות אין בכך כלום אבל לדבר הרשות אין מפליגין בספינה בפחות מג' ימים קודם השבת: הגה אבל קודם שלשה ימים שרי אפי' בספינה שמושכין אותו ע"י בהמות אפי' אין בגובה המים י' טפחים

[15] Shemos (20:9) - שֵׁשֶׁת יָמִים תַּעֲבֹד וְעָשִׂיתָ כָּל־מְלַאכְתֶּךָ

[16] See Bava Metzia (42a) - וא"ר יצחק לעולם יהא כספו של אדם מצוי בידו שנאמר וצרת הכסף בידך וא"ר יצחק לעולם ישליש אדם את מעותיו שליש בקרקע ושליש בפרקמטיא ושליש תחת ידו and Igros Moshe OC (2:111) - ולכן כיון שהשי"ת נתן דעה בדורות האחרונים שיהיה עסק זה של אינשורענס בעולם שהוא השארה לזקנותו ולירושה בדרך טבעי, הוא דבר טוב וראוי גם לאנשים כשרים יראי השי"ת ובוטחים רק על השי"ת שהוא הנותן עצה למיקני נכסין, דגם מי שקונה אינשורענס הוא נמי עצת השי"ת למיקני אינשורענס ובוטח על השי"ת שיוכל לשלם בהגיע הזמן בכל שנה וזהו הבטחון שאנו מחוייבין

[17] cf. Avos (2:7) - הוּא הָיָה אוֹמֵר מַרְבֶּה בָשָׂר מַרְבֶּה רִמָּה מַרְבֶּה נְכָסִים מַרְבֶּה דְאָגָה and Rav Bartenura - שֶׁמָּא יְגַזְּלוּהוּ מִבֵּית הַמֶּלֶךְ אוֹ שֶׁמָּא יָבֹאוּ עָלָיו לִסְטִים וְיַהַרְגוּהוּ וְחָסִיד אֶחָד הָיָה מִתְפַּלֵּל הַמָּקוֹם יַצִּילֵנִי מִפִּזּוּר הַנֶּפֶשׁ וְשָׁאֲלוּ מִמֶּנּוּ מַהוּ פִּזּוּר הַנֶּפֶשׁ אָמַר לָהֶם שֶׁיִּהְיוּ לוֹ נְכָסִים מְרֻבִּים מְפֻזָּרִים בִּמְקוֹמוֹת הַרְבֵּה וְצָרִיךְ לְפַזֵּר נַפְשׁוֹ לַחְשֹׁב לְכָאן וּלְכָאן

you don't learn despite making so much money, the Gemara[18] says Hashem will consider it a claim against you.

Q5. If you have enough money now, should you learn or continue working?

A: If you have the head to learn, then you should learn. However, if you don't have the head to learn then *l'chatchila* it's better to work and give at least a part of the money to *tzedakah*. However, if your work requires even a small amount of intelligence, the same Ribbono Shel Olam who gave you the intelligence to be successful at your work will give you intelligence to be able to learn.[19]

Q6. What *beracha* does one make on a deli roll or potato knish if you're *kove'ah seuda* on them?

---

[18] Yoma (35b) - ת"ר עני ועשיר ורשע באין לדין...עשיר אומרים לו מפני מה לא עסקת בתורה אם אומר עשיר הייתי וטרוד הייתי בנכסי אומרים לו כלום עשיר היית יותר מרבי אלעזר אמרו עליו על רבי אלעזר בן חרסום שהניח לו אביו אלף עיירות ביבשה וכנגדן אלף ספינות בים ובכל יום ויום נוטל נאד של קמח על כתיפו ומהלך מעיר לעיר וממדינה למדינה ללמוד תורה

[19] Midrash Tanchuma Vayeilech (2) - אָמַר אֵלִיָּהוּ זִכְרוֹנוֹ לִבְרָכָה, פַּעַם אַחַת הָיִיתִי מְהַלֵּךְ בַּדֶּרֶךְ וּמָצָאתִי אָדָם אֶחָד, וְהָיָה מַלְעִיג לִי וּמִתְלוֹצֵץ בִּי. אָמַרְתִּי לוֹ, מָה אַתָּה מֵשִׁיב לְיוֹם הַדִּין אַחַר שֶׁלֹּא לָמַדְתָּ תּוֹרָה. אָמַר, יֵשׁ לִי לְהָשִׁיב, בִּינָה וָדַעַת וָלֵב שֶׁלֹּא נִתְּנוּ לִי מִן הַשָּׁמַיִם. אָמַרְתִּי לוֹ, מַה מְּלַאכְתֶּךָ. אָמַר לִי, צַיָּד עוֹפוֹת וְדָגִים אֲנִי. אָמַרְתִּי לוֹ, מִי נָתַן לְךָ דַּעַת וָלֵב לִיקַּח פִּשְׁתָּן וְלִטְווֹתוֹ וְלְאָרְגוֹ וְלַעֲשׂוֹת הַמְּצוּדוֹת וְלָקַחַת בָּהֶן דָּגִים וְעוֹפוֹת וּלְמָכְרָם. אָמַר לִי, בִּינָה וָדַעַת שֶׁנִּתְּנוּ לִי מִן הַשָּׁמַיִם. אָמַרְתִּי לוֹ, לִיקַּח אֶת הַפִּשְׁתָּן לֶאֱרֹג וְלִטְווֹת וְלָקַחַת הַדָּגִים וְהָעוֹפוֹת, נָתְנוּ לְךָ בִּינָה וָדַעַת. אֲבָל לִקְנוֹת אֶת הַתּוֹרָה לֹא נָתְנוּ לְךָ בִּינָה. וּכְתִיב: כִּי קָרוֹב אֵלֶיךָ הַדָּבָר מְאֹד בְּפִיךָ וּבִלְבָבְךָ לַעֲשׂוֹתוֹ (דברים ל, יד). מִיָּד הִרְהֵר בְּלִבּוֹ וְהֵרִים קוֹלוֹ בִּבְכִי. אָמַרְתִּי לוֹ, בְּנִי, אַל יֵרַע לְךָ, שֶׁכָּל בָּאֵי הָעוֹלָם כֵּיוָן שֶׁבָּאִין וְנִמְשָׁכִין מִן הַתּוֹרָה, מוֹכִיחִין עֲלֵיהֶם, שֶׁנֶּאֱמַר: וּבֹשׁוּ עוֹבְדֵי פִשְׁתִּים שְׂרִיקוֹת וְאֹרְגִים חוֹרָי (ישעיה יט, ט), וְעָלָיו וְעַל כַּיּוֹצֵא בוֹ וְעַל הַדּוֹמִין לוֹ וְעַל הָעוֹשִׂין כְּמַעֲשָׂיו. וְאַחֲרִית דָּבָר, יִרְאַת ה'. וְעוֹשִׂין בֶּאֱמוּנָה, בּוֹ מוֹנֶה מְלַאכְתּוֹ וְרָאוּי לְחַיֵּי הָעוֹלָם הַבָּא

A: A deli roll and potato knish are both made from the five grains, so you make a *mezonos* if you eat them as a snack since both the deli roll and the potato knish are baked together with either the meat or the potatoes. If you are *kove'ah seuda* on them, then you say *homotzi* on them.[20] Puff pastry, like any baked *pas haba b'kisnin*, become *hamotzi* when *kove'ah seuda* on them. On the other hand, donuts are cooked in oil – not baked – and cannot be *kove'ah seuda.*[21] The *shiur* of being *kove'ah seuda* on the *pas haba b'kisnin* is the amount of *mezonos* normally set aside as a meal.

Q7. What should the *beracha* be on a granola bar?

A: The *beracha rishona* is *mezonos* and the *beracha achrona* is *al hamichya.*[22]

---

[20] Shulchan Aruch OC (168:6) - פת הבאה בכיסנין מברך עליו בורא מיני מזונות ולאחריו ברכה מעין שלש ואם אכל ממנו שיעור שאחרים רגילים לקבוע עליו אע"פ שהוא לא שבע ממנו מברך עליו המוציא וברכת המזון ואם מתחלה היה בדעתו לאכול ממנו מעט וברך בורא מיני מזונות ואחר כך אכל שיעור שאחרי' קובעי' עליו יברך עליו ברכת המזון אע"פ שלא ברך המוציא תחלה ואם אכל שיעור שאחרים אין קובעים עליו אע"פ שהוא קובע עליו אינו מברך אלא בורא מיני מזונות וברכה אחת מעין שלשה דבטלה דעתו אצל כל אדם

[21] Mishna Berura (168:38) - וכתבו הפוסקים דאותן שקורין בפראג וואלאפלאטקע"ס שנעשין ג"כ בלילתן רכה אך מפני שמתפשטין באפייתן נעשים דקין וקלושים הרבה יותר מאותן נאלסילקע"ס שנזכר לעיל אין לברך עליהם המוציא אפילו בדקבע דאין ע"ז תורת לחם כלל ודמיא לטריתא בסט"ו

[22] Shulchan Aruch OC (208:2) - חמשת מיני דגן ששלקן או כתשן ועשה מהם תבשיל כגון מעשה קדירה הריפות וגרש כרמל ודייסא אפילו עירב עמהם דבש הרבה יות' מהם או מינים אחרי' הרבה יות' מהם מברך עליו בורא מיני מזונות ולבסוף על המחיה

Q8. How far must one travel in order to be obligated in *tefillas haderech*[23]?

A: One must travel at least a *mehalech parsa*, which is a *shailah* if it's time or distance.[24] There are 4 mil in a *parsa*, and a mil is $\frac{7}{10}$ of a mile, so a *parsa* is about 2.8 miles. On the other hand, a *parsa* could be a distance of travel of 72 minutes – which traveling at 60 mph would be 72 miles. However, the 2.8 miles must be beyond the uninhabited region outside the city.[25] Therefore, if you are going to travel such a distance on a trip, you may say *tefillas haderech* even while still in the city limits. My Rosh Yeshiva in Lakewood is reported to have said *tefillas haderech* when he would reach County Line road. Although that is probably true, that has no bearing on when you should say *tefillas haderech* today since north of County Line Road, Route 9 used to be miles of fields. There was absolutely nothing there, but now the entire area is built up the entire way. In fact, there's a cemetery by Beis Feiga. Why would they put a cemetery in the middle of the city? They didn't – that part of Lakewood was originally the outskirts of the city. As Lakewood grew beyond County Line Road, the city grew past the cemetery.

Q9. When should you say *tefillas haderech* on an airplane?

A: There is a special *tefillas haderech* written for those traveling on planes. Who wrote such a *tefillah*? I don't think

---

[23] Shulchan Aruch OC (110:4) - היוצא לדרך יתפלל יהר"מ ה' אלהינו ואלהי אבותינו שתוליכנו לשלום וכו' וצריך לאומרה בלשון רבים ואם אפשר יעמוד מלילך כשיאמרנה ואם היה רוכב א"צ לירד

[24] Shulchan Aruch OC (110:7) - אומר אותה אחר שהחזיק בדרך ואין לאומרה אלא אם כן יש לו לילך פרסה אבל פחות מפרסה לא יחתום בברוך

[25] Mishna Berura (110:29) - ר"ל שלא יאמרנה כשעדיין הוא בתוך העיר שדר בה אף שמכין עצמו לצאת לדרך ועיבורה של עיר דהיינו שבעים אמה ומעט יותר סמוך לעיר לאחר שכבר כלו כל הבתים הרי הוא כתוך העיר

they had airplanes in the times of the Anshei Knesses Hagedola. Someone in the 1900s must have written it. Therefore, we don't know if the *tefillah* has any significance or not. On the other hand, the Rogatchover writes you should not say *tefillas haderech* while on the airplane since the Gemara[26] says דרך נשר בשמים isn't called a *derech* for people. Flying isn't called a *derech* for *tefillas haderech*, so we're *choshesh* for the Rogatchover and say the *tefillas haderech* on the way to the airport assuming it's out of the city. However, if you're in a place like Chicago where the airport is in the midst of the city, then the best time to say *tefillas haderech* is while you're on the plane taxiing onto the runway. Before the plane takes off, then you can say *tefillas haderech* even according to the Rogatchover. I think Interstate 695 is considered built up the whole way on both sides.

Q10. What should one do if he is in doubt whether he is obligated in *tefillas haderech*?

A: You should call your Rav and ask. If you don't have a phone with you, then we're lenient with a *safek berachos* and don't make the *beracha*.[27]

Q11. What is an appropriate hobby for a *bochur*?

A: A *bochur* should study the stars. The Rambam in Hilchos Kiddush HaChodesh[28] shows his intricate knowledge of the constellations of the stars. Also, observing the heavens allows you to better understand the moon which orbits the

---

[26] Chullin (139b) - אלא מעתה מצא קן בשמים דכתיב (משלי ל:יט) דרך נשר בשמים הכי נמי דמיחייב בשילוח הקן דרך נשר איקרי דרך סתמא לא איקרי

[27] Rema OC (210:2) - ספק ברכות להקל

[28] Rambam Kiddush HaChodesh (1:6) - בֵּית דִּין מְחַשְּׁבִין בְּחֶשְׁבּוֹנוֹת כְּדֶרֶךְ שֶׁמְּחַשְּׁבִים הָאִיצְטַגְנִינִים שֶׁיּוֹדְעִין מְקוֹמוֹת הַכּוֹכָבִים וּמַהֲלָכָם וְחוֹקְרִים וּמְדַקְדְּקִים עַד שֶׁיֵּדְעוּ אִם אֶפְשָׁר שֶׁיֵּרָאֶה הַיָּרֵחַ בִּזְמַנּוֹ שֶׁהוּא לֵיל שְׁלֹשִׁים אוֹ אִי אֶפְשָׁר

earth every 27 days. Why do we have a new moon every 29 or 30 days then? Even though it only takes 27 days, since the earth also revolves around the sun, the moon needs 29 days to circle around the earth to show its waxing and waning based on the sun. There's not too much of a *nafka minah* unless you need to say Kiddush Levana while on a satellite. If you're on the moon, then I don't think you can say Kiddush Levana. Also, this helps with knowing when to *daven* Shacharis, Mincha, and keeping Shabbos while on the space station. Another helpful hobby is studying botany. For instance, there are many questions about *orlah* – as papaya only gives its fruit for two years – which require an intricate practical knowledge of botany.[29] If animals did not exist, then one-third of the Shulchan Aruch wouldn't exist: *tzitzis* are from wool,[30] *tefillin* are from animal hide[31] as well as Sifrei Torah,[32] so none of that would exist. Many parts of Hilchos Shabbos are what you can and cannot do for your animals. *Basar b'cholov* and *melicha* are filled with *beheimos*, and much of *ta'aruvos* deals with animals. If you don't know anything about *beheimos*, then it's a sad story.

---

[29] Shulchan Aruch YD (294:1) - הנוטע עץ מאכל מונה לו ג' שנים מעת נטיעתו וכל הפירות שיהיו בו בתוך ג' שנים אסורין בהנאה לעולם בין עיקר הפרי בין הגרעינים בין הקליפות כגון קליפי אגוזים ורמונים והנץ שלהם והזגין והגרעינין של ענבים והתמד העשוי מהם והפגים והתמרים שאינם מתבשלים והענבים שלקו ואין נגמרים בבישולן כולם חייבים בערלה ופטורים מרבעי

[30] Shulchan Aruch OC (9:1) - אין חייב בציצית מן התורה אלא בגד פשתים או של צמר רחלים

[31] Shulchan Aruch OC (32:12) - יהיה הקלף מעור בהמה חיה ועוף הטהורים אפילו מנבלה וטריפה שלהם אבל לא מעור בהמה וחיה ועוף הטמאים דכתיב למען תהיה תורת ה' בפיך ממין המותר לפיך ולא מעור דג אפילו הוא טהור משום דנפיש זוהמיה

[32] Shulchan Aruch YD (271:1) - אין כותבין ספר תורה על עור בהמה חיה ועוף הטמאים ולא על עור דג אפי' טהור אבל כותבין על עור בהמה חיה ועוף הטהורים ואפי' עור נבילות וטריפות שלהן וצריך שיהו העורות מעובדין על ידי ישראל לשם ס"ת שיאמר בתחילת העיבוד כשמשים אותם לתוך הסיד עורות אלו אני מעבד לשם ספר תורה

The Shulchan Aruch[33] discusses finding milk in the stomach of a cow. Why would the Shulchan Aruch bring such a ridiculous case? Would the Shulchan Aruch discuss a question like an animal swallowing a television set, whether the television retains its *tumah* after it's excreted? (Which it doesn't) If you know that milk was really created for cows to drink, then you would understand many seemingly obscure cases of the Shulchan Aruch.

Q12. Is there an obligation for a person to check his *tefillin*?

A: Every day while you wear your *tefillin* for Shacharis, you check your *tefillin* by לטוטפות בין עיניך, פותח את ידך, and other places in *davening* where you check to ensure your *tefillin* are in the right place.[34] There's another *halacha* of checking your *tefillin* with a *sofer* to ensure everything is *b'seder*. *M'ikar hadin* you are not obligated to check *tefillin* ever.[35] The Shulchan Aruch[36] only writes the requirement of checking *mezuzos* twice in seven years, but checking *tefillin* isn't clearly said anywhere. *Mezuzos* are open and prone to being affected by the elements, sunshine, or insects. On the

---

[33] Shulchan Aruch YD (87:9) - חלב הנמצא בקיבה אינו חלב ומותר לבשל בו בשר אפילו בצלול שבה ויש מי שאוסר (וכן נוהגין) and Shulchan Aruch YD (87:10) - חלב הנמצא בקיבה (לכתחלה אין להניחו בקיבה עד שיצטנן החלב בתוך הקיבה אבל בדיעבד אין לחוש עד שנמלח בקיבתה או שעמד בו יום אחד (ואז) אסור להעמיד בו

[34] Shulchan Aruch OC (28:1) - חייב אדם למשמש בתפילין בכל שעה שלא יסיח דעתו מהם וימשמש בשל יד תחל' וכשיאמר וקשרתם לאות על ידך ימשמש בשל יד וכשיאמר והיו לטוטפות בין עיניך ימשמש בשל ראש

[35] Kitzur Shulchan Aruch (10:26) - תְּפִלִּין שֶׁהֻחְזְקוּ בְּכַשְׁרוּת מִן הַדִּין כָּל זְמַן שֶׁהַבַּיִת שָׁלֵם גַּם הַפָּרָשִׁיּוֹת הֲרֵי הֵן בְּחֶזְקָתָן וְאֵינָן צְרִיכִין בְּדִיקָה וּמִכָּל מָקוֹם נָכוֹן לְבָדְקָן מִפְּנֵי שֶׁלִּפְעָמִים מִתְקַלְקְלִין מִן הַזֵּעָה וְאִם אֵינוֹ מֵנִיחַ אוֹתָן אֶלָּא לִפְרָקִים צְרִיכִין בְּדִיקָה שְׁתֵּי פְּעָמִים בְּכָל שֶׁבַע שָׁנִים כִּי יֵשׁ לָחוּשׁ שֶׁמָּא נִתְעַפְּשׁוּ

[36] Shulchan Aruch YD (271:1) - מזוזת יחיד נבדקת פעמים בשבע שנים ושל רבים פעמים ביובל

other hand, *tefillin* which are closed and worn are not affected the way *mezuzos* are – unless the *tefillin* are subject to severe climate changes like a boiling hot car or if the *tefillin* were submerged in water. The weather forecast only tells you the heat in the shade – if they say it's 95 degrees outside, that only refers to the temperature in the shade. However, it could easily be 135 or 140 degrees in the sun. Therefore, if the sun shines directly on the *tefillin* while sitting in the car, it is subject to intense heat. Nonetheless, if you keep your *tefillin* in a normal area, then it's fine. The Achronim do say to check your *tefillin* twice every seven years to make sure none of the letters crack.[37] Many *medakdek sofrim* will count the letters in each *posuk* because very often you read the next letter in your head before seeing it. Also, there are two different ways *mezuzos* and *totafos* are spelled in Shema – the first time *mezuzos* has two *vavs* and *totafos* has one,[38] and the 2nd time *totafos* has no *vav* while *mezuzos* has only one *vav*.[39] A *sofer* would count for such letters. How many *gimmels* are in a *mezuza*? Only one: וְאָסַפְתָּ דְגָנֶךָ.[40] Therefore, a *sofer* will count how many letters are in each *parsha* to catch any extra or missing letter issues.

---

[37] Aruch HaShulchan OC (39:6) - תפילין שהוחזקו בכשרות אינם צריכים בדיקה לעולם ואם אינו מניחם אלא לפרקים צריכים בדיקה פעמיים בשבוע דחיישינן שמא נרקבו והוא הדין אם באו במים צריכים בדיקה אך אם אין לו מי שיוכל אחר כך לתופרן מוטב שלא לפותחם לבדוק ויניחם כך בלא בדיקה ודע דזהו מדינא אבל בזמנינו ידוע שהדיו שלנו במשך איזה שנים נקפצים מעל הקלף ולכן האידנא נראה לי דמדינא צריכים לבדוק אותם באיזה זמן וכן יש לנהוג

[38] Devarim (11:18; 20) – וְשַׂמְתֶּם אֶת־דְּבָרַי אֵלֶּה עַל־לְבַבְכֶם וְעַל־נַפְשְׁכֶם וּקְשַׁרְתֶּם אֹתָם לְאוֹת עַל־יֶדְכֶם וְהָיוּ לְטוֹטָפֹת בֵּין עֵינֵיכֶם... וּכְתַבְתָּם עַל־מְזוּזוֹת בֵּיתֶךָ וּבִשְׁעָרֶיךָ

[39] Devarim (6:8-9) – וּקְשַׁרְתָּם לְאוֹת עַל־יָדֶךָ וְהָיוּ לְטֹטָפֹת בֵּין עֵינֶיךָ. וּכְתַבְתָּם עַל־מְזוּזֹת בֵּיתֶךָ וּבִשְׁעָרֶיךָ

[40] Devarim (11:14) - וְנָתַתִּי מְטַר־אַרְצְכֶם בְּעִתּוֹ יוֹרֶה וּמַלְקוֹשׁ וְאָסַפְתָּ דְגָנֶךָ וְתִירֹשְׁךָ וְיִצְהָרֶךָ

Q13. Must one make a *beracha* on a *shul's tallis* when receiving an *aliyah* or serving as the *shliach tzibur*?

A: The Mishna Berura[41] writes a *shul tallis* is bought with the understanding that anyone who needs it can acquire it for *davening*. It's a partnership among the entire *shul*. Therefore, if one person forgot his *tallis* one day, he can take the *shul tallis* and make a *beracha* even though a borrowed *tallis* is exempt from *tzitzis* until you borrow it for 30 days since it says[42] עַל־כַּנְפֵי בִגְדֵיהֶם - it must be your *tallis*. Since borrowing a *tallis* for 30 days looks like it's yours, Chazal required you to put *tzitzis* on the *tallis* after borrowing it for that length of time.[43] However, the Mishna Berura brings the Lechem Chamudos who disagrees saying everything we just said is only if you need the *tallis* since you forgot yours at home. But if you're only wearing the *tallis* because of *kovod hatzibur*, then you don't make a *beracha*.[44] Although the Biur Halacha[45] questions this Lechem Chamudos, the

---

[41] Mishna Berura (14:11) - בטליתות של קהל כעין שלנו המצויות בבתי כנסיות צריך לברך עליו לכו"ע אפילו כשלובשו רק לעבור לפני התיבה או לעלות לתורה משום דטלית של קהל אדעתא דהכי קנוהו מתחלה שכל מי שלובש אותו שיהיה שלו כמו באתרוג

[42] Bamidbar (15:38) - דַּבֵּר אֶל־בְּנֵי יִשְׂרָאֵל וְאָמַרְתָּ אֲלֵהֶם וְעָשׂוּ לָהֶם צִיצִת עַל־כַּנְפֵי בִגְדֵיהֶם לְדֹרֹתָם וְנָתְנוּ עַל־צִיצִת הַכָּנָף פְּתִיל תְּכֵלֶת

[43] Shulchan Aruch OC (14:3) - השואל מחבירו טלית שאינה מצוייצת פטור מלהטיל בה ציצית כל ל' יום דכתיב כסותך ולא של אחרים אבל אחר שלשים יום חייב מדרבנן מפני שנראית כשלו

[44] Mishna Berura (14:11) - ודוקא אם שאל ממנו טלית המיוחד למצוה אבל אם הוא בגד העומד ללבישה ורק כיון שפתוח רובו עושין בו ציצית ולא נעשה בשביל מצות ציצית וכן אם שאל טלית לעלות לתורה או לעבור לפני התיבה או לדוכן שאינו אלא משום הכבוד אין מברכין עליו דאולי היה רצונו להשאילו רק למלבוש לחוד ולא להקנות לו ויש חולקין בזה וס"ל דבכל גווני מברכין ע"כ כתב בדרך החיים דיותר טוב שיכוין בכל אלו שלא לקנות כדי שלא יצטרך לברך לכו"ע לבד מהטלית ששאל בעת התפלה לצאת בו

[45] Biur Halacha (14:3) - ואולי טעם הדה"ח דפעמים העיר גדולה מאד ולא ימטי שוה פרוטה לכל חד וכעין שפירש"י בסוכה ע"ש ובספר שערי

minhag today is to not make a *beracha* if you are a *shliach tzibur* or getting an *aliyah*. If you need the *tallis* for your own *davening* since you don't have your personal *tallis*, then you make a *beracha*.

Q14. If you are at a large meal and cannot hear the *mezamen*, is it proper to make your own *zimun*?

A: The real *mitzvah* of *zimun* is to have one person be *motzi* the rest of the members of the *seuda* with *bentching*.[46] *B'dieved* you are *yotzei* if you just hear the first *beracha*, and you can say the rest of the *berachos* yourself. Today it's not the *minhag* for the *mezamen* to be *motzi* others since not every *mezamen* has *kavana* to be *motzi* others, and not all the

---

אפרים כתב דיותר טוב ליקח טלית שאולה בעת עלייתו לתורה מליקח טלית הקהל שבטלית הקהל נכנס לכלל ספק שמא מחוייב לברך ואם לקח טלית הקהל ורוצה לברך יכוין אז שרוצה ללבשו לשם מלבוש של ציצית ויעטוף בו ראשו כמו בשחרית וא"ץ אז לעמוד מעוטף שיעור הילוך ד' אמות וכו' ואם אינו רוצה לברך עליו לא יעטוף ראשו כלל רק עטיפת הגוף לבד ונתן טעם לדבריו בהפתחי שערים שלו וז"ל בטלית הקהל יש לברך עליו כמו בטלית של שותפין ומ"מ נראה דוקא כשמעטף בו ראשו כדרך עטיפת שחרית הא בלא"ה אין לברך אף שיש דעת קצת פוסקים החולקים ע"ז וס"ל דעיטוף הגוף סגי מ"מ אין כונתו להתעטף כלל רק לבישה לשעתו משום כבוד בעלמא לא קרינן אשר תכסה בה בעיטוף ארעי כזה ואף בטלית שלו אם זמנו בהול שאינו יכול להתעטף בו ממש ונותנו על הכתפיים לבד לשעה קלה בשעת הקריאה ודעתו להסירו מיד צ"ע בכה"ג עכ"ל ודבריו חלושים במקצת דהלא הסכמת השו"ע לעיל בסימן ח' דהעיטוף אינו לעיכובא וגם טעם השני שלו מרש"ל ומ"א וא"ר ושארי אחרונים משמע דבבגד שלו בודאי חייב לברך ולא חילקו כלל בין אם מעטף ראשו או לא משמע מדבריהם דבכל גווני חייב ע"י לבישה זו בציצית מ"מ מה שכתב בש"א הנ"ל דיכוין אז בלבישתו לשם מלבוש של ציצית ולא לכבוד בעלמא דבריו נכונים מאד מדינא מט"א דהלא קי"ל בסי' ס' ס"ד דמצות צריכות כונה ולעיכובא הוא כמבואר שם וכמש"ך בסי' ח' במ"ב סקי"ט עי"ש. אח"כ מצאתי חבר להשערי אפרים והוא מה שכתב בבה"ט בסימן י"ח סק"ד בשם הל"ח דהמתעטף מפני כבוד הציבור אין מברך ומסתמא טעמו כמש"כ השו"א דאפשר דזה אינו נקרא לבישה המחייבת בציצית

[46] Shulchan Aruch OC (183:7) - נכון הדבר שכל אחד מהמסובין יאמר בלחש עם המברך כל ברכה וברכה ואפי' החתימות

members of the *seuda* have *kavana* to be *yotzei* with him.[47] Nonetheless, we still allow the *mezamen* to be *motzi* the rest of the members with *zimun* despite him not being *motzi* their *bentching*. It would seem from the *shul* in Alexandria which allowed the *mispallelim* to say *amen* to the *berachos* they knew they were responding to, despite the fact they couldn't hear the actual *beracha*.[48] Here too, the people by the *seuda* can answer the *mezuman* along with everyone since you know where he is holding.

Q15. If three women eat together, should they make a *zimun*?

A: נשים מזמנות לעצמן רשות – they are not obligated to make a *zimun*, but may if they would like to.[49] I don't think it's the prevalent *minhag* to make a *zimun*, but if they do there's nothing wrong with that.[50]

Q16. What if there's a man eating with the women?

---

[47] Mishna Berura (183:27) - היינו אף דמדינא היה יותר נכון שישמעו המסובין כל הבהמ"ז מפי המזמן והוא יוציאם בברכתו ובעצמן לא יברכו כלל מ"מ בעבור שמצוי בעו"ה שהמסובין מסיחין דעתם ואינם מכוונין לדברי המברך כלל ונמצא שחסר להם בהמ"ז לגמרי ומבטלין עשה דאורייתא בידים לכך נכון כהיום יותר שהמסובין יאמרו בעצמן בלחש כל מלה ומלה עם המברך כדי שיברכו יחדו ונקרא עי"ז ברכת זימון ומתקיים מה שאמר הכתוב גדלו לה' אתי ונרוממה שמו יחדו דמזה ילפינן ברכת זימון

[48] Sukka (51b) - תניא רבי יהודה אומר מי שלא ראה דיופלוסטון של אלכסנדריא של מצרים לא ראה בכבודן של ישראל אמרו כמין בסילקי גדולה היתה סטיו לפנים מסטיו פעמים שהיו בה (ששים רבוא על ששים רבוא) כפלים כיוצאי מצרים והיו בה ע"א קתדראות של זהב כנגד ע"א של סנהדרי גדולה כל אחת ואחת אינה פחותה מעשרים ואחד רבוא ככרי זהב ובימה של עץ באמצעיתה וחזן הכנסת עומד עליה והסודרין בידו וכיון שהגיע לענות אמן הלה מניף בסודר וכל העם עונין אמן

[49] Shulchan Aruch OC (199:7) - נשים מזמנות לעצמן רשות אבל כשאוכלות עם האנשי' חייבות ויוצאות בזימון שלנו

[50] Biur Halacha (199:7) - ודעת הגר"א בביאורו שהעיקר כהרא"ש ותר"י שנשים מזמנות לעצמן חוב אך העולם לא נהגו כן

A: It doesn't make any difference. However, if there are three men at the *seuda*, then the women are obligated to answer to the men's *zimun*.[51]

Q17. Must one dip his bread in salt during the week?

A: We say שֶׁבְּכָל הַלֵּילוֹת אָנוּ מַטְבִּילִין פַּעַם אַחַת (Pesachim 10:4). Evidently, you don't need to dip bread into salt.[52] According to the *halacha*, having salt with the bread makes it taste better – and there is a *hiddur* in the *beracha* to cut the bread from the tastiest part.[53] In fact, if the bread isn't *shalem*, you should put on the butter and jam before the *hamotzi*. I'm not saying there's not an *inyan* to dip your bread in salt during the week – we find waters on earth complained that the upper waters were given more effort than the lower ones.[54] Hashem appeased the lower water by commanding salt to be placed on the *Mizbei'ach*, which parallels our tables. The bread companies put in salt anyway to make it taste better, and you wouldn't necessarily need to put salt on the bread made from fine flour unless it's whole wheat or bran bread. According to the Halachos Ketanos, you can even use sugar for *melicha* since both sugar and salt are small white particles and are considered salt.[55] Nonetheless, not everyone agrees with the

---

[51] Shulchan Aruch OC (199:7) - נשים מזמנות לעצמן רשות אבל כשאוכלות עם האנשי' חייבות ויוצאות בזימון שלנו

[52] Shulchan Aruch OC (167:5) - לא יבצע עד שיביאו לפניו מלח או ליפתן (פירש"י כל דבר הנאכל עם הפת) ללפת בו פרוסת הבציעה ואם היא נקייה או שהיא מתובל בתבלין או במלח כעין שלנו או שנתכוין לאכול פת חריבה אינו צריך להמתין: הגה ומ"מ מצוה להביא על כל שלחן מלח קודם שיבצוע כי השלחן דומה למזבח והאכיל' לקרבן ונא' על כל קרבנך תקריב מלח והוא מגין מן הפורענות

[53] Shulchan Aruch OC (167:1) - בוצע בפת במקום שנאפה היטב (ובפת דידן יש לבצוע בצד הפת ויחתוך מעט מצד העליון והתחתון)

[54] Rashi Vayikra (2:13) - שֶׁהַבְּרִית כְּרוּתָה לַמֶּלַח מִשֵּׁשֶׁת יְמֵי בְרֵאשִׁית שֶׁהֻבְטְחוּ הַמַּיִם הַתַּחְתּוֹנִים לִקָּרֵב בַּמִּזְבֵּחַ בַּמֶּלַח וְנִסּוּךְ הַמַּיִם בֶּחָג

[55] Avnei Nezer OC (532) and Minchas Chinuch (118) - ובס' הלכות קטנו' למהר"מ חאגיז סרי"ח כ' דמותר למלוח קרבן עם ציקור דהוא

Halachos Ketanos.[56] Some Poskim recommend dipping the bread in sugar where no salt is available.[57]

Q18. If you removed your *tzitzis* before entering the shower, must you make a new *beracha* when putting them on again?

מין מלח אף על פי שהוא מתוק. וכ' אף על פי דהוא פרי כמבואר בא"ח לענין ברכה ועובר משום דבש לא תקטירו נ"מ היכי דאין לו מלח אתי עשה ודל"ת דהקטרת דבש. והנה כבר כ' לעיל דאינו דבר ברור דאין עשה דוחה לא תעשה שבמקדש ע' זבחים צ"ו ויבואר במק"א.

[56] ולדברי הלכות קטנות המבואר באות הקודם גם הסוכר הוא מלח ומסלק זאת תורת העולה מכל האמור - See Tzitz Eliezer (9:36:12) .הדינים שאסור בהחלט למלוח הבשר בצוקער, ואפילו בדיעבד אם עברו ומלחו הבשר בצוקער ובישלוהו, הבשר טריפה והכלים טעונים הכשר. ומאידך אם מלחו הבשר בצוקער ונודע הדבר לפני שבישלוהו אין לאסור את הבשר כלל אלא יש להורות גם לכתחילה לחזור ולמלוח הבשר במלח כדת וכדין Shevet HaLevi (2:24) - אשר שאלת בענין מי שמלח במלח לימון וכן בענין מליחת צוקער, אשיב בקצור כי אין ספק בלבי שהצדק עם הגאונים אמרי אש וכ"ס וד"ח ישו"מ ודעמי' דמליחת סוכר אפילו דיעבד אסורה אלא דאם לא בישל עדיין אפשר לחזור ולמלוח, וסוגיות הש"ס במנחות (כא.) מוכחת להדיא דרק מלח ידוע כמו מלח של ים או מלח סדומית שנקרא גם אצלנו מלח סתם הוא המלח המכשיר, ומש"כ בשם תשובת אבני נזר או"ח (תקלב) עיינתי שם ובעניותי דאין דבריו מכריעים נגד כל הגדולים הנ"ל, דהוא מסתמך על דברי הלכות קטנות דמותר למלוח קרבנות בסוכר ודייק מיני' דהה"ד לענין מליחת בשר ודברי הלק"ט מן התמוהים כידוע וקשה לבנות עליו וכבר תמהו גדולים הנ"ל עליו, וגם אני עני בחידושי על המצות מצוה קי"ח יש לי קצת מו"מ באמונה בדברי הד"ח והלק"ט הנ"ל וכו'...עכ"פ פשיטא לי דאסור למלוח בסוכר או במלח לימון וכיו"ב, דיכול אני לספור עוד כמה וכמה מינים דנקראים מלח ואין להם טבעית מלח סתם השכיח בינינו, והיות כי זמני מוגבל אקצר בפשוט

[57] Kaf HaChaim OC (167:37) - ומ"ש היפ"ל אות יו"ד דאם אין לו מלח יטבול בסוכר אחר הס"ר מכת"ר אינו נראה דמה שייך סוכר במקום מלח בענין זה כיון שהטעם היא כדי למתק הדין והסוכר אינו דין לא בשמו ולא בטעמו לא כן המלח או הלחם

A: No.[58]

Q19. Doesn't Rav Elyashiv say you need to make a new *beracha* if your *tzitzis* were off for two hours?

A: Yes, but if it takes you two hours to take a shower then you have some problems.

Q20. If you sleep for two hours and remove your *tzitzis*, must you make a new *beracha*?

A: It's not the *minhag* to make a new *beracha* on the *tzitzis*.[59] Nonetheless, you can put your *tzitzis* over your blanket in order to certainly not require a new *beracha*.

Q21. If you remove your *tzitzis* to exercise, is there a time limit to how long you don't need to make a new *beracha* for them?

A: As long as you had *kavana* to put them back on again, the *minhag* is to not make another *beracha*.[60]

---

[58] Biur Halacha (8:14) - ועיין בספר ארצות החיים בשם תשובת קול אליהו דלפי זה היוצא מבית המרחץ צריך ברכה שנית על הטלית קטן דאיכא הפסק גדול והביא כן בשם רבני קשישי דירושלים עכ"ל. והעולם אין נוהגין ליזהר בזה ואפשר שטעמם דלא שייך בזה היסח הדעת שמוכרח הוא לחזור וללבוש את בגדיו ולכאורה נראה דלא מהני בזה אפילו אם יכוין בבוקר בעת הברכה שיפשטנו ויחזור וילבשנו כיון דמטעם הפסק אתינן עלה ואפשר לומר דכשמכוין לזה בעת ברכה בבוקר לא שייך בזה הפסק בין הפשיטה והלבישה דהברכה קאי על לבישה השנית

[59] Mishna Berura (8:42) - הישן ביום שינת הצהריים ומסיר מעליו הטלית קטן יש דעות בין הפוסקים אם זה בכלל היסח הדעת. על כן מהנכון שעל כל פנים יכסה בו בשעת השינה וכשלובשו אחר כך אין צריך ברכה לכולי עלמא

[60] Shulchan Aruch OC (8:14) - ואם פשט טליתו אפי' היה דעתו לחזור ולהתעטף בו מיד צריך לברך כשיחזור ויתעטף בו: הגה וי"א שאין מברכין אם היה דעתו לחזור ולהתעטף בו וי"א דוקא כשנשאר עליו טלית קטן והכי נוהגין

Q22. Should one make a *beracha* on a fruit cup salad served as an appetizer at the beginning of a meal?

A: An appetizer is the first thing served in the meal, therefore you do not make a *beracha* on it.[61]

Q23. Should one make a *beracha* on wine one drinks after eating fish served as an appetizer?

A: I would think it's the same thing as one who drinks wine after eating meat served as an appetizer.[62] I don't understand the question. If you want to clean out your mouth, then it's cheaper to clean it out with water.

Q24. May one make a *beracha* on *tzitzis* after *davening* Maariv if it's still light outside?

A: Yes, you can still make a *beracha*.[63]

Q25. How much light must there be?

---

[61] Shulchan Aruch OC (177:3) - ואם קובע ליפתן סעודתו על הפירות הוו ליה הפירות כדברים הבאים מחמת הסעודה ואפי' אם אוכל מהפירות בתחלת סעודתו בלא פת אינו מברך לא לפניהם ולא לאחריהם ויש חולקין ולכן טוב שיאכל בתחלה מהפירות עם פת ואז אפילו אם אח"כ יאכל מהם בלא פת אינם טעונים ברכה כלל

[62] Shulchan Aruch OC (174:1) - יין שבתוך הסעודה מברך עליו בורא פרי הגפן ואין הפת פוטרו

[63] cf. Rema OC (18:1) - ואחר תפלת ערבית אע"פ שעדיין יום הוא אין לברך עליו and Mishna Berura (18:7) - אבל אם איחר להתעטף עד לילה שוב לא יברך דשמא הלכה כהרמב"ם ומשמע מדברי המ"א בסק"ד דאפילו בין השמשות מותר לברך עד צה"כ וטעמו דהלא בציצית לא כתיב יום רק וראיתם אותו משמע כל זמן שנוכל לראות וכן פסק בעל דרך החיים ובספר מטה אפרים ראיתי שמחמיר בזה. אך אם זה גופא הוא מסתפק אם כבר הגיע בין השמשות נראה דבודאי יוכל לברך דבלא"ה דעת התוספות והרא"ש דכסות יום חייב בלילה והגר"א בביאוריו מצדד ג"כ לשיטה זו עי"ש

A: Enough light to be able to see the difference between the aqua green color of *techeiles* and the regular *tzitzis* strings not made of *techeiles*.[64]

Q26. If one was an אונס and couldn't put on *tefillin* until after nightfall, may he put on *tefillin*?

A: No. The Chachamim made a *takana* not to put on *tefillin* at night.[65]

Q27. If one did not eat or drink the entire day before Mincha, may he say Aneinu?

A: No, don't say Aneinu unless you didn't eat or drink with the *kavana* to fast until after Mincha.[66] If you intend to fast for half of the day, then you may say Aneinu at Mincha as long as you have not broken your fast yet.[67]

Q28. Should one wear the strings of his *tzitzis* out?

---

[64] Shulchan Aruch OC (18:3) - מאימתי מברך על הציצית בשחר משיכיר בין תכלת שבה ללבן שבה

[65] Shulchan Aruch OC (30:2) - אסור להניח תפילין בלילה שמא ישכחם ויישן בהם

[66] Shulchan Aruch OC (562:5) - כל תענית שלא קבלו עליו היחיד מבעוד יום אינו תענית: הגה להתפלל עננו ולא לענין אם חייב תענית סתם והתענה כך לא יצא ידי נדרו (מיהו) יש אומרים דמתפלל עננו וכן נראה לי לנהוג בתענית יחיד ולכולי עלמא המתענה תענית חלום מתפלל עננו אע"פ שלא קבל עליו מאתמול

[67] Mishna Berura (562:6) - היינו אם פירש בשעת קבלה שלא להשלים אפילו התענה רק עד מנחה גדולה מתפלל עננו אבל אם קיבל תענית סתם צריך להשלים עד צאת הכוכבים כדלקמן בס"ג

A: The Arizal[68] seems to say it is better to leave them in, and the Mishna Berura[69] says it's better to leave them out. The Mishna Berura brings from the *pesukim* in Zecharia that ten people from the seventy nations will hold onto the corners of each *yid* and say, "We want to follow you because we heard Hashem is with you."[70] We'll have 2,800 servants in the future based on this *posuk.*[71] I understand when the world realizes Hashem runs the world and we are His nation that everyone will want to be connected with us to be connected with Hashem, but what are you supposed to do with more than just a few servants? It's the *chashivus* of *tzitzis* that each person will grab onto the *tzitzis* which will be seen by everyone. If you wear a *kapota,* then there doesn't appear to be an *inyan* to wear *tzitzis* out since no one will see them. However, even if you wear your *tzitzis* inside your pants, you must make sure the *tzitzis* aren't sitting in a *makom tinofes.*

Q29. Should one wear the knots of his *tzitzis* out?

A: You don't need to wear the knots out.

---

[68] Mishna Berura (8:25) - ובכתבים איתא דטלית קטן תחת בגדיו. וכתב המגן אברהם, דעל כל פנים צריך שיהיו הציצית מבחוץ, ולא כאינך שתוחבין אותן בהכנפות. אך האנשים שהולכים בין העכו"ם יוצאין בזה. ומכל מקום בשעת הברכה יהיו מגולין [כדי הילוך] ארבע אמות

[69] Mishna Berura (8:26) - כמה דכתיב "וראיתם אותו וזכרתם" וגו'. ואותן האנשים המשימין הציצית בהמכנסים שלהם לא די שמעלימין עיניהם ממאי דכתיב "וראיתם אותו וזכרתם" וגו' עוד מבזין הן את מצות השם יתברך ועתידין הן ליתן את הדין על זה. ומה שאומרין שהולכים בין הנוכרים לזה היה די שישימו הציצית בתוך הכנף

[70] Zecharia (8:23) - כֹּה אָמַר ה' צְבָאוֹת בַּיָּמִים הָהֵמָּה אֲשֶׁר יַחֲזִיקוּ עֲשָׂרָה אֲנָשִׁים מִכֹּל לְשֹׁנוֹת הַגּוֹיִם וְהֶחֱזִיקוּ בִּכְנַף אִישׁ יְהוּדִי לֵאמֹר נֵלְכָה עִמָּכֶם כִּי שָׁמַעְנוּ אֱלֹקִים עִמָּכֶם

[71] Shabbos (32b) - אמר ריש לקיש כל הזהיר בציצית זוכה ומשמשין לו שני אלפים ושמונה מאות עבדים שנאמר כה אמר ה' [צבאות] בימים ההמה אשר יחזיקו עשרה אנשים מכל לשונות הגוים [והחזיקו] בכנף איש יהודי לאמר נלכה עמכם

Q30. Why don't we wear a *tallis* by Mincha or Maariv?

A: Mincha is a time when you need to stop in the middle of your working. It's more difficult to *daven* Mincha than Shacharis or Maariv, hence Eliyahu was answered by Mincha specifically.[72] Despite the fact you might lose a couple customers during that time, you stop to *daven* Mincha.[73] Therefore, we didn't accept upon ourselves to wear a *tallis* by Mincha. We don't wear a *tallis* by Maariv[74] because night is not the *zman* for *tzitzis*.[75]

Q31. Should one make a *beracha* on seeing the Grand Canyon?[76]

A: I don't think there's a *beracha* on seeing the Grand Canyon. It's not mentioned anywhere. You cannot say *oseh maaseh bereishis* because we don't know if that's the way it looked at the time of *maaaseh bereishis*. It appears to have been formed later on by rain and erosion. When you see the Mississippi River, you make the *beracha oseh maaseh bereishis* because all the large rivers famous for their size

---

[72] Berachos (6b) - ואמר רבי חלבו אמר רב הונא לעולם יהא אדם זהיר בתפלת המנחה שהרי אליהו לא נענה אלא בתפלת המנחה שנאמר ויהי בעלות המנחה ויגש אליהו הנביא ויאמר וגו' ענני ה' ענני

[73] Tur OC (232) - והטעם מפני שתפלת השחר זמנה ידוע בבקר בקומו ממטתו יתפלל מיד קודם שיהא טרוד בעסקיו וכן של ערב בלילה זמנה ידוע בבואו לביתו והוא פנוי מעסקיו אבל של מנחה שהיא באמצע היום בעוד שהוא טרוד בעסקיו צריך לשום אותה אל לבו ולפנות מכל עסקיו ולהתפלל אותה ואם עשה כן שכרו הרבה מאד

[74] Mishna Berura (18:4) - ובתענית צבור כשלובשין טלית במנחה יסיר את הטלית כשיגיע לברכו מאחר דעכשיו אין לובשין הטלית אלא למצות ציצית אם יהיה עליו יראה כאילו סובר דלילה זמן ציצית הוא

[75] Shulchan Aruch OC (18:1) - לילה לאו זמן ציצית הוא דאמעיט מוראיתם אותו להרמב"ם כל מה שלובש בלילה פטור אפי' הוא מיוחד ליום

[76] Shulchan Aruch OC (228:1) - על ימים ונהרות הרים וגבעות ומדבריות אומר ברוך אתה ה אמ"ה עושה מעשה בראשית

receive a *beracha*.[77] The Nile is the largest river, the Yangztee River in China is the 2nd largest, and the Mississippi is the 5th largest in the world. The Amazon River carries more water than the Yangtzee River due to its tributaries, but it is not longer. We assume these rivers were there since maaseh bereishis. In fact, the Mississippi River starts in Canada as a small stream, and continues all the way down to the Gulf of Mexico. Although it receives a different name along various borders, it's the same large river.

Q32. The Gemara Tamid notes Alexander reaching the entrance of Gan Eden[78] – does that mean it's a physical place?

A: Gan Eden is on earth as it says in the Torah[79] – the lower Gan Eden parallels the upper Gan Eden.[80] The lower Gan Eden is where Adam HaRishon lived on earth. Hashem wanted to protect it to prevent people from entering, so He created the revolving sword to stand by the entrance.[81] The

---

[77] Mishna Berura (228:4) - כמו חדקל ופרת - לאו דוקא אלו אלא ה"ה כל הנהרות שהן גדולות כמו אלו הד' נהרות ושיהיו ידועים שהם מימי בראשית כמו אלו ולא נתהוו אח"כ מברך

[78] Tamid (32b) - אנא אלכסנדרוס מוקדון הויתי שטייא עד דאתיתי למדינת אפריקי דנשיא ויליפת עצה מן נשיא כי שקיל ואתי יתיב אההוא מעיינא קא אכיל נהמא הוו בידיה גולדני דמלחא בהדי דמחוורי להו נפל בהו ריחא אמר ש"מ האי עינא מגן עדן אתי

[79] Bereishis (2:15) - וַיִּקַּח ה' אֱלֹקִים אֶת־הָאָדָם וַיַּנִּחֵהוּ בְגַן־עֵדֶן לְעָבְדָהּ וּלְשָׁמְרָהּ

[80] Shelah Ki Seitzei Torah Ohr (45) - דע כי יש גן עדן תחתון וגן עדן עליון and Ramban Sha'ar HaGamul (52) - גן עדן בעולם הזה התחתון הוא מה שכר הנשמות שם ואין תועלתם בדבר גשמי ולא במקום ממקומות הארץ ועולם התחתונים כבר פרשתי שהעניין כפול וזה הגן והעדן התחתונים הן ציורים לסודות העליונים והדברים ההם העליונים הרמוזים באלה גם כן נקראים "גן ועדן" שאלו התחתונים מהן תופסין השם הזה

[81] Bereishis (4:24) - וַיְגָרֶשׁ אֶת־הָאָדָם וַיַּשְׁכֵּן מִקֶּדֶם לְגַן־עֵדֶן אֶת־הַכְּרֻבִים וְאֵת לַהַט הַחֶרֶב הַמִּתְהַפֶּכֶת לִשְׁמֹר אֶת־דֶּרֶךְ עֵץ הַחַיִּים

Ramban[82] writes that there were many explorers looking for plants needed for *refuah* and saw the revolving sword. Parenthetically, most animals produce their own vitamin C without the need of potatoes or fruits, while we only produce our own Vitamin D. Hashem made all the *refuos* for every sickness in creation, which was figured out and transcribed by Shlomo HaMelech until his descendant Chizkiyahu hid the book.[83] When people would get sick, they would just eat the right combination of foods and weren't worried. This was problematic because Hashem created sicknesses in order to humble us to pray to Him.[84] We generally don't find animals getting sick in the forest – there's no such thing as animal dentists or doctors. We only have veterinarians in our society in order to make money, but animals in the wild don't have these problems. Now, Gan Eden is in Burma and was recorded by Bnei Tzion (14) in order to pinpoint what time Adam HaRishon was created, which required knowing exactly where sunrise began in that location.

---

[82] Sha'ar HaGamul (50) - ובספרי הרפואות ליונים הקדמונים וכן בספר אסף היהודי יספר כי אספקלינוס חכם מקדוני וארבעים איש מן החרטומים מלומדי הספרים הלכו הלוך בארץ ויעברו מעבר להודו קדמת עדן למצוא קצת עצי הרפואות ועץ החיים למען תגדל תפארתם על כל חכמי הארץ ובבואם אל המקום ההוא ויברק עליהם להט החרב המתהפכת ויתלהטו כולם בשביבי אש הברק ולא נמלט מהם איש ותשבות חכמת הרפואה מן הגויים ההם ימים רבים עד מלוך ארתחששתא המלך ואחרי כן נתחדשה בהם דעת הרופאים על ידי הנקובים בשם במלאכה ההיא וכל אלה דברי אמת ידועים ומפורסמים גם היום כי רבים מבאי הארץ הלזו ארצה בני קדם יראו מרחוק הלהט המתהפכת

[83] Pesachim (56a) - תנו רבנן ששה דברים עשה חזקיה המלך על שלשה הודו לו ועל שלשה לא הודו לו גירר עצמות אביו על מטה של חבלים והודו לו כיתת נחש הנחשת והודו לו גנז ספר רפואות והודו לו

[84] Rambam Mishna Pesachim (4:9) - שלמה חבר ספר רפואות כשיחלה שום אדם או יקרנו שום חולי מן החולים היה מתכוין לאותו הספר והיה עושה כמ"ש בספר והיה מתרפא וכאשר ראה חזקיה כי בני אדם לא היו סומכין על הש"י הסיר אותו וגנזו

Q33. Is the Sambatyon a physical location that we can locate by satellite?

A: The *Harei Choshech* are massive mountains which block out the sun within 10 miles of them.[85] We sing in *zemiros* that the Sambatyon testifies to Shabbos as it tosses up stones the entire week but is tranquil on Shabbos.[86] In fact, Eldad Hadani was one person who crossed the Sambatyon on Shabbos from the inhabitants on the other side of the river since it was a case of *pikuach nefesh*.[87] He explained the *mesorah* they had across the river, and it seems they *poskin* like Beis Shamai. Nonetheless, we don't follow most of the things he says.[88] They still have *arba misos* Beis Din, hence no one crossed the river on Shabbos. There is no such thing as Reform Judaism on the other side either. In the 1930s, an American Rav wrote Kol Mevaser, a *sefer* providing exact directions to find the Sambatyon. The map began in Tibet and explained "1½ days travel by donkey from this city, then follow North a certain amount of time." Although we know

---

[85] Tamid (32a) - אמר להן בעינא דאיזל למדינת אפריקי אמרו ליה לא מצית אזלת דפסקי הרי חשך אמר להן לא סגיא דלא אזלינא אמטו הכי משיילנא לכו אלא מאי אעביד אמרו ליה אייתי חמרי לובאי דפרשי בהברא ואייתי קיבורי דמתני וקטר בהאי גיסא דכי אתית (באורחא) נקטת בגוייהו ואתית לאתרך עבד הכי ואזל מטא לההוא מחוזא דכוליה נשי

[86] Rashi Sanhedrin (65b) - נהר סבטיון יוכיח - נהר אחד של אבנים ובכל ימות השבת שוטף והולך וביום השבת שוקט ונח

[87] Otzar Midrashim (1:13) - בעסק ר' אלדד הדני ששלחתם לפנינו ואשר שמעתם ממנו ספרו לנו חכמים ששמעו מן רבנא יצחק בן מר ורבנא שמחה שראו ר' אלדד הדני זה והיו תמהים מדבריו שהיו במקצתן נראים כדברי חכמים שלנו ומקצתם היו מופלגין

[88] Bach YD (19:2) - שחט ולא בירך וכו' פי' בין בשוגג בין במזיד וכ"כ הרמב"ם בפ"א וכן כתב סמ"ג דלא כהלכות אלדד הדני שכתב דשחיטתו פסולה מיהו אפשר דר"ל דלאחרים שרינן לאכלו אבל הוא עצמו אסור לו לאכלו אם הזיד ולא בירך כמ"ש המרדכי פרק כיסוי הדם ע"ש ראבי"ה בשם הגאונים דקנסינן ליה שלא יאכל הוא ממנה וגם מלקין אותו מכת מרדות אבל בשוגג שרי אף לדידיה וגם אין מלקין אותו והאגור הביא דברי ראבי"ה לפסק הלכה וגם הביא מ"ש המחברים לחלוק אהלכות אלדד הדני אלמא דתרווייהו הילכתא נינהו ומחלקים בין לדידיה ובין לאחריני

what's happening on the moon and Mars, there are still many unexplored regions on earth today. We just don't know about those locations yet because a war wasn't fought there, or there was no economic advantage to exploring that area. You can try to find the Sambatyon on Google Earth, but many areas are still covered with trees.

Q34. Why do we say *shehakol* on orange juice?

A: Would you rather say בורא מאורי האש on orange juice? The oranges we eat are different than the oranges used for juicing, which makes the question even stronger. Meaning, if the oranges used for juicing are primarily grown for orange juice, then we should certainly make a *ha'eitz* on the drink. However, orange producers would rather sell the juice fruits to be eaten and sold at a higher cost than used for a cheaper juice.[89] Therefore, these oranges are designed to be eaten, and the leftover unbought fruit are juiced.[90] The same is true for milk – famers make much more money from selling milk to be drunk rather than the powder form. Farmers only powder the leftover milk they couldn't sell. That's why you can make *non-Cholov Yisroel* milk powder for a fraction of the price. On the other hand, *Cholov Yisroel* powdered milk is more expensive than the milk itself because the company must pay for the *mashgiach* from the time the milk is

---

[89] Mishna Berura (202:52) - מיהו בפירות שרוב אכילתן הוא ע"י בישול או כבישה מי שליקתן וכבישתן כמותן ומברך עלייהו בפה"ע לכו"ע וכ"ז בפירות שמתחלת נטיעתם נטעי להו אדעתא לאוכלם מבושלים או כבושים אבל בפירות שדרכן לאוכלן חיים רק שיש שמיבשין אותן ואח"כ מבשלין אותן אין מברך על רוטבן לעולם רק שהכל אע"ג דדרך כולן לבשלן כשהן יבשין מ"מ תחלת נטיעתן לא נטעי להו אדעת ליבשן אלא לאוכלן חיין ולענין פלוימי"ן יבשים או קרשי"ן כתב הח"א דבמדינות שגדילים שם הרבה מסתמא נטעי להו ברובא אדעתא ליבשן וא"כ ברכתן של רוטבן בפה"ע

[90] Shulchan Aruch OC (202:10) - פירות ששראן או בשלן במים אע"פ שנכנס טעם הפרי במים אינו מברך על אותם המים אלא שהכל והרא"ש כתב דאפשר שאם נכנס טעם הפרי במים מברך בפה"ע

produced, and it must be milked initially to be made into powder.

Q35. Can one buy coffee from a gas station without a *hechsher*?

A: Does the coffee come out of the gas pump that you are only asking about gas stations? This question is really the same broad question of buying coffee from any location without a *hechsher*. If a facility has a machine dedicated to coffee without any added flavor, then it is kosher because coffee doesn't have *bishul akum* issues.[91] The Shach[92] says this is true because the main part of coffee is the hot water, which doesn't have a *din* of *bishul akum* since water is edible raw and not fit for a royal table.

Q36. What if the facility currently doesn't sell flavored coffee but might have in the past?

A: What do you do if you don't know? You have every right to stay away from something when you don't know, but the *halacha* tells us "*stam keilim aino b'nei yoman*" and therefore the flavor imparted from the utensil is negative, so we don't need to suspect they used flavored coffee in the past.[93] This is especially true if you are traveling on the road and stopped off by a Howard Johnsons or the like. The *Poskim* say such a situation is considered *b'dieved* where you need coffee, and you can therefore be more lenient.

---

[91] Chochmas Adam (66:14) - יין תפוחים ושאר פירות מותר דדבר שאינו מצוי ל"ג וכן קאווע ושאקאלדע מותר לשתות בביתו

[92] Shach YD (114:1) - ואין לאסור משום בישולי עובדי כוכבים דאסור בכל ענין כדלעיל סי' קי"ג ס"א לפי שאינו עולה על שלחן מלכים ועוד דכי היכי דהתבואה בטילה לגבי מים לענין ברכת שהכל נהיה בדברו ה"נ בטלה לענין איסור בש"ע כ"כ התוס' והרא"ש ושאר פוסקים ומ"ש הב"ח בכאן לא ירדתי לסוף דעתו בכל דבריו ע"ש

[93] Shulchan Aruch YD (122:7) - כשם שסתם כליהם של עובדי כוכבים אינם בני יומן כך סתם כלים שלנו בחזקת שאינן בני יומן

Q37. Should we be concerned the facility will wash the non-kosher *keilim* with the coffee utensils?

A: My experience has been that they never wash the *keilim*. All the leftover coffee each day adds to the next day's flavor. Nonetheless, you should insist on a disposable cup. If you know they do wash the *keilim*, then you shouldn't drink the coffee.[94]

[94] Rema YD (87:6) - עוד כתבו דאין לערב מים שהדיחו בהם כלי בשר עם מים שהדיחו בהם כלי חלב וליתן לפני בהמה דאסורים בהנאה עוד כתבו דהכלי שעושין בו מים לחפיפת הראש אין לשמש בו דעושין אותה מאפר שעל הכירה ורגילות הוא להתערב שם בשר וחלב ולכן יש לאסור גם כן להשתמש מן הקדרות של התנורים שבבית החורף משום דנתזים עליהם לפעמים בשר וחלב מן הקדרות שמבשלים בתנורים

Chapter 5: Shonim Tammuz 5772

Q1. What does it mean to make fun of avoda zara?

A: If you think anything can help or hurt you other than the Ribbono Shel Olam, that is avoda zara.[1] Therefore, if you think driving around with a Lexus will give you *chashivus*, then your Lexus becomes an avoda zara. Only Hashem can give you *chashivus*. We're not just talking about someone who prays to a Lexus. We know a Lexus is helpful with driving you places just like a fire hydrant is helpful to put out forest fires. However, despite seeing the strength of the fire hydrant in its ability to stop destruction, we don't put faith in it to do other things. We see the Nevi'im insult avoda zaras saying, "One side of a plank of wood you use for firewood, and the other side you serve."[2] If people bow to the sun or moon, we don't make fun of the things Hashem created, rather we make fun of those who pray to those objects.

Q2. May one buy a lottery ticket?

A: There is no *issur* to buy one as long as you pay for the ticket at the time you acquire it. The only issue would be if you don't give the money upfront because as soon as you pay for the ticket, you were *mayayesh* from the money.[3]

---

[1] Rambam Shavuos (11:2) - וְאָסוּר לְהִשָּׁבַע בְּדָבָר אַחֵר עִם שְׁמוֹ. וְכָל הַמְשַׁתֵּף דָּבָר אַחֵר עִם שֵׁם הַקָּדוֹשׁ בָּרוּךְ הוּא בִּשְׁבוּעָה נֶעֱקָר מִן הָעוֹלָם. שֶׁאֵין שָׁם מִי שֶׁרָאוּי לַחְלֹק לוֹ כָּבוֹד שֶׁנִּשְׁבָּעִין בִּשְׁמוֹ אֶלָּא הָאֶחָד בָּרוּךְ הוּא

[2] Sanhedrin (63b) - אמר רב נחמן כל ליצנותא אסירא חוץ מליצנותא דעבודת כוכבים דשריא דכתיב כרע בל קרס נבו קרסו כרעו יחדו לא יכלו מלט משא

[3] Rema CM (203:13) - ויש אומרים דג' חלוקין בדיני אסמכתא דכל מה שאין בידו ותלוי ביד אחרים כגון שא"ל קנה לי יין ממקום פלוני ואם לא תקנה תחייב לי בכך וכך דזה אינו תלוי בו דדילמא לא ירצו למכור לו הוי אסמכתא בכל ענין ולא קנה ומה שיש בידו לעשות אם לא גזים כגון שאמר אם אוביר ולא אעבוד אשלם במיטב לא הוי אסמכתא וקניא אבל אי

Once you put down the money in the hands of a third party, then you are *meyayesh*. However, this is not *hishtadlus* for *parnasa* because *hishtadlus* is what people generally do in order to make money. Since the chances of winning the lottery are like one-in-a-million, that is not considered legitimate *hishtadlus* that people do to make money. If you win the lottery, it may very well come off the end-of-the-year *parnasa* Hashem assigned for you,[4] but it's still not considered *hishtadlus*. It's like saying going out into the middle of the street to say, "I'm available for work." If employers are around listening, then that would be considered *hishtadlus*. However, if no one hiring is there, then it's not considered *hishtadlus* for *parnasa*. Yes, someone might be listening from an open window in a neighboring house, but it's not the normal method of *hishtadlus*. If Hashem said you're supposed to make $80,000 this year, then you'll receive your *parnasa* as long as you complete the normal *hishtadlus*. On the other hand, if you don't do the normal *hishtadlus*, then you won't receive the money designated to come to you.

Q3. Must stickers be removed from *keilim* prior to *tevilla*?

A: *Min HaTorah*, the only *chatzitza* is something which is *rubo* and *makpid*.[5] Meaning, the *chatzitza* must cover most

---

גזים ואמר אם לא אעבוד אשלם אלפא זוזי הוי אסמכתא ולא קניא לפיכך כשמוכר מקנה ללוקח על תנאי אם תעשה לי כך תקנה הוי אסמכתא כיון שקיום התנאי אינו תלוי ביד המוכר רק ביד הלוקח אבל אם אין בידו לגמרי ולא ביד אחרים כגון המשחק בקוביא וכיוצא בו שאינו יודע אם ינצח או לא ואפילו הכי התנה ודאי גמר ומקני מספק בד"א כששוחקין במעות מוכנים אבל אם שוחקים באמנה אין מוציאין ממנו מה שהפסיד

[4] Beitza (16a) - תני רב תחליפא אחוה דרבנאי חוזאה כל מזונותיו של אדם קצובים לו מראש השנה ועד יום הכפורים חוץ מהוצאת שבתות והוצאת י"ט והוצאת בניו לתלמוד תורה שאם פחת פוחתין לו ואם הוסיף מוסיפין לו

[5] Shulchan Aruch YD (202:2) - כל דבר שדרך להקפיד עליו חוצץ ואם לאו אינו חוצץ אא"כ היה חופה את רובו

of the utensil and you must be *makpid* not to have the sticker there. A sticker which covers less than most of the utensil, or covers most of the utensil which you're not *makpid* on, is not a *chatzitza d'oraysa*. However, the Rabanan decreed that either having an object on *rov* or *makpid* is considered a *chatzitza. Tevillas keilim* might help *d'oraysa* if it's just a small sticker, but *mid'rabanan* the *tevilla* wouldn't help.[6] Nonetheless, if you have a utensil like a pitcher which has a sticker on the bottom of its base where you don't see the sticker, then it could potentially not be a *chatzitza* if you're not *makpid*.[7] If the owner will remove the sticker sooner or later because he is *makpid*, then he would need to remove the sticker before *tevilla*.

Q4. If the husband isn't *makpid* on the sticker, but his wife is, is the sticker a *chatzitza* when he *tovels* the *keli*?

A: If a person's wife is *makpid* on the sticker, then why wouldn't the husband be *makpid* on it? You should be *makpid* if your wife is *makpid*. It doesn't matter whether he would be *makpid* with or without his wife.

Q5. Is a ring a *chatzitza* if a woman doesn't mind wearing it during washing?

A: Although a woman might not currently be *makpid* on the ring during washing, it would still be a *chatzitza* if she removes it while making dough since she doesn't want the

---

[6] Kitzur Shulchan Aruch (37:10) - צְרִיכִין לְהַשְׁגִּיחַ קֹדֶם הַטְּבִילָה שֶׁיְּהֵא הַכְּלִי נָקִי וְלֹא יְהֵא עָלָיו שׁוּם לִכְלוּךְ אוֹ חֲלוּדָה (אַךְ רֹשֶׁם חֲלוּדָה אוֹ שַׁחֲרוּרִית בְּעָלְמָא שֶׁדַּרְכּוֹ בְּכָךְ וְאֵין מַקְפִּידִין עָלָיו אֵינוֹ מַזִּיק) וּצְרִיכִין לְהַטְבִּיל כָּל הַכְּלִי בְּבַת אַחַת שֶׁיְּהֵא כֻּלּוֹ בַּמַּיִם. וּכְלִי שֶׁיֵּשׁ לוֹ יָד צָרִיךְ לִהְיוֹת עִם הַיָּד בְּבַת אַחַת כֻּלּוֹ בַּמַּיִם וְהָאָדָם הַמַּטְבִּיל וְאוֹחֵז הַכְּלִי בְּיָדוֹ צָרִיךְ לְהַטְבִּיל מִתְּחִלָּה יָדוֹ בְּמָקוֹם שֶׁהוּא מַטְבִּיל וְלֹא יֶאֱחוֹז אֶת הַכְּלִי בְּכֹחַ בְּדִבּוּק בֵּינוֹנִי

[7] Shulchan Aruch YD (120:13) - צריך להעביר החלודה קודם טבילה ואם לא העביר אם מקפיד עליו חוצץ ואם שפשף ונתן בגחלים ונשאר עדיין מעט של חלודה שלא יכול לעבור על ידי כך הוי מיעוטו שאינו מקפיד עליו ואינו חוצץ

dough to get stuck inside the ring.[8] If a woman is *makpid* occasionally, then she is considered to be *makpid* at all times on such a *chatzitza*.[9] On the other hand, if a woman wants the ring on while she is washing, then it is not a *chatzitza* even if she takes it off at other times.[10]

Q6. How much of a leak would make a *keli* unfit for *netilas yadayim*?

A: The *shiur* is כונס משקה.[11] Meaning, if you would submerge this *keli* into water and water would enter - as opposed to releasing water - then it would be considered כונס משקה. A small hole lets out water, but a larger hole is needed to let water in.[12] On the other hand, we invalidate a *keli* with a crack on the wall since we're concerned the crack will get larger over time. The *keli* is only good until the hole. Therefore, if the hole is on the upper part of the *keli*, then

---

[8] Shulchan Aruch OC (161:3) - צריך להסיר הטבעת מעל ידו בשעת נטילת ידים: ואפי' הוא רפוי ואפי' אינו מקפיד עליו בשעת נטילה הואיל ומקפיד עליו בשעה שעושה מלאכה שלא יטנפו

[9] Mishna Berura (161:19) - ומסקי האחרונים דדוקא אשה שדרכה להקפיד להסיר הטבעת בשעת מלאכה [היינו בשעת לישה] אבל איש שאין דרכו להקפיד להסירו בשעת מלאכה כי אין דרכו ללוש אין צריך להסיר אותו בשעת נטילה אפילו אם אינו רפוי רק אם יש בו אבן טוב שגם איש דרכו להקפיד להסיר בשעת נטילה שלא יתלכלך מהמים אז יש לחוש להסירו משום חציצה

[10] Mishna Berura (161:12) - והיו ידיו צבועות - ר"ל מקצת ממקום הנטילה דאלו היה רובו הא קי"ל דאפילו אינו מקפיד חוצץ אכן בסיפא לענין נשים שדרכן לצבוע ידיהן לנוי שם אפילו כל ידיהן צבועות נמי כיון שמתכוונות לעשות כן ורוצות בזה הרי הוא כגופן ממש ולא חייצי

[11] Shulchan Aruch OC (159:1) - ואם ניקב בכונס משקה דהיינו שאם ישימו אותו על משקים יכנסו בתוכו דרך הנקב והוא גדול מנקב שהמשקים שבתוך הכלי יוצאים בו אז בטל מתורת כלי ואין נוטלים ממנו לידים ואפילו אם הוא מחזיק רביעית מן הנקב ולמטה

[12] Mishna Berura (159:8) - דאם לא היה רק נקב קטן שהמשקין יוצאין בו אבל לא נכנסין מבחוץ לתוכו חשיב ככלי שלם ונוטלין דרך פיו

you can pour out the water onto your hand entirely through the hole.[13]

Q7. Can one be *tovel takanas Ezra* while wearing shorts since shorts are neither *rubo* nor *makpid*?

A: The concept of *chatzitza* applies in the *halachos* of *takanas Ezra*.[14] You can be *tovel* in shorts for *takanas Ezra* if you want. If it's *rubo u'makpid*, then I'm not so sure about allowing *tevilla*, but if it's not *rubo* or not *makpid* then you can be *tovel takanas Ezra* in shorts. Therefore, you don't need to shave before being *tovel* for *takanas Ezra* either.

Q8. Should one make another *beracha* again on his *tefillin* if he originally made the *beracha* on them with the intention of removing them before going to the bathroom, and then he removes them for the bathroom?

A: Since you cannot go to the bathroom with *tefillin* on, it's considered a *hesech hada'as*.[15] Consequently, when you put on *tefillin* again then you need to make a new *beracha* on each of the *tefillin* you removed.[16] On the other hand, since you're allowed *m'ikar hadin* to wear your *tallis* in the

---

[13] Shulchan Aruch OC (159:2) - והני מילי כשנוטל דרך פיו למעלה שמה שממנו מן הנקב ולמעלה אינו חשוב ככלי ונמצאו שאין המים באים על ידו מהכלי אבל אם נוטל דרך הנקב שרי כיון שמחזיק רביעית ממנו ולמטה

[14] Biur Halacha (88:1) - ודע עוד דמה שמסתפק בשע"ת לענין חציצה בטבילת בע"ק מצאתי בספר האשכול שזכינו עתה לאורו שכתב בהדיא דאין פוסל חציצה בזה. אך ביש חציצה ברוב גופו משמע שם דפוסל גם בזה

[15] Shulchan Aruch OC (43:1) - אסור ליכנס לבית הכסא קבוע להשתין בתפילין שבראשו גזרה שמא יעשה בהם צרכיו ואם אוחזן בידו מותר להשתין בהם בבית הכסא קבוע

[16] Shulchan Aruch OC (25:12) - אם מניח תפילין כמה פעמים ביום צריך לברך עליהם בכל פעם נשמטו ממקומם וממשמש בהם להחזירן למקומן צריך לברך

bathroom,[17] you shouldn't make a new *beracha* after putting the *tallis* back on. Going to the bathroom isn't a *hesech hada'as* for *tallis*.

Q9. May one own or wear clothing depicting the face of the Greek goddess Medusa?

A: How do they know what she looks like? I would say you shouldn't wear such clothing. If this image which people think depicts the face of Medusa, then it would pose an issue. Similarly, you shouldn't make clothing with the image of a sun, but it's permitted to own such clothing.[18] Although wearing it might be an issue that others will think you worship the sun, we're not concerned for that nowadays since people generally don't serve the sun today.[19]

Q10. May one own or wear clothing with the logo of a crocodile, horse, or man?

A: I have no problem with that – I only have a problem with avoda zara. It doesn't make a difference whether the image

---

[17] Shulchan Aruch OC (21:3) - מותר ליכנס בציצית לבית הכסא

[18] Shulchan Aruch YD (141:4) - אסור לצייר צורות שבמדור שכינה כגון ד' פנים בהדי הדדי וכן צורות שרפים ואופני' ומלאכי השרת וכן צורת אדם לבדו כל אלו אסור לעשותם אפילו הם לנוי ואם עובד כוכבים עשאם אסור להשהותם: הגה ומיהו אם מוצא אותם מותרים מלבד בחמה ולבנה שדרך העובד כוכבים לעבדם או שיש הוכחה שעשאן לעבדם שאז אסור ככל הצלמים כמו שנתבאר בריש הסימן: במה דברים אמורים בבולטת אבל בשוקעת כאותם שאורגים בבגד ושמציירים בכותל בסמנין מותר לעשותם וצורת חמה ולבנה וכוכבים אסור בין בולטת בין שוקעת ואם הם להתלמד להבין ולהורות כולן מותרות אפי' בולטות (ויש מתירין בשל רבים דליכא חשדא)

[19] Pischei Teshuva YD (141:6) - ושנית אלו הצורות הורגל באותן מדינות שנדפסו שלא לשם עבודת כוכבים כו' ואף שכתב ר' ירוחם (הובא בבה"ט סק"כ) דאף דליכא חשדא ברבים מכוער הדבר לא דבר ביריעות האלה שהרבה מהן נמכרין בחנות ומכ"ש שחותכין אותה ואם נטה החתך באותן צורות לא מדקדקים ודאי אין ביטול גדול מזה אף לחכמים דס"ל אם מכרו לצורף ישראל אין זה ביטול היינו בעבודת כוכבים ממש

is embroidered, woven, or dyed into the cloth, even the image of a man.[20]

Q11. Is there a *maris ayin* to *daven* with money in front of you?

A: Are you *davening* to the coins? It says, 'In G-d we trust'. That means the money is their god which they invest their trust into, but no one actually bows to the money. People just want to have it. No one thinks you're bowing to the money or the face on the currency, so it's fine. It's permitted to bow to a person – the reason Mordechai didn't bow to Haman was because of the *avoda zara* worn around his neck.[21] Technically, it was permitted for everyone to bow to Haman since they were paying their respects to a man of such power.[22] However, Mordechai went beyond the letter of the law by not wanting to even appear as if he were bowing to an *avoda zara*.[23] That is why Klal Yisroel had tremendous

---

[20] Shulchan Aruch YD (141:4) - אסור לצייר צורות שבמדור שכינה כגון ד' פנים בהדי הדדי וכן צורות שרפים ואופני' ומלאכי השרת וכן צורת אדם לבדו כל אלו אסור לעשותם אפילו הם לנוי ואם עובד כוכבים עשאם אסור להשהותם: הגה ומיהו אם מוצא אותם מותרים מלבד בחמה ולבנה שדרך העובד כוכבים לעבדם או שיש הוכחה שעשאן לעבדם שאז אסור ככל הצלמים כמו שנתבאר בריש הסימן: במה דברים אמורים בבולטת אבל בשוקעת כאותם שאורגים בבגד ושמציירים בכותל בסמנין מותר לעשותם וצורת חמה ולבנה וכוכבים אסור בין בולטת בין שוקעת ואם הם להתלמד להבין ולהורות כולן מותרות אפי' בולטות (ויש מתירין בשל רבים דליכא חשדא)

[21] Esther Rabba (7:5) - מֶה עָשָׂה הָמָן, עָשָׂה לוֹ צֶלֶם מְרֻקָּם עַל בְּגָדָיו וְעַל לִבּוֹ, וְכָל מִי שֶׁהָיָה מִשְׁתַּחֲוֶה לְהָמָן הָיָה מִשְׁתַּחֲוֶה לַעֲבוֹדַת כּוֹכָבִים

[22] Sanhedrin (61b) - איתמר העובד עבודת כוכבים מאהבה ומיראה אביי אמר חייב רבא אמר פטור

[23] Tosafos Sanhedrin (61b) - אי נמי משום קידוש השם כדאמרינן בירושלמי דשביעית כגון פפוס ולוליינוס אחים שנתן להם מים בזכוכית צבועה ולא קיבלו and Tosafos Avoda Zara (3a) - שלא השתחוו לצלם - אומר ר"ת דצלם דנבוכדנצר לאו עבודת כוכבים הוא אלא אנדרטי עשוי לכבוד המלך ובהכי ניחא דנקט גבי אברהם שלא עבד עבודת כוכבים

ta'anos on Mordechai despite the fact that he was a prophet. Mordechai knew there was a Divine decree that Klal Yisroel deserved the decree from Haman.

Q12. May one waste his time taking the 30 hour driving classes when he could get off with a shorter illegal class?

A: I'm not so sure it's a waste of time to take a 30-hour class for driving lessons. There was a time in Lakewood that they would not rent a car to Yeshiva *bochurim* because they got into too many accidents. Why? *Bochurim* didn't necessarily have the required driving experience because they felt it was *bittul* Torah to practice driving. It's not a waste of time. I spoke to a *choshuv shochet* from Europe who was also a *ba'al seichel*. Before taking on a student to prepare for the *bechinos* for *kabbala* in *shechita*, he would first give the prospective *shochet* a hammer, nail, and a wooden 2x4. If the individual couldn't hammer in the nail without struggling, then he wouldn't be a good *shochet* because he needs precision to sharpen the *chalif* knife on the stone at the correct angle. If you lack the dexterity to maintain the *chalif* at the same constant angle, then it won't work well. Some people can do it and some people can't. Some people might

---

ובחנניה מישאל ועזריה שלא השתחוו לצלם וניחא נמי הא דאמרינן בפרק אלו נערות (כתובות דף לג:) אלמלי נגדו לחנניה מישאל ועזריה פלחו לצלמא ואילו היה עבודת כוכבים ממש חס ושלום כי מדאגת שום יסורין שבעולם לא היו משתחוים לצלם כר' חנינא בן תרדיון (לקמן עבודה זרה יח.) ששמו ספוגין על לבו ליסרו ור"ע (ברכות סא:) שסרקו בשרו במסרקות פיות והיינו הא דפריך פרק מקום שנהגו (פסחים דף נג:) מה ראו חנניה מישאל ועזריה שמסרו עצמן לתוך כבשן האש פירוש היה להם להשתחוות לצלם כיון שלא היה עבודת כוכבים ממש ועוד ראיה מפ"ק דמגילה (דף יב.) מפני מה נתחייבו שונאיהם של ישראל כלייה מפני שהשתחוו לצלם וכו' הם לא עשו אלא לפנים ואם היתה עבודת כוכבים היה להם למסור עצמן על קידוש השם ולישנא דקרא נמי משמע הכי דכתיב לאלקיך לית אנן פלחין ולצלמך לית אנן סגדין משמע דתרי מילי הוו and see Targum Esther (3:4) - די להמן לא הוה סגיד על דהוה עבדיה דאזדבן ליה בטולמת לחם ולאנדרטא די הקים בחדייה לא הוה גחין על דהוה יהודי ויהודאי לא פלחין ולא גחנין ליה

be able to figure out how to drive in less than 30 hours, while others might need 30 hours. However, we don't know who needs what, and we certainly don't consider it a waste of time to practice driving. The second issue is taking such an illegal class. When you purchase driver's insurance, the company provides you with a policy assuming you are legally allowed to drive. However, if the company would know you didn't gain the legally required experience, then they wouldn't insure you. Finally, the government has the right to make the rules of the roads which they own. The government can tell all drivers that it only wants people driving who achieve a certain level of experience. If you don't meet their requirements yet you drive anyway, then you are trespassing on their property. At the same time, any law which the government does not enforce even though they know it is violated is not considered a law. Therefore, if the speed limit is 30 MPH yet police officers will allow you to drive 35 MPH, then you are allowed to drive 35 MPH since they are not *makpid*. However, if they are *makpid* on driving 50 MPH on such a road, then you are not allowed to drive that fast. If the government knows about such a class but doesn't mind, then it would be OK. However, if the government would be *makpid* on having fewer hours of driving experience, then you cannot take a course which offers less.

Q13. May one photograph another person without the other's permission?

A: If you just photograph someone else, and won't show the picture to others, then I don't see a way for someone to be *makpid* – he's standing there for everyone to see right now. However, if you will show the picture to others, then perhaps the individual would be *makpid* not to have his picture taken. For instance, someone might be walking on a street which he wouldn't want his in-laws in a different state to see him walking on. If the person being photographed is in a private location, then you certainly need his permission. Nonetheless, if you entered a building seeing that there was a camera taking pictures, then you can't say you are *makpid* not to have the pictures available for others since you put yourself into the position to have your picture taken. Therefore, the owner of the camera would be allowed to use your photograph.

Q14. Must a photographer ask permission from a *gadol* before taking a picture?

A: Yes, I think he must ask permission. I know a story of a photographer who wasn't really making a *parnasa*. When he went to Rav Moshe to ask if he could take his picture, Rav Moshe said no. When the photographer told Rav Moshe that he was having difficulty making a *parnasa*, and the sale of Rav Moshe's picture would help him make a *parnasa,* Rav Moshe said, "To help a *yid* make a *parnasa*? Of course!" and proceeded to ask how he should pose for the best picture. The Steipler didn't want anyone to take a picture of him since he held that as long as anyone has a picture of you in this world, your *neshama* cannot be completely attached to Olam Haba. However, he allowed his own picture for a *dvar mitzva* which would help him gain more merits for Olam Haba.[24] In fact, I had a picture of the Steipler as he was exiting his car. One of my children put the picture in his shirt pocket and had his shirt accidentally washed with it inside. The picture emerged from the washing machine completely bleached white with the exception of the Steipler's face – and not a single hair of his face was affected. All the buildings, cars, etc. around the Steipler were washed off except for the Steipler's face.

---

[24] Ben Ish Chai Masei (2:9) - ודע כי בזמן הזה לוקחים צורת האדם כמו שהיא ע"י המאכינה (מכונה) החדשה הנעשית באירופ"א שקורי פותוגרא"ף וזו עדיפה מצבע קל על נייר שאין בה בליטה אפלו משהו ונתפשטה מלאכה זו בכל העולם ודשו בה רבים ואע"ג דגם בזה יש מידת חסידות מכל מקום אם יש צורך גדול בדבר יקחו צורת הפנים בלבד בלא ידים ורגלים ואז גם אדם חשוב אין לו לחוש בכך ומעשה שלקחו צורת חכמים במלאכה זו צורת הפנים בלבד ואמרתי לאחד אין לו להרהר בזה כיון דלא מצא ידיו ורגליו בבית המדרש, וכל שכן היכא דהיה צורך גדול בכך

Q15. May one wear earplugs or a Band-Aid outside of an *Eruv* on Shabbos?

A: A Band-Aid is considered *batel* to the body as far as carrying is concerned. Although it is a *chatzitza* for washing *netilas yadayim*,[25] for Hilchos Shabbos it's *tafel* to the body.[26] Similar to *tachshitim* being *batel* to the body since you want them to look nicer and aren't considered carrying.[27] On the other hand, earplugs are only *batel* to the body if you need them medically because you cannot take the outside noises. However, if you don't need them for your health, rather you don't want to hear *lashon hara* or other things, then they're not *batel* to your body and you cannot wear them outside on Shabbos without an *Eruv*.

Q16. Must one remove a Band-Aid from one's finger before *netilas yadayim*?

A: The Mishna Berura says that if you would put the bandage back on after washing because the wound has not healed yet, then you are not obligated to remove it. However, if the wound is essentially healed and you just left the Band-

[25] Shulchan Aruch OC (161:1) - צריך ליזהר מחציצה שכל דבר שחוצץ בטבילה חוצץ בנטילה כגון צואה שתחת הציפורן שלא כנגד הבשר ובצק שתחת הציפורן אפילו כנגד הבשר ורטיה שעל בשרו וטיט היון וטיט היוצרים אבל במיעוטו שאינו מקפיד אין לחוש

[26] Shulchan Aruch OC (303:15) - יוצאת בקשר שעושין לרפואת קיטוף עין הרע שלא ישלוט ובמוך הקשור ומהודק באזנה ובמוך שבסנדלה הקשור בסנדלה ובסנדל ומנעל הסתומים מכל צד אפי' אינו קשור מותר ובמוך שהתקינה לנדתה

[27] Shulchan Aruch OC (303:18) - ומיהו טבעת שיש עליה חותם לאשה ושאין עליה חותם לאיש דתנן בה חייב חטאת אף בכרמלית אסור אפי' לדידן וה"ה לכל מאי דאתמר ביה חיוב חטאת ויש מי שאומר שבזמן הזה שנהגו האנשים לצאת בטבעת שאין עליה חותם הרי זה להם כתכשיט ושרי

Aid on as an added level of caution, then you are obligated to remove it before washing.[28]

Q17. May one offer his mother his suit jacket if she is cold?[29]

A: There is a *machlokes haPoskim* of what the *issur* of לֹא־יִלְבַּשׁ גֶּבֶר is based on.[30] Rashi writes it's an issue of trying to look like a man.[31] Others say the Torah forbade it even if such a person is not trying to look like a member of the

---

[28] Mishna Berura (161:5) - ואף דמבואר לקמן בסימן קס"ב ס"י דא"צ ליטול כלל על מקום הרטיה ומטעם דכיון שאינו יכול ליטול באותו מקום הוי כמו שנקטעה אצבעו דא"צ ליטול רק שאר מקום היד התם הלא מיירי ביש לו מכה ולכך לא חיישינן שיסיר מקום הרטיה ויגע בבשרו להאוכלין דכאיב ליה אבל הכא מיירי שאין לו מכה רק מיחוש בעלמא במקום הנטילה ואין לו צער בנטילתו ויוכל להסיר הרטיה מתי שירצה א"כ יש לחוש שיסיר הרטיה בתוך הסעודה ויגע בבשרו להאוכלין ולכך צריך להסיר הרטיה וליטול ידיו דאם יטול כשהרטיה על ידו יהיה חציצה

[29] See Shraga HaMeir (7:124) - בדבר שאלתו באיש הרוצה ללבוש בגד אשה, כגון מעילה מיוחד לאשה מפני הקור וצינה, או אשה הרוצית ללבוש בגד איש מפני הך טעמא אם יש בזה איסור הלאו של לא תלבש אשה כלי גבר ולא ילבש איש בגד אשה, וכת"ה מביא דברי הב"ח והש"ך מסי' קפ"ב, וכן סובר הטו"ז שם בס"ק ד שאם עושה כן מפני החמה או צנה או גשמים אין איסור עש"ה, רק כת"ה פלפל בדברי הב"ח וכן מביא בשם ספר בינת אדם כלל צ' אות צ"ד שהאריך לסתור דברי הב"ח. הנה כיון דהטו"ז וגם הש"ך מסכים לדברי הב"ח שאינם חולקים על הב"ח רק בדין לובש כל המלבושים שאינם לקישוט כו' אלא כיושב בין הנשים אבל אם אינו לובש הבגד רק להציל מן הצינה גם הש"ך מודה שמותר, וכן פסק כשו"ת אבני צדק (מסיגוט) חיו"ד סי' ע"ב כן להלכה, דכיון דמחשבת הלבישה אינה להתדמות לאיש רק מתכוין להציל מן הצנה, וא"כך יש כאן המעשה והמחשבה לטובה ולא התדמות לאיש, בכה"ג לא אסרה תורה בפרט במקום צער צנה דכל מקום שכוונתו להציל מן הצער לא מיקרי לא תלבש

[30] Devarim (22:5) - לֹא־יִהְיֶה כְלִי־גֶבֶר עַל־אִשָּׁה וְלֹא־יִלְבַּשׁ גֶּבֶר שִׂמְלַת אִשָּׁה כִּי תוֹעֲבַת ה אֱלֹהֶיךָ כָּל־עֹשֵׂה אֵלֶּה

[31] Rashi Devarim (22:5) - שֶׁתְּהֵא דּוֹמָה לְאִישׁ כְּדֵי שֶׁתֵּלֵךְ בֵּין הָאֲנָשִׁים שֶׁאֵין זוֹ אֶלָּא לְשֵׁם נִאוּף

opposite gender. For this reason, the Targum Yonasan[32] writes that Yael killed the sleeping Sisera using a tent spike rather than a sword in order to be *makayem* לֹא־יִהְיֶה כְלִי־גֶבֶר עַל־אִשָּׁה,[33] since a sword is a man's weapon. Would she have looked like a man by taking the sword? No. She would have looked like the same woman as before, but the Targum[34] seems to hold that there is an inherent problem of using the *keilim* of the opposite gender – in contrast to Rashi. The Rema[35] writes a man may dress up like a woman on Purim because that's only for *simcha.* It seems the Rema follows Rashi since if it was an *issur* whether you want to look like a woman or not, then it should be forbidden on Purim as well. Now this question is dependent on this *shailah*. His mother will not look like a man for wearing a man's suit jacket. Therefore, *b'dieved* you can rely on the *Poskim* who follow Rashi, but it's not the *da'as* of all the *Poskim* to allow this.[36]

---

[32] Targum Yonasan Shoftim (5:27) - טַבְתָּא יָעֵל אִתַּת חֶבֶר שַׁלְמָאָה דְקַיְמַת מַה דִכְתִיב בִּסְפַר אוֹרַיְתָא דְמֹשֶׁה לָא יֶהֱוֵי תִקוּן זֵין דִגְבַר עַל אִתְּתָא וְלָא יִתַקַן גְבַר בְּתִקוּנֵי אִתְּתָא אֱלָהֵן יְדָהָא לְסִכְתָא אוֹשִׁיטַת וִימִינָא לְאַרְזַפְתָּא דְנַפְחִין לְמִתְבַּר רַשִׁיעִין וַאֲנוּסִין מַחְתֵיהּ לְסִיסְרָא תַּבְרַת רֵישֵׁיהּ פַּצְעַת מוֹחֵיהּ אַעֲבָרַת סִכְתָא בְּצִדְעֵיהּ

[33] Shoftim (5:27) - יָדָהּ לַיָּתֵד תִּשְׁלַחְנָה וִימִינָהּ לְהַלְמוּת עֲמֵלִים וְהָלְמָה סִיסְרָא מָחֲקָה רֹאשׁוֹ וּמָחֲצָה וְחָלְפָה רַקָּתוֹ

[34] Targum Onkelos Devarim (22:5) - לָא יְהֵי תִקוּן זֵין דִגְבַר עַל אִתְּתָא וְלָא יְתַקַן גְבַר בְּתִקוּנֵי אִתְּתָא אֲרֵי מְרַחַק קֳדָם יְיָ אֱלָהָךְ כָּל עָבֵד אִלֵין

[35] Rema OC (696:8) - מה שנהגו ללבוש פרצופים בפורים וגבר לובש שמלת אשה ואשה כלי גבר אין איסור בדבר מאחר שאין מכוונין אלא לשמחה בעלמא

[36] Shulchan Aruch YD (182:5) - לא תעדה אשה עדי האיש כגון שתשים בראשה מצנפת או כובע או תלבש שריון וכיוצא בו (ממלבושי האיש לפי מנהג המקום ההוא) או שתגלח ראשה כאיש ולא יעדה איש עדי אשה כגון שילבש בגדי צבעונים וחלי זהב במקום שאין לובשין אותם הכלים ואין משימין אותו החלי אלא נשים: הגה ואפילו באחד מן הבגדים אסור אף על פי שניכרים בשאר בגדיהם שהוא איש או אשה

Q18. Is it better if his mother doesn't put her arms through the sleeves?

A: No, it's the same *machlokes haPoskim* whether or not she puts her arms through sleeves or merely allows the suit jacket to drape over her shoulders.

Q19. May a man dye his hair?

A: There was a story in Europe that a Rav had half a white beard and half a black beard. He wrote to all the *gedolei haPoskim* to find out whether he would be allowed to dye his beard since he wasn't changing the color to appear like a woman – women don't have black beards, but they do occasionally dye their white hair black. In addition to the *shailah* of לֹא־יִלְבַּשׁ, this was also a Choshen Mishpat *shailah* since some employers might be tricked into hiring him since he appears younger with a dyed black beard than he truly is.[37] The Divrei Chaim[38] - the Chassidishe Rebbe of Tzanz -

---

[37] Igros Moshe YD (2:61) - ובאם כוונת צביעתו הוא לא ליפוי אלא כדי שיקבלוהו למשרה באופן שאין איסור אונאה כגון שיודע שיעשה המלאכה כצעיר מסתבר שיש להתיר כמו בלובש מפני החמה והצנה שהתיר הב"ח כדהביאו הט"ז סק"ד והש"ך סק"ז והסכימו לזה כיון שהוא רק דבר אחד ולא מתדמה בזה לאשה. אחרי כתבי זה נזדמן לי לראות ספר המאור להגרא"מ פרייל שמדבר בזה וכן תשובה מהגאון ר' משה מרדכי עפשטיין הר"מ דסלאבאדקא והעלו ג"כ להתיר לצבוע בשביל השגת משרה כשליכא איסור אונאה עיי"ש

[38] Divrei Chaim YD (1:62) - ע״ד שאלתו אם מותר לאיש שנתלבנו חצי זקנו וגבות עיניו וחצי השני נשארו שחור אם מותר לצבעם ומעכ״ת נוטה להקל ותמוה לי טובא הלא כל ההיתר של הרשב״א ותו׳ [הובא בב״י קפ״ב] בצריך לרפואה או כל גופו הוא רק משום דס״ל העברת שער הוי מדרבנן אבל אם הי׳ מדאו׳ אסור לעבור על לאו והנה במלקט שחירות מתוך לבנית כ׳ הרמב״ם ז״ל [פי״ב מעכו״ם ה״י] דלוקה וכ״פ הראב״ד דבהרבה שערות לוקה כמבואר בהשגות וכ״פ הטור ביו״ד קפ״ב א״כ בודאי אין חכמה ואין עצה אפי׳ במקום כבוד הבריות אסור והנה בחפזי לא מצאתי מי שיחלוק על הרמב״ם והראב״ד והטור הנ״ל א״כ בודאי אסור לצבוע שחור ולוקה משום לא ילבש אך תקנתו שיצבע שיהי׳ כולו לבן דבזה אין שום

said it's better to shave off one's beard than color the white part of the beard black. Even the Chassidim know having a beard is a *middas chassidus*, but dying the hair is a potential *issur d'oraysa*.[39]

Q20. May this man dye his black beard white?

A: Dying the black part of the beard white would be permitted because women generally don't dye their hair white.[40] Nonetheless, it's very difficult to keep a darker

---

איסור כלל כמבואר בב"י סי' קפ"ב וז"ב וגם תמהתי איך עלה על דעתו להתיר אפי' איסור דרבנן במקום שיכול להסיר חרפתו במה שיגלח ע"י סם כמו שנוהגין בכל מדינות אשכנז דאין בזה שום איסור כלל וגם בגבות עיניו יוכל להתחבל שלא יוכר היטב אבל ח"ו להתיר איסור לאו בתורה והרבה יש להסתפק אם הוא מביזרא דג"ע דיהרג ואל יעבור להרבה שיטות ולכן והשתא דאתית להכא - and see Minchas Elazar (4:23) ח"ו להקל שי"ל שאינו רק איסור דרבנן וכמ"ש בערך ש"י כנ"ל וא"כ שפיר יש לדמותו למ"ש שם (קפב) בד"מ בשם המרדכי דבני אדם שיש בהם ריבוי שערות ביד מותר להסירם דאין לך צער גדול מזה עכ"ל ולא שייך לחלק דהתם בשאר אברים להסיר השערות לכ"ע לא הוי רק דרבנן וכמ"ש הרמב"ם בזה (פרק יב מהל' ע"ז הלכה ט) וע"כ מותר משום צער שמתבייש וכנז' משא"כ הכא דהוי איסור תורה וכמו שחילקו בזה במהר"י אשכנזי ובערך ש"י. וז"א כיון דאיירינן השתא די"ל שפיר דאינו רק איסור דבריהם גם בצובע זקנו במינכר. אם נאמר דטעמא של הראב"ד הואיל ומינכר אינו עיקר אצלו כנ"ל רק כיון דהכונה בש"ס רק אסור מדבריהם וא"כ בזה יש להתיר לו לצבוע להסיר צער בשתו כנז' דומיא דהתם בשערות שעל ידיו שהתירו כיון שאינו רק מדבריהם

[39] Shulchan Aruch YD (182:6) - אסור (לאיש) ללקט אפילו שער אחד לבן מתוך השחורות משום לא ילבש גבר וכן אסור לאיש לצבוע (שערות לבנות שיהיו) שחורות אפילו שערה אחת

[40] Beis Yosef YD (182:9) - וכן כתב הרמב"ם גבי צבע מי ששערו שחור וצבעו לבן חייב אפי' בשער אחת נוסחא זו אינה מכוונת דלשון הרמב"ם בסוף הלכות ע"ז כך הוא וכן אם צבע שערו שחור משיצבע לבנה אחת לוקה והדברים מבוארים דבבא לצבוע לבנות שבו בצבע שחור כדי להראות בחור מיירי וקאמר דמשיצבע לבנה אחת משערות לבנות שבו וישחירנו לוקה דאילו בגוונא שכתב רבינו לאו נוי הוא לו להראות זקן ואע"ג דאיש הדר הוא לו מ"מ כיון דגבי אשה לאו נוי הוא אלא גריעות תו

beard white since the darker color comes through the dye. Someone told me he needed to paint his newly acquired house with seven coatings of white paint in order to prevent the black paint from coming through. On the other hand, it would take only one coat of black paint to cover the white wall.

Q21. May one be *meyached* with his grandmother?

A: This is a *din* in the Shulchan Aruch. You are allowed to be *meyached* with your grandmother, great grandmother, and all the previous generations of grandmothers all the way back to Sarah Imeinu even *b'derech kevius*.[41] Similarly, it's permitted for you to be *meyached* with your daughter,[42]

לית ביה משום לא ילבש שמלת אשה. ומשמע לי דאפי' לכתחלה שרי ללבן שערותיו כיון דלית ביה משום תקוני אשה

[41] Igros Moshe EH (4:65:8) - אבל מה שנמנעות הקרובות דהוא מפני שאין להן תאוה אין טעם שגם היא שאינה קרובתו ואית לה תאוה שתמנע מלזנות עמו מ"מ כיון דאין כוונת בושה זו מצד שתתבייש לעשות מעשה איסור לפניה אלא מצד בושה טבעית שלא תעיז לעשות פריצות כזו להבעל בזנות והפקרותא בפני אינשי אף להכנס בפניהם לזנות להדר אחר לא שייך לחלק שלכן אף בקרובות כיון שהן לא יזנו הוא שמירה שגם האחרות לא יזנו ואין לאסור

[42] Shulchan Aruch EH (22:2) - אסור להתייחד עם ערוה מהעריות בין זקנה בין ילדה שדבר זה גורם לגלות ערוה חוץ מהאם עם בנה והאב עם בתו and Pischei Teshuva EH (22:2) - עיין בב"ח אות א' שכתב דכל יוצאי חלציו דינן שוה בת בתו ובת בת בתו נמי שרי כמו בתו עכ"ל (ע' לעיל סי' נ"א בבה"ט סקי"ד ומ"ש שם סק"ה ועיין בנו"ב תניינא סי' י"ח ויובא לקמן סי' קע"ח סק"י) וע' בס' זכור לאברהם אות י' יחוד הביא ג"כ דברי הב"ח אלו. וכ' עוד ולכאורה נראה דכ"ז הוא דוקא להתייחד עמה לבדה אבל אם יש שם אשה אחרת אפי' עם בתו או בת בתו שם אסור דהא בב' נשים אסור להתייחד לכ"ע וכמו כן אב ובתו ההולכים בדרך ויש ישראל אחר עמהם אסור דדוקא בעיר מהני ב' אנשים ולא בדרך ומטעם שמא יצטרך א' לנקביו וכאן נמי יש חשש שמא יצטרך האב ותשאר בתו ביחוד עם ישראל האחר. ומזה הטעם אשה ההולכת בדרך ובנה עמה לא תוכל לילך עם עגלון אא"כ יש ישראל אחר דהוי ג' עם העגלון. באופן דנראה דאין חילוק בין אם הוא בנה או אביה וכדומה דלעולם בעינן ג' דדוקא בבעל

granddaughter,[43] and all future generations of daughters. There is also no *issur negiah.*

Q22. May one hold or hug his 5-year-old niece?

A: The Rambam[44] says hugging your aunt, sister, or niece is considered a *maaseh tipshus* and forbidden since they are considered *arayos*. Although a niece isn't necessarily considered an *ervah*, the Rambam still says it's forbidden. Even if she starts crying, you should comfort her without touching.

Q23. When is the cut-off age for touching one's niece?

A: We find in the Gemara[45] that Rav Acha put the *kallah* on his shoulders. When his *talmidim* asked him if they could do the same, he replied, "When you consider the *kallah* like a piece of wood, then you may." Meaning, you have no *hirhurim* when picking her up. The *Poskim* say nowadays we don't have anyone who can say they can truly feel women are like a piece of wood. Nonetheless, you see from here that something which is a normal form of *hiskarvus* is problematic, but if it's not a normal form of *hiskarvus* then

---

ואשה אמרו דמשמרין זא"ז ולא באחר וע' ת' מהרי"ו סי' נ"ה. וע"ש עוד שכתב בשם חכם אחד דאף אי נימא דהבן מהני לשמור אמו משום דהבן מקפיד שלא תזנה אמו משא"כ אב עם בתו דהבת אינה מקפדת כ"כ אם יזנה אביה ע"ש

[43] Pischei Teshuva EH (22:2) - והאב עם בתו. עיין בב"ח אות א' שכתב דכל יוצאי חלציו דינן שוה בת בתו ובת בת בתו נמי שרי כמו בתו חוץ מהאב לבתו. וה"ה and Chelkas Mechokek EH (21:10) - עכ"ל לבת בתו כדאמרינן בגמ' שם הכל לש"ש

[44] Rambam Isurei Biah (21:6) - הַמְחַבֵּק אַחַת מִן הָעֲרָיוֹת שֶׁאֵין לִבּוֹ שֶׁל אָדָם נוֹקְפוֹ עֲלֵיהֶן אוֹ שֶׁנִּשֵּׁק לְאַחַת מֵהֶן כְּגוֹן אֲחוֹתוֹ הַגְּדוֹלָה וַאֲחוֹת אִמּוֹ וְכַיּוֹצֵא בָּהֶן אַף עַל פִּי שֶׁאֵין שָׁם תַּאֲוָה וְלֹא הֲנָאָה כְּלָל הֲרֵי זֶה מְגֻנֶּה בְּיוֹתֵר וְדָבָר אָסוּר הוּא וּמַעֲשֵׂה טִפְּשִׁים הוּא. שֶׁאֵין קְרֵבִין לְעֶרְוָה כְּלָל בֵּין גְּדוֹלָה בֵּין קְטַנָּה חוּץ מֵהָאֵם לִבְנָהּ וְהָאָב לְבִתּוֹ

[45] Kesubos (17a) - רב אחא מרכיב לה אכתפיה ומרקד אמרי ליה רבנן אנן מהו למיעבד הכי אמר להו אי דמיין עלייכו ככשורא לחיי ואי לא לא

it is permitted. Therefore, incidentally touching another passenger's hand on the subway is not a problem[46] as well as taking change from a cashier – assuming you're not touching with any *kavana* to have *hana'ah* or *hirhurim.*[47] Rav Moshe[48] has a *teshuva* about adopted children where he

---

[46] Igros Moshe EH (2:14) - הנה מצד הנגיעה ודחיפה בנשים אז ליכא שום איסור משום דאין זה דרך תאוה וחבה וכל איסור נגיעה בעריות הוא אף להרמב"ם שסובר שהוא בלאו דלא תקרבו דאורייתא דוקא דרך תאוה כמפורש בדבריו ריש פכ"א מאי"ב ומשמע שבלא דרך תאוה ליכא אף איסור מדרבנן שלא הזכיר זה ומפורש כן בש"ך יו"ד סימן קנ"ז סק"י שהרי כתב הש"ך ראיה ממה שמצינו האמוראים היו מחבקים ומנשקים לבנותיהם ואחיותיהם

[47] Shach YD (195:20) - ודאי אף להרמב"ם ליכא איסור דאורייתא אלא כשעושה כן דרך תאוה וחיבת ביאה

[48] Igros Moshe EH (4:64:2) - במי שמגדל יתום או יתומה שאשכחן שהוא מצוה גדולה וכן מה שהרבה אינשי שלא זכו לבנים משיגים בן ובת ומגדלים אותם באופן שלא ידעו כלל הרבה שנים עד שיגדלו שאינם אביהם ואמם ממש ויש שאין רוצים לגלות להם כלל אבל זה הוא דבר אסור דהא אפשר שישאו קרוביהם האסורות להם...עכ"פ כשעושין כדין ודאי צריך לדון בדבר היחוד אף שנקל בזו מפני הסתם והצורך גם עד בת ח' וט' הא מגדלין אותן כל השנים כמו בן ובת ממש והיחוד הוא יותר מוקשה מהחיבוק ונישוק דאין זה דרך תאוה וחיבת ביאה אלא דרך חיבוק ונישוק לבניו ובנותיו שלא נאסר כדאיתא בש"ך יו"ד סימן קנ"ז סק"י ומשמע שם דליכא איסורא כלל ומשמע מסוטה סוף דף מ"ג מהא דא"ר יצחק א"ר יוחנן משום ראב"י חורגתא הגדילה בין האחין אסור לינשא לאחין דמתחזיא כי אחתייהו דלא היה היכר בהנהגת האב עם החורגתא מהנהגתו עם בתו ואם לא היה נוגע בה ולא היה מתייחד עמה כמו עם בתו היה זה ניכר לעלמא דהא דוחק לומר דהוא דמתחזיא לאלו שרואין רק שהיא נמצאת שם בבית יאמרו שהיא בת להאב ואחות להאחין וכי יסברו כן גם על משרתת שכורה כמה שנים אצלם שאסורה לינשא לאחין שא"כ משמע שהוא דוקא מחמת שמתנהג עמה כהנהגת האב עם בתו ממש ואם היה זהיר מלהתייחד עמה שלא כהנהגת כו"ע עם בתם היה זה היכר גדול שאינה אחותם ולא היה שייך לאסור והגמ' דמסיק דאין הלכה כן הוא משום דקלא אית לה למלתא הוא מידיעת בני העיר שבשעה שנשא את אשתו זו היה לה בת שקבל עליו לזונה ולפרנסה ולהשיאה כמו לבתו שמהם ידעו אף האינשי הנולדים והבאים אח"כ להעיר אבל גם הם סברי שהנהגת האב עם החורגתא היתה כהנהגתו עם בתו ממש ודוחק לומר דאיירי באיש עבריין לאיסור יחוד ולכאורה הא

discusses telling them when they become Bar or Bas Mitzvah that they were adopted or *megayer*. Rav Moshe addresses in that *teshuva* about treating the child like a regular child – including hugging and *yichud*. The adopted boy's mother is allowed to hug him because that's not *hiskarvus* for *arayos*, rather it's considered motherly love. However, hugging a sister isn't the same natural feeling of being cared for by hugging his sister. If she hugs you anyway, then you can just stand still like a piece of wood as *karka olam*. *Yichud* for your niece would start at three years old[49] as an *isha penuya* which Dovid HaMelech was *gozer* on,[50] but you can have a *yotzei v'nichnas* or give the key to a neighbor.[51]

תמוה זה וצריך לומר דיירא מאשתו שתהא חושדתו שבחזרתה תחקור ותדרוש לבתה ולהיתומה ויגלו לה שלכן מאלו שנמצאין בבית תדיר עמו ועם אשתו אין לאסור אף אם נזדמן איזה זמן קצר שלא היתה אשתו ונשאר הוא לבדו עם בתה ועם היתומה שמגדלין וכן להיפוך אם היא נשארה זמן קצר עם בנו ועם יתום שמגדלין ואם מתה אשתו בעצם יש לו ליזהר שלא יתייחד עם בתה ועם היתומה שמגדלין ומה שיש שאין נזהרין אולי סומכין מפני הדחק ע"ז שכיון שמגדל אותה כבתו לא ירצה לקלקלה מצד שרוצה בטובתה וכן כשהוא מת ונשאר בנו מאשה אחרת אצלה לא תתפתה לו כיון שרוצה בטובתו אבל ודאי אין לסמוך ע"ז וצריכין ליזהר שלא להתייחד עם אלו שמגדלין כשמת אחד מהם

[49] Shulchan Aruch EH (22:11) - תינוקת שהיא פחותה מבת שלש ותינוק פחות מבן ט' מותר להתייחד עמהן שלא גזרו אלא על יחוד אשה הראויה לביאה ואיש הראוי לביאה

[50] Avoda Zara (36b) - כי גזרו בית דינו של חשמונאי ביאה אבל ייחוד לא ואתו אינהו גזור אפי' ייחוד ייחוד נמי בית דינו של דוד גזרו

[51] Shevet Halevi (9:261) - ולענין אם יש לכל בני בית מפתחות שהם יוכלים לבא מבחוץ עיין תשובת דובב מישרים סו"ס ה' שהגאון מטשיבין זצ"ל דן בזה ומדמה זה לשיטת המקילים בדלת סתומה ולא נעולה וכ' דנדון זה כדין דלת נעולה ולא סגורה כיון דאפשר לשמוח מבחוץ ולא באתי לחלוק על בעל דובב מישרים אבל הדבר שקול אם הנושאים דומים וגם אני בענייי בשבט הלוי ח"ה סי' ר"ג-ד נטיתי להחמיר בפלוגתא זו של הפוסקים מכ"מ אין להרהר למי שמקיל כנ"ד כיון שיש גדולי פוסקים מקילים בזה ובצירוף עכ"פ כמה סניפים

Q24. How close must one be in a city for it to be considered *ba'alah ba'ir*?

A: As long as the adjacent city the husband is currently working in does business with the city of the *yichud*, then it is still considered *ba'alah ba'ir*.[52] On the other hand, if the two areas don't do business together then it's not *ba'alah ba'ir* even if it's one large city. For instance, Far Rockaway and Washington Heights in New York are at least an hour distance from one another without traffic. The stores in Far Rockaway won't necessarily send leaflet advertisements to Washington Heights about a sale. Pikesville is certainly a part of Baltimore, and Columbia is part of Baltimore as well since stores there send advertisements to Baltimore. However, the Vaad HaRabbonim of Washington has a deal with the Vaad HaKashrus of Baltimore that neither of us give *hashgacha* to establishments in the other's location without permission. Our agreement is that Columbia is included in the area of Baltimore, but any region beyond Columbia is considered Washington.

---

[52] Shulchan Aruch EH (22:8) - אשה שבעלה בעיר אין חוששין להתייחד עמה מפני שאימת בעלה עליה ואם היה זה גס בה כגון שגדלה עמו או שהיא קרובתו או אם קינא לה בעלה עם זה לא יתייחד עמה אע"פ שבעלה בעיר

Chapter 6: Shonim 5779

Q1. Does toothpaste need to be checked for non-kosher ingredients?

A: You don't really eat toothpaste. Therefore, *pashtus* it doesn't matter whether it's kosher or not.[1] The problem is that even though you don't have *kavana* to eat toothpaste, there is still a small amount of toothpaste which remains in your mouth and is swallowed. I would think *m'ikar hadin* since you don't have intention to eat it and it's not *ra'ui l'achila* – people don't eat toothpaste and don't even give it to a dog – then it would not be considered *treif*. However, it is a *middas chassidus* not to eat anything which comes from a non-kosher source even though it is not forbidden.[2] In former times, babies were only fed by their mothers through nursing – they didn't have formula. Baby bottles were only used by older babies who would drink milk from a cow. In fact, they would use a *shofar* to feed these older babies by making a small hole in the narrow end. Of course you needed to be careful to make sure the wide end of the *shofar* was tilted up otherwise all the milk would spill out, but eventually the babies would figure it out. It says in the Megillas Antiochus that one of the decrees the Yevanim made was כִּתְבוּ עַל קֶרֶן הַשּׁוֹר - you must write on the horn of the ox that you have nothing to do with the Ribbono Shel

---

[1] Pischei Teshuva YD (98:1) - ועיין בשו"ת צמח צדק סי' מ"ז שנשאל אם מותר לטעום הבורית אם יש בו מלח כל צרכו והשיב דאע"ג דדבר שהוא פגום. מדרבנן מיהא אסור לכתחלה וטעימה היינו דוקא לאכילה אבל לטעימה שרי לכתחלה וטעימה אינו אסור אלא מדרבנן ובדרבנן לא גזרו ע"ש. והמובן מדבריו דס"ל דה"ה בכל איסורי דרבנן שרי טעימה ואף לטעום בפיו ממש

[2] Shach YD (108:24) - אבל אסור לטועמו. אע"פ שאינו בולע ע"ש בריב"ש שכת' דבכל איסורי אכילה אפי' שאינם אסורים בהנאה נמי אסור לטועמן

Olam.[3] Why write that on the *keren hashor*? I would understand if you would need to write that on the wall of your house. Rav Kulefsky *zecher tzaddik l'vracha* said the *keren hashor* we're talking about is the baby bottle. The Yevanim said that already at such a young age the child needed to be *mechunach* that he has nothing to do with the Ribbono Shel Olam as part of their goal to steer people away from Yiddishkeit. In former times, if you couldn't nurse a child yourself then you would need to give it someone else. It says in the Shulchan Aruch that if a woman can't nurse her child, she should not give her child to a non-Jewish nursing mother because she eats *treif* food.[4] What's the problem with that? Chazal say the child can taste what the mother ate in the milk. Since the child will taste the *ta'am issur*, it's like giving him *issur*. If another nursing mother is available who is Jewish, then you cannot go to the non-Jew. Not only that, but the Shach says that if a Jewish mother needed to eat something *treif* for *pikuach nefesh* – which she is allowed and obligated to do – she shouldn't nurse her child after that because of *timtum halev*.[5] That doesn't mean to say it is forbidden for the child to drink milk with a taste of *issur*. Although cows *pashtus* eat only kosher food as grass is kosher, but chickens love eating earthworms yet we eat them and their eggs. We don't even say *l'chatchila* to avoid eating chickens which get their energy from worms. It's not forbidden, but there's an *inyan* not to taste *ta'am issur*. Therefore, there's an *inyan* to buy kosher toothpaste, but if

---

[3] Bereishis Rabba (2:4) - וְחֹשֶׁךְ זֶה גָּלוּת יָוָן שֶׁהֶחֱשִׁיכָה עֵינֵיהֶם שֶׁל יִשְׂרָאֵל בִּגְזֵרוֹתֵיהֶן שֶׁהָיְתָה אוֹמֶרֶת לָהֶם כִּתְבוּ עַל קֶרֶן הַשּׁוֹר שֶׁאֵין לָכֶם חֵלֶק בֵּאלֹקֵי יִשְׂרָאֵל

[4] Rema YD (81:7) - חלב מצרית כחלב ישראלית ומ"מ לא יניקו תינוק מן המצרית אם אפשר בישראלית דהחלב עובדת כוכבים מטמטם הלב ומוליד לו טבע רע

[5] Shach YD (81:25) - כלומר אע"פ שאסור לה בלא"ה לאכול דברים האסורים מ"מ גם בשביל התינוק לא תאכל ונ"מ אם היא חולה בענין שצריך להאכילה דברים האסורי' לא יתן האב לתינוק לינק ממנה אלא ישכור לו מינקת אחרת ישראלית

it's not available then you can't say non-kosher toothpaste can't be used.

Q2. Do e-cig drops need to be checked for non-kosher ingredients?

A: E-cigarettes are not even eaten at all. I believe they are only inhaled. There is no *halacha* anywhere which says you cannot inhale non-kosher smoke.[6] There are *issurei hana'ah* - like maybe *chametz* on Pesach - which are problematic to smell,[7] but I don't think e-cigarettes are a problem from a *kashrus* perspective. However, I don't think e-cigarettes are too healthy to smoke, so if there is a question regarding it being habit forming and bad for your health, then you shouldn't smoke e-cigarettes. I heard they might be worse for your health than normal cigarettes, so time will tell to see how long people live after smoking e-cigarettes and how long people live after smoking regular cigarettes. Then we'll find out the truth.

Q3. If a *shiur* that is recorded is sold by the Yeshiva, and one records it on his own device, can he distribute it to his friends and family for free?

---

[6] Pischei Yeshuva YD (108:3) - אף לדעת רובא דרבוותא שפסקו דסתם יינם אסור בהנאה מ"מ שרי לשאוף הטאב"ק דזה ממש כההיא דבת תיהא דשרי לכ"ע והלכה פסוקה היא זולת סברת איכא מ"ד שכתב הרי"ף וכ"ש בנ"ד דאיכא לספוקי שמא יש ס' נגד היין שמזלפין דבהא לכ"ע ריחא לאו מלתא

[7] Biur Halacha (443:1) - כתבו האחרונים בסי' תמ"ח דלפ"ז אסור להריח גם פת חמה של עכו"ם. ובח"מ מפקפק בעיקר דינא דריח פת חמץ ואפילו בישראל לפי מה דקי"ל ביורה דעה סימן ק"ח דדבר שאינו עומד לריח מותר להריח בו וכמו כן לענין פת עיין בדבריו אכן באמת לא ברירא עיקר דבר זה אם פת אינו עומד לריח עיין לעיל סי' רי"ד בהג"ה ב' דעות בזה ועיי"ש בביאור הגר"א גם ביורה דעה סי' ק"ח גופא איתא לחד מ"ד דבחמץ בפסח דאיסורא במשהו אמרי' ריחא מילתא עיי"ש ובר מן דין יש לאסור מטעם אחר דשמא יבא לאכלו

A: If it's sold by the Yeshiva, and the Yeshiva writes a *siman* that it's copyrighted, you should assume they are *makpid* and you would not be allowed to record it on your own device,[8] and certainly cannot share it with friends or family even for free. However, if the Yeshiva does not say it's copyrighted, then you can assume they are not *makpid.* The rights to a *shiur* given by a Rosh Yeshiva which is recorded by the Yeshiva is owned by the Yeshiva because they pay the Rosh Yeshiva to be *mechadesh chiddushim.* If the Rosh Yeshiva wants to put out the *shiur* himself, he will need to have a Din Torah with the Yeshiva regarding who has the rights to his *chiddushim.* It probably depends on the understanding from when he was originally hired. Either way, one of them has the intellectual rights to the property of the *shiur*, so if they are *makpid* then you cannot record the *shiur*. The Chofetz Chaim wrote that he gives permission to anyone who wants to reprint the Mishna Berura. However, today we have a Mishna Berura with *hagahos* and *peirushim*, like when the Mishna Berura says something in Polish which is translated into another language. Therefore, the person who invested the work into those additions might have a claim against copying that particular Mishna Berura, so you would only be able to copy over the original Mishna Berura.

Q4. Is an Ashkenazi allowed to eat non-glatt meat?

A: There is a *machlokes* between the Mechaber and the Rema which generally boils down to a *machlokes* between Sefardim and Ashkenazim as the Mechaber was a Sefardi and the Rema was an Ashkenazi. The Mechaber wrote in the

---

[8] Igros Moshe OC (4:40:19) - בדבר אחד שעשה טייפ מדברי תורה וכותב שאוסר לעשות מטייפ שלו עוד טייפס ודאי אסור כי הוא ענין שוה כסף ועשה הטייפ להרויח מזה שאחרים שירצו יצטרכו לשלם לו שא"כ ליכא משום מדת סדום ממילא כיון שהוא חפצו אין רשאין ליקח אותו להשתמש בו שלא ברשות ואף כשלא שמעו ממנו שאינו נותן רשות אסור להעתיק ממנו בסתמא כל מן שלא הרשה בפירוש...וליתן גם לאחרים יכול לעכב שלא יעשו כלל אבל עכ"פ הוא ענין איסור אחר ולא איסור גזלה אבל לעשות טייפ אחר מטייפ אחד שלא ברשות הוא איסור גזל

hakdama to the Beis Yosef[9] that he wrote the Shulchan Aruch with the *hachra'ah* of his Beis Din – which is the Rambam, Rif, and the Rosh – and whenever the three agree that's how he *poskins* unless all the other Rishonim disagree, which is not usually the case. The Rema says the Ba'alei Tosafos - who numbered in the hundreds is more than the Rosh, the Rif and the Rambam - so he *poskins* like Tosafos against the other Rishonim. The Ashkenazi *yidden* follow the Ba'alei Tosafos which is where most of them lived. The Rambam was a Sefardi who lived in Spain and went to Egypt, the Rif was in North Africa in Morocco, and the Rosh was initially a Sefardi who eventually went to Ashkenaz. That being said, the if there is a hole in the lung then the animal is *treif.*[10] Everyone agrees to that and there is no *machlokes*. The question is what happens if this hole repairs itself naturally with scar tissue growing over this hole?[11] The Mechaber[12] says the animal is *treif* because the hole isn't

---

[9] Beis Yosef Introduction - ועלה בדעתי שאחר כל הדברים אפסוק הלכה ואכריע בין הסברות כי זהו התכלית להיות לנו תורה אחת ומשפט אחד וראיתי שאם באנו לומר שנכריע דין בין הפוסקים בטענות וראיות תלמודיות הנה התוספות וחידושי הרמב"ן והרשב"א והר"ן ז"ל מלאים טענות וראיות לכל אחת מהדיעות. ומי הוא זה אשר יערב ליבו לגשת להוסיף טענות וראיות ואיזהו אשר ימלאהו ליבו להכניס ראשו בין ההרים הררי א-ל להכריע ביניהם על פי טענות וראיות לסתור מה שביררו הם או להכריע במה שלא הכריע הם כי בעוונותינו הרבים קצר מצע שכלינו להבין דבריהם כל שכן להתחכם עליהם. ולא עוד אלא שאפילו היה אפשר לנו לדרוך דרך זה לא היה ראוי להחזיק בה לפי שהיא דרך ארוכה ביותר ולכן הסכמתי בדעתי כי להיות שלושת עמודי ההוראה אשר הבית בית ישראל נשען עליהם בהוראותיהם הלא המה הרי"ף והרמב"ם והרא"ש ז"ל אמרתי אל ליבי שבמקום ששנים מהם מסכימים לדעה אחת נפסוק הלכה כמותם

[10] Shulchan Aruch YD (35:1) - ריאה שניקבה טריפה

[11] Shulchan Aruch YD (36:3) - ניקבה ועלה בו קרום ונסתם טריפה

[12] Shulchan Aruch YD (39:10) - כל מקום שאסרו סרוכת הריאה אין הפרש בין שתהא הסירכא דקה כחוט השערה בין שתהא עבה וחזקה ורחבה כגודל ולא כאותם שממעכים ביד ואם נתמעכה תולים להקל וכל הנוהג כן כאלו מאכיל טרפות לישראל

completely repaired. The Rema[13] says if you can peel off the scar tissue so there is no more scar tissue after peeling it off and the hole is no longer there, then the lung is repaired and the animal is no longer *treif*. That is the *machlokes*. Typically after *shechting* an animal, especially a large animal like a bull, steer, or cow - but it's also true by smaller animals like calves or lambs - the *shochet* cuts open the skin near the outside of the lung and puts his hand in between the wall of the animal and the lung. If there is any scar tissue which has grown between the lung and the side of the animal, or between the different lobes of the lungs, then the Mechaber[14] says the animal is *treif*. On the other hand, the Rema[15] says you can take out the lung, peel off the scar tissue, and check the lung by blowing it up the same way you blow up a car tire to see where the air is leaking. Then you place it into water to see where the bubbles emerge from. That's a *siman muvhak* to see whether there's a hole in the lung or not. If there is a hole in the lung, then it's *treif*. If there is no hole,

---

[13] Rema YD (39:13) - ויש מתירין למשמש בסרכות ולמעך בהם ואומרים שסרכא אם ימעך אדם בה כל היום לא תנתק ולכן כל מקום שיתמעך תולין להקל ואומרים שאינו סרכא אלא ריר בעלמא ואע"פ שהוא קולא גדולה כבר נהגו כל בני מדינות אלו ואין למחות בידם מאחר שיש להם על מה שיסמכו ומכ"מ צריך להיות הבודק ירא אלהים שיודע ליזהר למעך בנחת שלא ינתק בכח ויש מקומות שאין נוהגין למעך ולמשמש בסרכות הורדא אם נסרכה למקום אחר וכל מקום שתסרך טריפה ויש מקומות שנהגו להקל גם בזה ולי נראה כסברא הראשונה שלא למעך בורדא ובכל סרכות שהם שלא כסדרן מאחר שסירכא שלא כסדרן טריפה מוזכר בגמ' ואין חולק עליו אין לסמוך אדברי מקילין בענין המעוך והמשמושים אבל המנהג בעירנו למשמש ולמעך בכל הסרכות ואין חלוק בין סרכא לסרכא ונכון לחוש למה שכתבתי אם לא בהפסד מרובה עוד נהגו בעירנו להטריף כל סרכות גדיים וטלאים ועגלים הרכים ולא למעך בהם כלל כי יש קבלה בזה להטריף כי הסירכא עדיין רכה ומתנתקת על ידי מיעוך

[14] Shulchan Aruch YD (39:1) - אין צריך לבדוק אחר שום טריפות מן הסתם חוץ מן הריאה צריך לבדוק בבהמה וחיה אם יש בה סירכה וכל הפורץ גדר לאכול בלא בדיקה ישכנו נחש

[15] Rema YD (39:1) - ונהגו ג"כ לנפוח כל ריאה אפילו לית בה ריעותא ובקצת מקומות מקילין שלא לנפחה רק אם היתה בה סירכא עוברת על ידי משמוש וכן עיקר

then the Rema says it's kosher. That is the *din*, and that was the *minhag* in Europe for hundreds of years. Not only that, I spoke to a Rosh Yeshiva from Paris, Rav Yaakov Toledano, who was a big *talmid chacham* and moved his Yeshiva to Eretz Yisroel. He told me his family was from Toledano, which was in either Spain or Portugal – which are both Sefardi regions. Sometimes the family name was the place where you came from since countries became gradually more *makpid* for people to have a last name. If a person's name is Berlin, then you know he moved from Berlin to somewhere else. Let's say he moved from Berlin to Frankfurt, then the people in Frankfurt would call him Berlin. They wouldn't call him Berlin if he lived in Berlin since they would all have the same name. Some people were called London – a lot of names from cities. So Rav Toledano told me his family escaped to Morocco which was owned by France. They had a big *machlokes* with the people who lived in Morocco regarding the *shechita* because the people there were *noheg* like the Mechaber while the people from Toledano were *noheg* like the Rema. This was before there even was a Mechaber or Rema - the cities had this *machlokes* already! The citizens of Morocco complained this Rav Toledano came with a bunch of *kulos*. The Mechaber and Rema weren't *mechadesh* the idea. Glatt is really a compromise between the Mechaber and Rema where the Rema says you can peel off every adhesion, inflate the lungs, and see if any air comes through. Glatt is very thin, about the thickness of a regular needle, and it could be peeled off easily. However, if it took time to remove the *sircha* then they were not lenient it because they were afraid some people might not test it properly. In America, it's much easier to be stringent on glatt-kosher than it is in Europe. In Europe, a butcher hardly had any kosher slaughterhouses the same way there are today. The butcher would take a few animals to the *shochet* and the Rav. The butcher was concerned the *shochet* would be stringent, so he wanted the Rav to *poskin* the *shailah* as he knew more of Hilchos Shechita with the *lamdus* of the Rishonim enough to potentially formulate a leniency. Since the entire *parnasa* of the butcher was dependent on what the Rav *poskined*, Rabbonim were lenient like the Rema. Moreover, if the three animals the butcher brought to be *shechted* were found not to be kosher, then not only would the butcher not have *parnasa* for that week, but no one in the town would have kosher meat that week either. That *sha'as hadchak* situation allowed the Rabbonim to be more lenient. In America today (around 5776), there are less than ten slaughterhouses where they actually *shecht* the animals. All of those slaughterhouses are owned by non-Jews except for one. Even the one owned by the *yid* can sell the animals which aren't kosher, so he still can make a *parnasa* by selling it to one of the three hundred million non-Jews in America. No one loses much by *poskining* an animal is considered *treif* in America, but in Europe they were more lenient. We are not stringent for Beis Yosef glatt kosher nowadays because the more people eat only glatt kosher, the scarcer the glatt kosher will become. The scarcer the Beis Yosef glatt kosher meat becomes, the more pressure the *shochtim* have on them to make more meat glatt kosher. It's not so simple. We know there are certain types of animals which will statistically produce more kosher animals than others. Even among the animals which generally come out more kosher than others, we can get about 35% of them glatt kosher, maybe 55% regular kosher, and 10-15% Beis Yosef kosher. If everyone eats Beis Yosef, then we would need to *shecht* almost seven times more animals than we need in order to get enough Beis Yosef glatt kosher. If everyone wants Beis Yosef glatt, then the *shochtim* will need to water down what glatt kosher means – which already started happening in Eretz Yisroel because the Sefardim need to eat Beis Yosef glatt. In Eretz Yisroel, 60% of the Jewish population are Sefardim. There isn't enough Beis Yosef glatt to go around, so they need to water down the definition of glatt or *shecht* significantly more animals – which raises the price of meat for the added number of animals, people, and time required to produce more glatt Beis Yosef. Therefore, when you ask whether an Ashkenazi can eat non-glatt kosher meat, the answer is that he is allowed to. The old *minhag* of the Ashkenazim was to eat non-glatt kosher meat. Nonetheless, if a person eats glatt kosher meat three times with the intention of doing so in the future, then it is like a *neder*.[16] However, if that's not his *minhag* and he's not *mekabel* it on himself, then he's not obligated to do that.

Q5. Is there a *ma'alah* to Chassidishe *shechita*?

A: Does that mean the *shochet* is a *chassid* or he belongs to a group called *Chassidim*? It depends who you ask. Some people say it is not enough to have just *Chassidish shechita*, but it must be your type of *chassid*. So if you're a Lubavitcher *chassid*, then it must be Lubavitcher *shechita*, and if you're a Satmar *chassid* then it must be Satmar *shechita*. If you're not Lubavitch, Satmar, Belz, or the like, then it doesn't really make any difference. As long as the *shochet* is an *ehrliche yid* and a *yirei shamayim*, then the *shechita* is good. If he's not a *yirei shamayim*, then it doesn't help what kind of *chassid* he is because his *shechita* should be rejected. It's all dependent on what kind of *yirei shamayim* you are. The Shulchan Aruch[17] says he should be a *yirei shamayim b'rabim* – not a *stam yirei shamayim* – because so much depends on the *shochet*. If he stops anywhere for a split second in the middle of the *shechita* then

---

[16] Kitzur Shulchan Aruch (67:7) - מִי שֶׁנָּהַג אֵיזֶה חֻמְרָא בִּדְבָרִים הַמֻּתָּרִים מִדִּינָא מֵחֲמַת סְיָג וּפְרִישׁוּת כְּגוֹן תַּעֲנִיּוֹת שֶׁבִּימֵי הַסְּלִיחוֹת אוֹ שֶׁלֹּא לֶאֱכוֹל בָּשָׂר וְשֶׁלֹּא לִשְׁתּוֹת יַיִן מִשִּׁבְעָה עָשָׂר בְּתַמּוּז וָאֵילָךְ וְכַיּוֹצֵא בָּזֶה אֲפִלּוּ לֹא נָהַג כֵּן רַק פַּעַם הָרִאשׁוֹנָה אֶלָּא שֶׁהָיָה בְּדַעְתּוֹ לִנְהוֹג כֵּן לְעוֹלָם אוֹ שֶׁנָּהַג כֵּן שָׁלֹשׁ פְּעָמִים אַף עַל פִּי שֶׁלֹּא הָיָה בְּדַעְתּוֹ לִנְהוֹג כֵּן לְעוֹלָם וְלֹא הִתְנָה שֶׁיְּהֵא בְּלִי נֶדֶר וְרוֹצֶה לַחֲזוֹר מִפְּנֵי שֶׁאֵינוֹ בָּרִיא, צָרִיךְ הַתָּרָה וְיִפְתַּח בַּחֲרָטָה שֶׁהוּא מִתְחָרֵט עַל מַה שֶּׁנָּהַג כֵּן לְשֵׁם נֶדֶר. לָכֵן מִי שֶׁהוּא רוֹצֶה לִנְהוֹג בְּאֵיזֶה חֻמְרוֹת לִסְיָג וּפְרִישׁוּת יֹאמַר בַּתְּחִלָּה שֶׁאֵינוֹ מְקַבֵּל עָלָיו כֵּן בְּנֶדֶר וְגַם יֹאמַר שֶׁאֵין בְּדַעְתּוֹ לִנְהוֹג כֵּן אֶלָּא בַּפַּעַם הַהִיא אוֹ בִּפְעָמִים שֶׁיִּרְצֶה וְלֹא לְעוֹלָם

[17] Shulchan Aruch YD (39:11) - יש מי שכתב שמכניס אצבעו תחת הסירכא ומגביה קצת אם נפסקה מחמת הגבהה כל שהוא סירכא בת יומא היא וכשרה ואין להקל בכך אלא בבהמת ישראל ואין סומכין על קולא זו אלא בבודק כשר וירא את ה' מרבים

it is *treif* according to our *minhag.*[18] Also, if while he was *shechting* he banged his hand against the wall, the animal is *treif* because we assume he paused for a split second during the *shechita*. If the knife isn't completely smooth, then we consider the animal *treif.*[19] Some *shochtim* might be a little lenient regarding what is considered smooth, so you need to make sure to have a *yirei shamayim*. I'm not talking about any specific *shechita*. These are all general rules. You need to ask your Rav or particular person who knows about these things to use a specific *shechita* or not. Even that can change from one week to another since it depends on who the *shochet* is for that *shechita*. In general, we say most *shochtim* know what they're doing, but if you know the *shochet* is someone who doesn't wear *tzitzis* or doesn't wear a head covering, then he's not a *yirei shamayim* and you should not consider eating from his *shechita*. The bigger *yirei shamayim* the *shochet* is, the better the *shechita* is – it doesn't make any difference whether he is a *chassid* or not.

Q6. If one was away from home for an extended time, is he allowed to hug his sisters upon return?

A: It doesn't make any difference regarding hugging your sister whether you were away from home for a while or not. It's the same *halacha*. The Rambam[20] says that if someone is *mechabek um'nashek* his relatives, then it's a *ma'aseh*

---

[18] Rema YD (23:2) - והמנהג פשוט במדינות אלו להטריף כל שהייה אפי' משהו בין בעוף בין בבהמה ואין לשנות ואם נמצא לאחר שחיטה גמי או כיוצא בו מונח בוושט או בקנה ונשחט עמו טריפה דודאי הוצרך להשהות מעט בחתיכת הדבר ההוא לאחר ששחט הסימן והוי שהייה במשהו וטרפה

[19] Shulchan Aruch YD (18:10) - סכין שיש לה פגימה אסור לשחוט בה אפי' אם מכוין לשחוט שלא כנגד הפגימה

[20] Rambam Issurei Biah (21:6) - הַמְחַבֵּק אַחַת מִן הָעֲרָיוֹת שֶׁאֵין לִבּוֹ שֶׁל אָדָם נוֹקְפוֹ עֲלֵיהֶן אוֹ שֶׁנִּשֵּׁק לְאַחַת מֵהֶן כְּגוֹן אֲחוֹתוֹ הַגְּדוֹלָה וַאֲחוֹת אִמּוֹ וְכַיּוֹצֵא בָּהֶן אַף עַל פִּי שֶׁאֵין שָׁם תַּאֲוָה וְלֹא הֲנָאָה כְּלָל הֲרֵי זֶה מְגֻנֶּה בְּיוֹתֵר וְדָבָר אָסוּר הוּא וּמַעֲשֵׂה טִפְּשִׁים הוּא. שֶׁאֵין קְרֵבִין לְעֶרְוָה כְּלָל בֵּין גְּדוֹלָה בֵּין קְטַנָּה חוּץ מֵהָאֵם לִבְנָהּ וְהָאָב לְבִתּוֹ

boris, *tipshus*, and *issur* because the sister is forbidden to him. The brother isn't allowed to do hug his sister, but the question is whether the sister needs to run away from him. That's something to think about.

Q7. Must a married woman cover her hair in front of her father, brothers, and children?

A: There are two *halachos* in this question. One is saying *dvarim shebikedusha* in front of a woman whose hair is uncovered – that would be forbidden even for her husband.[21] If they are not saying *dvarim shebikedusha*, then it's an *inyan* of *tznius*.[22] The Gemara says that Kimchis said, "My hair was never uncovered,"[23] and the Zohar says a woman's hair must be covered at all times.[24] According to the *din* of the Gemara, if a woman is in the *chatzer* then it is *Das Yehudis* to cover her hair since there are a few other people there. If she is in the marketplace, then it is forbidden *min HaTorah* to walk outside with her hair uncovered, and in her house she is allowed to have her hair uncovered regardless of who is at home.[25] If the man has a problem, then he should

---

[21] Shulchan Aruch OC (75:2) - שער של אשה שדרכה לכסות אסו' לקרות כנגדו: הגה (אפי' אשתו)

[22] Shulchan Aruch EH (115:4) - איזו היא דת יהודית הוא מנהג הצניעות שנהגו בנות ישראל ואלו הם הדברים שאם עשתה אחת מהם עברה על דת יהודית יוצאת לשוק או למבוי מפולש או בחצר שהרבים בוקעים בו וראשה פרוע ואין עליה רדיד ככל הנשים אע"פ ששערה מכוסה במטפחות

[23] Yoma (47a) - ת"ר שבעה בנים היו לה לקמחית וכולן שמשו בכהונה גדולה אמרו לה חכמים מה עשית שזכית לכך אמרה להם מימי לא ראו קורות ביתי קלעי שערי אמרו לה הרבה עשו כן ולא הועילו

[24] Magen Avraham (75:4) - ועסי' קט"ו בא"ע שם משמע דוקא בשוק אסור אבל בחצר שאין אנשים מצויים שם מותרים לילך בגילוי הראש וכ"כ התו' בכתובות אבל בזוהר פ' נשא ע' רל"ט החמיר מאוד שלא יראה שום שער מאשה וכן ראוי לנהוג

[25] Kesubos (72b) - אמר רבי אסי אמר ר' יוחנן קלתה אין בה משום פרוע ראש הוי בה רבי זירא היכא אילימא בשוק דת יהודית היא ואלא

leave. However, the Mishna Berura[26] says to be careful for the Zohar which writes to keep your hair covered at all times unless it is necssary. The Mishna Berura[27] *poskins* that if a woman's elbow is uncovered, then a person who wants to say Divrei Torah or *daven* must not only not look, but must also turn around. We know a woman's hair is considered an *ervah* because the *posuk* in Shir HaShirim says "שַׂעְרֵךְ כְּעֵדֶר הָעִזִּים"[28] – you see woman's hair is a *taiva*. On the other hand, when it comes to uncovered hair, the Mishna Berura[29] says

---

בחצר אם כן לא הנחת בת לאברהם אבינו שיושבת תחת בעלה אמר אביי ואיתימא רב כהנא מחצר לחצר ודרך מבוי

[26] Mishna Berura (75:14) - ובזוהר פרשה נשא החמיר מאוד שלא יתראה שום שער מאשה דגרמא מסכנותא לביתא וגרמא לבנהא דלא יתחשבון בדרא וסטרא אחרא לשרות בביתא וכ"ש אם הולכות בשוקא כך ע"כ בעאי איתתא דאפילו קורות ביתה לא יחמון שערה חדא מרישאה ואי עבדית כן מה כתיב בניך כשתילי זיתים מה זית וכו' בנהא יסתלקון בחשובין על שאר בני עלמא ולא עוד אלא דבעלה מתברך בכל ברכאן דלעילא וברכאן דלתתא בעותרא בבנין ובני בנין עכ"ל בקיצור וכתב המ"א דראוי לנהוג כהזוהר וביומא איתא במעשה דקמחית בזכות הצניעות היתירה שהיתה בה שלא ראו קורות ביתה אמרי חלוקה יצאו ממנה כהנים גדולים

[27] Mishna Berura (75:1) - מפני שזה מביא לאדם לידי הרהור כשמסתכל בו בכלל ערוה היא ואסור לקרות או להזכיר שום דבר שבקדושה נגד זה כמו נגד ערוה ממש ולפי מה שביארנו לקמן סעיף ו' בשם האחרונים דנגד ערוה ממש אסור אפילו בעוצם עיניו עד שיחזיר פניו ה"ה בזה ויש מתירין בזה אם הוא נזהר מלראות כלל. וכשא"א בענין אחר נראה דיש לסמוך ע"ז

[28] Shir HaShirim (4:1) - הִנָּךְ יָפָה רַעְיָתִי הִנָּךְ יָפָה עֵינַיִךְ יוֹנִים מִבַּעַד לְצַמָּתֵךְ שַׂעְרֵךְ כְּעֵדֶר הָעִזִּים שֶׁגָּלְשׁוּ מֵהַר גִּלְעָד

[29] Shulchan Aruch OC (76:6) - היתה ערוה כנגדו והחזיר פניו ממנה או שעצם עיניו או שהוא בלילה או שהוא סומא מותר לקרות דבראייה תלה רחמנא והא לא חזי לה and Mishna Berura (76:29) - והאחרונים הסכימו דכל אלו העצות לבד מהחזרת פנים לא מהני דלא כתיב ולא תראה אלא ולא יראה ר"ל לא יראה הרואה ואפילו החזרת פנים שהותר הוא רק דוקא אם החזיר כל גופו ועומד בצד אחר דנעשית הערוה מצידו אבל אם החזיר פניו לבד לא מהני וא"כ בהוא עצמו ערום לא יצוייר שום עצה שיהא מותר לדבר ד"ת וכתב במשבצות זהב דאם הוא ברשות אחד ואדם ערום הוא ברשות אחר כנגדו והוא עוצם עיניו מלראותו י"ל דשרי בזה לכו"ע

it's enough just not to look. Hair isn't inherently an *ervah*. Even in a place where they have a balcony along three sides of the *shul* where the men can see the women sitting, then it's fine as long as you don't look at them since they are considered to be in a different *reshus*. Therefore, it is not inherently forbidden for family members to see a married woman's hair uncovered as long as they don't get pleasure from seeing her hair, but they cannot say Divrei Torah, *berachos*, or *daven* if they see her hair.[30]

Q8. Is a man allowed to hear his daughter sing? What about his sister?

A: No, he is not allowed to hear his daughter or sister sing.[31] However, if she is a young girl then as long as she is below the age of when she would get her period then you are allowed to hear them sing.[32] Once she reaches that age, you shouldn't try to listen to her sing. The Sdei Chemed writes בשירי קודש לא חיישינן להרהור – it's permitted to hear women singing *zemiros*, but it's not widely accepted.[33] Also, the

---

וכן משמע קצת בדרך החיים ובסימן ע"ט אות ח' באשל אברהם משמע דחזר מזה וכן בח"א כלל ד' אות ט' לא משמע כן אכן אם חלון של זכוכית מפסיק בינו לערוה ועוצם עיניו מלראותו מהני לכו"ע כיון דיש עכ"פ איזה חציצה המכסה נגד הערוה. מותר להרהר בד"ת כשהוא ערום וא"צ לומר כנגד ערוה אחרת שנאמר ערות דבר דיבור אסור הרהור מותר ומ"מ אין לו לשמוע אז ברכה מחבירו לצאת ידי חובה כי א"א לומר שומע כעונה כיון שא"א לו לענות

[30] Shulchan Aruch OC (75:2) - שער של אשה שדרכה לכסות אסו' לקרות כנגדו: הגה (אפי' אשתו)

[31] Shulchan Aruch OC (75:3) - יש ליזהר משמיעת קול זמר אשה בשעת ק"ש הגה ואפי' באשתו אבל קול הרגיל בו אינו ערוה

[32] Rav Eliyashiv quoted in Avnei Yoshfei (2:5:8) as starting at 11-years-old

[33] See Teshuvos Chasam Sofer CM (190) - ומ"ט לא יספדו כל איש עם אשתו יחדיו אע"כ דגם זה אסור דגורם הרהור ובטול הכוונה וכיון דבררנו דקול באשה ערוה א"כ הקול המתהלך מעזרת נשים לעזרת אנשי' מעורר הרהור ובטול הכוונה בתפלה והודאה ואנחנו מאמינים לפי דתינו

Sridei Eish[34] saying two voices aren't heard[35] isn't so widely accepted either. If your daughter does want to sing, then ask a *shailah*.

Q9. Is one allowed to take pictures of celestial bodies?

A: No, you're not allowed to take pictures of the sun, moon, or stars.[36] אֱלֹהֵי כֶסֶף וֵאלֹהֵי זָהָב – you shouldn't make "with Me" means in the heavens.[37] Normally it's not forbidden to take a picture of an idol since it's just a flat surface, but the Rishonim say that since the sun and the moon look to us as flat, two-dimensional images from our perspective, it's also

---

שזאת התפלה וזה השבח לא יקובל לפני שומע תפלה וכיון שכן ראוי ומחיוב עלינו לשום עינא פקיחא לבלתי היות שם ערוב ביום תת שבח ותהלה לי"ת ע"י ביאת הקיר"ה לשלום ובעת שפיכת שיח ותפלה לאל חי לחיי' מלכא ובנוהיי בכדי שתהי' תפלתינו ראוי להתקבל לפני ממליך מלכים ומושיב מלכים לכסא ית"ש ותהא ארכא לשלותי' ירום הודו וקרנו דאדונינו הקיר"ה ועיני עבדיו רואות ושמחות. זהו הנלע"ד בזה לבטל קול זמירות הנשים בבה"כ שלהן בשעה שהאנשי' בבה"כ שלהם ושלום לכם בכל גבולכם כאות נפשם היפה ונפש נענה מטופל ביסורי' מצפה לרחמי שמי' הרופא חנם ית"ש הכ"ד א"נ and Tzitz Eliezer (14:7) - מה מקום לבוא להקיש וללמוד משם בד"כ לשירת אנשים ונשים יחדו בשירי קודש שגילוי שכינה ודאי שליכא שם ואפילו אם יש מתחילה כוונה לשם שמים ברור הדבר שלאחר מכן היא מתבטלת ויצא השכר בהפסד והפרוץ בזה יהא עפ"י רוב מרובה על העומד

[34] Sridei Eish (1:77) - ואולם אחרי חקירה ודרישה נאמר לי כי הגאון הצדיק ר"ע הילדסהיימר ז"ל וכן הגרש"ר הירש ז"ל בפרנקפורט על נהר מיין התירו בזמירות קודש לזמר יחד והטעם משום דתרי קלא לא משתמעי וכיון שמזמרים יחד אין חשש איסור

[35] Rashi Megilla (21b) - ובלבד שלא יהא אחד קורא ושנים מתרגמין - וכל שכן שאין שנים קורין וטעמא משום דתרי קלי לא מישתמעי

[36] Shulchan Aruch YD (141:4) - אסור לצייר צורות שבמדור שכינה כגון ד' פנים בהדי הדדי וכן צורות שרפים ואופני' ומלאכי השרת וכן צורת אדם לבדו כל אלו אסור לעשותם אפילו הם לנוי ואם עובד כוכבים עשאם לו אסור להשהותם

[37] Shemos (20:20) - לֹא תַעֲשׂוּן אִתִּי אֱלֹהֵי כֶסֶף וֵאלֹהֵי זָהָב לֹא תַעֲשׂוּ לָכֶם

forbidden to take a two-dimensional picture of them.[38] It's not forbidden to have these pictures unless there is a concern that people might think you are worshiping them, but I don't think there is too much of a concern in our country.[39] What does a star look like? Is it something with points sticking out of it? No, that's not really a picture of a star. However, the moon is more of a *shailah* that you shouldn't take a picture.

Q10. Can a DNA test be used to determine if a child is a *mamzer*?

A: The question is that there is a married woman whose husband claims that this child isn't from him. The mother says the child is from this father. The truth is that you can determine the identity from a DNA test as long as it's taken by an independent person who is not *noge'ah* to the *shailah*, but without a DNA test the wife has a *chezkas kashrus*[40] and the child would be kosher as long as the husband does not know if it is his child or not. However, if the husband says, "This is not my child," the Torah believes him, and the child would be a *mamzer*. In a case where there is a doubt who the father of the child is, the DNA test would be the deciding factor because the DNA test is like two witnesses.[41] So too, we can rely on DNA testing to verify the identity of someone

---

[38] Pischei Teshuva YD (141:8) - עיין בשו"ת דברי יוסף סימן ח' שנשאל אם ציירו בדלתות ההיכל של בית הכנסת מבפנים צורת כוכבים בסממנים ועפרות זהב אם יש צד היתר לקיימם ואף דזה אינו לא בולט ולא שוקע וכמ"ש מהר"ם מ"מ מדברי הרמב"ם נראה דהציור בצבע דין אחד לו כמו שוקעת ויש להחמיר כדבריו and Rambam Avoda Zara (3:11) - וְכֵן אָסוּר לָצוּר דְּמוּת חַמָּה וּלְבָנָה כּוֹכָבִים מַזָּלוֹת וּמַלְאָכִים שֶׁנֶּאֱמַר לֹא תַעֲשׂוּן אִתִּי

[39] Shulchan Aruch YD (141:4) - וצורת חמה ולבנה וכוכבים אסור בין בולטת בין שוקעת ואם הם להתלמד להבין ולהורות כולן מותרות אפי' בולטות [ויש מתירין בשל רבים דליכא חשדא]

[40] Kesubos (13a) - היתה מעוברת ואמרו לה מה טיבו של עובר זה מאיש פלוני וכהן הוא רבן גמליאל ורבי אליעזר אומרים נאמנת

[41] כך שמעתי ממו"ר רב יוסף שלום אלישוב זצ"ל

who died in a fire as well as a dentist being able to match the teeth identically.

Q11. Can security cameras be used to break *yichud*?

A: I believe that security cameras can be used to break *yichud*, but it depends how you use it. We say פתח פתוח לרשות הרבים - an entrance open to the public view breaks *yichud*,[42] so even though there are only two people here right now – the man and the woman – we say since anyone can walk in then the two are afraid to do anything wrong out of the fear someone may walk in. Similarly, if there is a camera which would expose them in case they do something wrong, then they won't do something in front of the monitored camera the same way they wouldn't do something in front of someone else. Even though someone is not watching the camera at all times, it still works because *pesach pasuach* doesn't mean there are always people there. Rather, it's good enough to have the potential for someone to come in. If the camera is one which the husband put up and connects to his cellphone, then I think it's equal to *ba'alah ba'ir*. However, that doesn't work if the video is only sent to one person who isn't her husband since *pesach pasuach* must be open to at least three people.[43] You would need to have the camera connected to the cellphones of three people in such a case, and *yichud* would only be permitted in the view of the camera.

Q12. What about for *Cholov Yisroel* and *kashrus*?

A: This actually was a question which arose in Eretz Yisroel because they could get inexpensive milk from New Zealand

---

[42] Shulchan Aruch EH (22:9) - בית שפתחו פתוח לרשות הרבים אין חשש להתייחד שם עם ערוה

[43] Rema EH (22:5) - הגה וי"א דאשה אחת מתייחדת עם שני אנשים כשרים אם הוא בעיר וסתם אנשים כשרים הם אבל אם הם פרוצים אפילו עם י' אסור וכ"ז בעיר אבל בשדה או בלילה אפילו בעיר בעינן ג' אפילו בכשרים ויש מתירין איש א' עם נשים הרבה אם אין עסקו עם הנשים

and import it to Eretz Yisroel. Milk in Eretz Yisroel is particularly expensive because they don't have any pastureland, so they need to feed the cows grain which is much more expensive than grass since grass grows for nothing. Most of the milk used in Eretz Yisroel is imported, but they're *makpid* on *Cholov Yisroel*, so having a *mashgiach temidi* in New Zealand wasn't practical since there are no *yidden* in that part of the country. They asked Rav Elyashiv if they could put a camera on the farm in New Zealand, and he said it would be considered *Cholov Yisroel.*[44] It was a big *chiddush* to me that you could do such a thing. It wasn't a *chiddush* to me that it would be considered *Cholov Yisroel* since it doesn't matter how you know this milk is *Cholov Yisroel*. In fact, the Rema says if you milk an animal for cheese then you know for sure it's from a kosher animal since only kosher animal milk makes cheese even if there is no *yid* watching.[45] So too, if you know this milk is from a kosher animal because of the camera, it should also be good for *Cholov Yisroel* too. The *chiddush* to me was that the milk this dairy farm in New Zealand is sending you can be trusted to be the milk which was watched. The camera can't tell you which milk is being shipped and there's no plumba on milk. There are only non-Jews there without any *yidden*, so maybe they are bringing the milk from somewhere else completely. I went to Rav Elyashiv and asked him why we're not worried that the milk being imported isn't the milk which was watched by the camera. He said, "They were *mavti'ach* me that the government has the most advanced intelligence and has ways of tracking which milk was sent from this farm."

---

[44] See Nesiv HaChalav 3 (p.29)

[45] Rema YD (115:2) - ואם ראה עשיית הגבינות ולא ראה החליבה יש להתיר בדיעבד כי אין לחוש שמא עירב בו דבר טמא מאחר שעשה גבינות מן החלב כי דבר טמא אינו עומד ובודאי לא עירב בו העובד כוכבים מאחר שדעתו לעשות גבינות ומכל מקום אסור לאכול החלב כך

Q13. Do couches and chairs need to be checked for *shatnez*?

A: It's not the *minhag* to check them for *shatnez*. There is a *machlokes* whether the actual material which they use to upholster the couch and the chair is unusual to have *shatnez*. Besides, it's not really forbidden if it's like a rug since the Torah[46] writes לֹא יַעֲלֶה עָלֶיךָ – don't let *shatnez* go on top of you.[47] Shag rugs might pose a problem if you walk on them barefooted since it would be forbidden if you know for sure there is *shatnez* as the shag rug can cover your feet. However, the regular rugs are permitted. Besides that, the only real concern for wool and linen together in a chair is that the tapes used to hold the upholsltery together might have linen in them. The wool and linen generally are not attached to one another since linen is a tough thread. It's a *machlokes* Rishonim if you have a woolen cloth on one end of a garment and linen thread on the other end of the garment whether that's considered a *beged shatnez* if they are sewed into the garment.[48] Maybe since they are not touching each other then it would be permitted. Some are stringent, but the Rema is lenient.[49] Most people are lenient since that whole

---

[46] Vayikra (19:19) - אֶת־חֻקֹּתַי תִּשְׁמֹרוּ בְּהֶמְתְּךָ לֹא־תַרְבִּיעַ כִּלְאַיִם שָׂדְךָ לֹא־תִזְרַע כִּלְאָיִם וּבֶגֶד כִּלְאַיִם שַׁעַטְנֵז לֹא יַעֲלֶה עָלֶיךָ

[47] Shulchan Aruch YD (301:1) - מותר מן התורה לישב על מצעות של כלאים שנא' לא יעלה עליך אבל אתה מציעו תחתיך

[48] Rambam Kilyaim (10:3) - תָּפַר בֶּגֶד צֶמֶר בְּשֶׁל פִּשְׁתָּן וַאֲפִלּוּ תְּפָרָן בְּמֶשִׁי אוֹ שֶׁתָּפַר בֶּגֶד צֶמֶר בְּחוּטֵי פִּשְׁתָּן אוֹ בֶּגֶד פִּשְׁתִּים בְּחוּטֵי צֶמֶר אוֹ קָשַׁר חוּטֵי צֶמֶר בְּחוּטֵי פִּשְׁתִּים אוֹ גְּדָלָן אֲפִלּוּ נָתַן צֶמֶר וּפִשְׁתִּים בְּשַׂק אוֹ בְּקֻפָּה וּכְרָכָן הֲרֵי אֵלּוּ כִּלְאַיִם. וַאֲפִלּוּ קָשַׁר גְּדִיל שֶׁל צֶמֶר בִּגְדִיל שֶׁל פִּשְׁתָּן אַף עַל פִּי שֶׁהָרְצוּעָה בְּאֶמְצַע. וְכֵן אִם כָּפַל בִּגְדֵי צֶמֶר וּפִשְׁתָּן וּקְשָׁרָן הֲרֵי אֵלּוּ כִּלְאַיִם שֶׁנֶּאֱמַר "צֶמֶר וּפִשְׁתִּים יַחְדָּו" מִכָּל מָקוֹם כֵּיוָן שֶׁנִּתְאַחֵד נֶאֱסַר and Rash Mishna Kilayim (9:1) - כשבאו החוטים של צמר ושל פשתן זה אצל זה אבל אם זה בצד אחד של חלוק שכולו צמר גמלים וזה בצד אחר מותר

[49] Shulchan Aruch YD (300:2) - העושה בגד כולו צמד גמלים או ארנבים או קנבוס וארג בו חוט של צמר מצד זה וחוט של פשתן מצד זה הרי זה אסור משום כלאים: הגה וי"א דשרי בכה"ג אלא אם כן ארג חוט

machlokes is only if you know there is *shatnez*, but if you don't know then it's not usual to have wool on the lining of a chair since nowadays they are usually composed of wood, the padding is usually from synthetic fibers, and if it's sewed together then it's often synthetic fibers which are stronger and cheaper than linen. Therefore, we are not obligated to check whether chairs or couches have *shatnez* in them.

של צמר אצל החוט של פשתים אבל אם אינם נוגעים יחד שרי ועיין לקמן סימן ש דנוהגין להקל

Chapter 7: Cicadas

(5768) – When the Yidden were in Mitzrayim, there was a Makkah of Kinim and there was Arbeh. The cicadas are not Arbeh, and they are not *chagavim* – you are not allowed to eat them. וְכָל־הַשֶּׁרֶץ הַשֹּׁרֵץ עַל־הָאָרֶץ שֶׁקֶץ הוּא לֹא יֵאָכֵל (Vayikra 11:41) – they don't jump around or eat anything. They live for maybe a week or two, and then they disappear. However, it is *Hashgacha Min Hashamayim* that there is such a thing as a *briah* which is *nischadesh* every 17 years. We don't find that in the regular *briah*. Most of the insects are *nischadesh* every year or less – where do we find something in the *teva* which is *nischadesh* every 17 years? Insects in general go through a cycle. For instance, the fly lays an egg, it becomes a maggot, then it enters another stage until it becomes a fly. The lifecycle of a fly might be 10 days or so – whatever it is – and then it lays eggs and continues the cycle. On the other hand, for an insect to enter the ground for 17 years is שלא כדרך הטבע. The Ramban says that *negaim* are a *siman* of Hashgacha Pratis.[1] It doesn't come in the natural world and

---

[1] Ramban Vayikra (13:47) - והבגד כי יהיה בו נגע צרעת זה איננו בטבע כלל ולא הווה בעולם וכן נגעי הבתים אבל בהיות ישראל שלמים לה' יהיה רוח השם עליהם תמיד להעמיד גופם ובגדיהם ובתיהם במראה טוב וכאשר יקרה באחד מהם חטא ועון יתהוה כיעור בבשרו או בבגדו או בביתו להראות כי השם סר מעליו ולכך אמר הכתוב (ויקרא יד:לד) ונתתי נגע צרעת בבית ארץ אחוזתכם כי היא מכת השם בבית ההוא והנה איננו נוהג אלא בארץ שהיא נחלת ה' כמו שאמר כי תבאו אל ארץ כנען אשר אני נותן לכם לאחוזה ואין הדבר מפני היותו חובת קרקע אבל מפני שלא יבא הענין ההוא אלא בארץ הנבחרת אשר השם הנכבד שוכן בתוכה ובתורת כהנים (מצורע ה:ג) דרשו עוד שאין הבית מטמא אלא אחר כבוש וחלוק ושיהא כל אחד ואחד מכיר את שלו והטעם כי אז נתישבה דעתם עליהם לדעת את ה' ותשרה שכינה בתוכם וכן אני חושב בנגעי הבגדים שלא ינהגו אלא בארץ ולא הוצרך למעט מהן חוצה לארץ כי לא יארעו שם לעולם ומפני זה עוד אינם נוהגים אלא בבגדים לבנים לא בצבועים כי אולי הצבע הוציא הכיעור ההוא במקום ההוא כטבעו ולא אצבע אלהים היא ולפיכך

is a *siman* that the Ribbono Shel Olam cares about us. Actually, on the posuk כִּי תָבֹאוּ אֶל־אֶרֶץ כְּנַעַן אֲשֶׁר אֲנִי נֹתֵן לָכֶם לַאֲחֻזָּה,[2] Rashi brings from a Chazal that it's a *besurah tovah* because the Emoriyim hid treasures in the walls of the house and Klal Yisroel would have never found it if they didn't knock down the house due to the *negaim*.[3] However, other Meforshim explain *besurah tovah* refers to the Hashgacha Pratis that when someone does a חטא like *lashon hara* then he is punished. The Ribbono Shel Olam is holding him by the hand and telling this person, "Don't do this *aveirah*." There is a *maaseh* which I heard from my Rosh Yeshiva Rav Aharon Kotler *zecher tzaddik l'vracha*, with Rav Chaim Volozhiner that he lost five rubles. That was a sizeable amount of money – maybe it was about $50 today (2003) – and Rav Chaim Volozhiner was very upset. His children said to him, "Don't worry about the $50, the Ribbono Shel Olam will take care of us. Why are you getting so upset about it?" He told them, "I'm not upset about the fact that I lost five rubles. I'm upset about what חטא did I do that I deserved this punishment of losing that money." He made a *cheshbon* and realized that since he used to give one-fifth of his income for *tzedakah*,[4] he gave five rubles too little. Rav Chaim Volozhiner set aside five rubles for *tzedakah* and then found

---

הצבועים בידי שמים מטמאין כדברי רבי שמעון (נגעים יא:מג) ועל דרך הפשט מפני זה יחזירו הכתוב בכל פסוק ופסוק "הבגד או העור או השתי והערב" כי הדבר נס ולרבותינו בהם מדרשים וכולם בתורת כהנים

[2] Vayikra (14:34) - כִּי תָבֹאוּ אֶל־אֶרֶץ כְּנַעַן אֲשֶׁר אֲנִי נֹתֵן לָכֶם לַאֲחֻזָּה וְנָתַתִּי נֶגַע צָרַעַת בְּבֵית אֶרֶץ אֲחֻזַּתְכֶם

[3] Rashi Vayikra (14:34) - ונתתי נגע צרעת. בְּשׂוֹרָה הִיא לָהֶם שֶׁהַנְּגָעִים בָּאִים עֲלֵיהֶם; לְפִי שֶׁהִטְמִינוּ אֱמוֹרִיִּים מַטְמוֹנִיּוֹת שֶׁל זָהָב בְּקִירוֹת בָּתֵּיהֶם כָּל אַרְבָּעִים שָׁנָה שֶׁהָיוּ יִשְׂרָאֵל בַּמִּדְבָּר, וְעַל יְדֵי הַנֶּגַע נוֹתֵץ הַבַּיִת וּמוֹצְאָן (ויקרא רבה י"ז)

[4] Shulchan Aruch YD (249:1) - שיעור נתינתה אם ידו משגת יתן כפי צורך העניים ואם אין ידו משגת כל כך יתן עד חומש נכסיו מצוה מן המובחר ואחד מעשרה מדה בינונית פחות מכאן עין רעה וחומש זה שאמרו שנה ראשונה מהקרן מכאן ואילך חומש שהרויח בכל שנה

five rubles on the street. He realized that the Ribbono Shel Olam is holding him by the hand, so when he figured out what he did wrong then he was able to do *teshuva* and get the money back right away. That is the *inyan* of *negaim*: Hashgacha Pratis that if you do something wrong, then you are told right away so that you are close to the Ribbono Shel Olam to realize that He cares about us. That is the *besura tovah.*

Now we have these cicadas which are שלא כדרך הארץ, and not only are they שלא כדרך הארץ but they are primarily in Baltimore. It's almost as if the Ribbono Shel Olam targeted this town to have cicadas. Where do you have such a thing that only one place in the world has this? When the locusts came to Mitzrayim, the Torah says לֹא־הָיָה כֵן אַרְבֶּה כָּמֹהוּ וְאַחֲרָיו לֹא יִהְיֶה־כֵּן – it was never like this before, and it never will be.[5] If this Makkah will be again in the future, then it's not such a big miracle. Even though Rashi says there was one plague of locust in the times of Yoel, he explains that was with many species of locust but in Mitzrayim there was only species.[6] Makkas Dam happened throughout the whole Egypt except by the Yidden,[7] so it was Hashgacha Pratis. It was a miracle – a clear Makkah against Mitzrayim – and it never happened again. When it says the water split, נִבְקְעוּ הַמַּיִם כָּל מַיִם שֶׁבָּעוֹלָם

---

[5] Shemos (10:14) - וַיַּעַל הָאַרְבֶּה עַל כָּל־אֶרֶץ מִצְרַיִם וַיָּנַח בְּכֹל גְּבוּל מִצְרָיִם כָּבֵד מְאֹד לְפָנָיו לֹא־הָיָה כֵן אַרְבֶּה כָּמֹהוּ וְאַחֲרָיו לֹא יִהְיֶה־כֵּן

[6] Rashi Shemos (10:14) - ואחריו לא יהיה כן. וְאוֹתוֹ שֶׁהָיָה בִּימֵי יוֹאֵל שֶׁנֶּ' "כָּמוֹהוּ לֹא נִהְיָה מִן הָעוֹלָם" (יואל ב'), לָמַדְנוּ שֶׁהָיָה כָּבֵד מִשֶּׁל מֹשֶׁה. (אוֹתוֹ שֶׁל יוֹאֵל הָיָה) עַ"יְ מִינִין הַרְבֵּה, שֶׁהָיוּ יַחַד אַרְבֶּה, יֶלֶק, חָסִיל, גָּזָם, אֲבָל שֶׁל מֹשֶׁה לֹא הָיָה אֶלָּא מִין אֶחָד, וְכָמוֹהוּ לֹא הָיָה וְלֹא יִהְיֶה

[7] Shemos Rabbah (9:10) - אָמַר רַבִּי אָבִין הַלֵּוִי בְּרַבִּי, מִמַּכַּת דָּם הֶעֱשִׁירוּ יִשְׂרָאֵל, כֵּיצַד, הַמִּצְרִי וְיִשְׂרָאֵל בְּבַיִת אֶחָד וְהַגִּיגִית מְלֵאָה מַיִם, וּמִצְרִי הָלַךְ לְמַלְאוֹת הַקִּיתוֹן מִתּוֹכָהּ מוֹצִיאָהּ מְלֵאָה דָּם, וְיִשְׂרָאֵל שׁוֹתֶה מַיִם מִתּוֹךְ הַגִּיגִית, וְהַמִּצְרִי אוֹמֵר תֵּן לִי בְּיָדְךָ מְעַט מַיִם וְנוֹתֵן לוֹ וְנַעֲשׂוּ דָּם, וְאוֹמֵר לוֹ נִשְׁתֶּה אֲנִי וְאַתָּה מִן קְעָרָה אַחַת, וְיִשְׂרָאֵל שׁוֹתֶה מַיִם וְהַמִּצְרִי דָּם, וּכְשֶׁהָיָה לוֹקֵחַ מִיִּשְׂרָאֵל בְּדָמִים, הָיָה שׁוֹתֶה מַיִם, מִכָּאן הֶעֱשִׁירוּ יִשְׂרָאֵל.

– all the water in the world split as well.[8] It only happened at one time, so it was recognized as a נס נגלה when the Yidden needed it. But if it happened every 17 years then it wouldn't be such a miracle – people would just think, "Okay, it happens." The *mann* came down *Min Hashamayim* and it was clear Hashgacha Pratis for the Yidden. There was nothing to eat, Moshe Rabbeinu was *mispalel*, and the Ribbono Shel Olam sent down the *mann*. The *mann* came down every day for 40 years.[9] There were people who were born in the Midbar, and from the day they ever opened their eyes they saw the *mann* in the morning. For them, seeing the *mann* every day for 40 years, it would seem to be a natural occurrence. However, since it stopped once the Yidden were no longer in the Midbar, then all of a sudden they realized it was a miracle. Until then only the *Zekeinim* who came out of Mitzrayim realized it wasn't normal. The Meiri[10] says the *lashon* of טבע comes from the *lashon* of טֻבְּעוּ בְיַם – something which is sunk[11] – because after a while you get used to the

---

[8] Mechilta D'Rebbi Yishmael (14:21:3) - וישם את הים לחרבה עשאו כמין חרבה: ויבקעו המים, כל מים שבעולם נבקעו ומנין אתה אומר אף המים שבבורות ושבשיחין ושבמערות ושבכד ושבכוס ושבצלוחית ושבחבית נבקעו שנ' ויבקעו המים כאן [ויבקע הים אין כתיב כאן אלא ויבקעו המים מלמד שכל המים שבעולם נבקעו] ומנין אתה אומר אף המים העליונים והתחתונים נבקעו שנ' ראוך מים אלהים ראוך מים יחילו אף ירגזו תהומות (תהלים עז) ראוך מים אלו שעברו ישראל שנחרבו בדבר הקב"ה שנ' הים ראה וינס ראוך מים יחילו אלו העליונים אף ירגזו תהומות אלו התחתונים וכן הוא אומר זורמו מים עבות קול נתנו שחקים אלו העליונים אף חצציך יתהלכו (תהלים עז) אלו התחתונים [וכתיב תהום אל תהום קורא לקול צינוריך (תהילים מ"ב:ח')] ואומר נתן תהום קולו וגו' (חבקוק ג) וכשחזרו למקומם כל מים שהיה בעולם חזרו שנ' וישובו המים מלמד שכל מים שבעולם חזרו להם למקומם. And see Gevuros Hashem (42)

[9] Shemos (16:35) - וּבְנֵי יִשְׂרָאֵל אָכְלוּ אֶת־הַמָּן אַרְבָּעִים שָׁנָה עַד־בֹּאָם אֶל־אֶרֶץ נוֹשָׁבֶת אֶת־הַמָּן אָכְלוּ עַד־בֹּאָם אֶל־קְצֵה אֶרֶץ כְּנָעַן

[10] See Shem M'Shmuel Bereishis (10:4)

[11] Shemos (15:4) - מַרְכְּבֹת פַּרְעֹה וְחֵילוֹ יָרָה בַיָּם וּמִבְחַר שָׁלִשָׁיו טֻבְּעוּ בְיַם־סוּף

דרך הטבע and say, "That's just how things are – it doesn't mean there's a Ribbono Shel Olam in the world." Therefore, the Ribbono Shel Olam sends this kind of reality to the world once in 17 years in such a limited area. It's not a נס נגלה since it happens every 17 years, but it is a change in the דרך הטבע to show there is a Ribbono Shel Olam in the world. I think that it is a *Hashgacha Min Hashamayim* that He has a special feeling for this city.

There used to be a time when Baltimore was called the Yerushalayim of America. The one who coined that phrase was Rav Elchonon Wasserman *zecher tzaddik l'vracha* הי"ד. What was so special about Baltimore? This was the only town where there was no Conservative or Reform at that time. Everything was Orthodox. Of course it didn't keep up, but at that time Baltimore was the only place in America which did not have any Conservative or Reform in the town. Why that happened I don't know, but I do know that the first Rav in America was in Baltimore – Rabbi Rice – who was a *talmid* of the Aruch LaNer, Rav Yaakov Ettlinger. I don't know what he was able to accomplish here because the people were so far removed from any Yiddishkeit in those days even though there were quite a few Yidden here – they even built a *shul* downtown, it's still there, and there was a *mikva* in the *shul*, a *matza* bakery there. It was not the first *shul* in America, but he was the first ordained Rabbi with *semicha* in the United States. He must have done some good things over here which gave the Yidden some *ko'ach*. He was buried in a cemetery in Baltimore, and around his *kever* there was fence ten *tefachim* high. I assume he asked for that in his *tzava'ah* because you are not supposed to bury a Shomer Shabbos together with Mechalelei Shabbos.[12]

---

[12] Shulchan Aruch YD (362:5) - אין קוברין רשע אצל צדיק אפילו רשע חמור אצל רשע קל וכן אין קוברין צדיק וכשר ובינוני אצל חסיד מופלג (אבל קוברים בעל תשובה אצל צדיק גמור) and Igros Moshe

Everyone else at that time were Mechalelei Shabbos, so the only way he could be buried there was by surrounding his *kever* with a fence. His children did not turn out to be *frum*, nor his grandchildren or great-grandchildren, but his great-great-grandchildren are *frum* and learning in Kollel. The Yidden at that time were so far away from anything in *ruchniyus* that I don't even think he was able to accomplish anything with *shechita*. I don't know what he did, but I must say that there is a *yid* here in town – Rav Pesach Diskind – who is a *choshuv yid* and takes care of the Russians who came here. There are Russians who came to America and Russians who came to Eretz Yisroel. The Russians who went to Eretz Yisroel did so because they chose to have a connection to Yiddishkeit, and for those Yidden it was relatively easy to work with them to send their children to Yeshivos. The Russian Jews who came to America came because they wanted a good life. They weren't interested in Yiddishkeit, and it was especially difficult to work with them. His job was to work with them to be *mekarev* these Yidden to Yiddishkeit. He learned the Russian language – he speaks it fluently – and works with them. He told me, "My job is not to make them into Satmar Chassidim or Bnei Torah. I'm not even trying to make them into Shomrei Mitzvos. They're too far away from that. All I'm trying to do is make them *ma'aminim* in the Ribbono Shel Olam. If I have accomplished that, then I have accomplished a lot." The truth is that not only did he accomplish that, but once

---

YD (2:152) - ואם ציוה יש לקיים מצותו אבל אם הוא מפורסם למחלל שבת משום שהוא מחלל השבת בפהרהסיא אין צורך לקבלת עדות בפניו ובפני ב"ד ואסור לקוברו אצל סתם אנשים שנחשבים לכשרים וצריך להרחיק מלקבור אדם כשר ממנו שמנה אמות של תורה שהם לענין זה חמשה יארד במדת מדינתנו ורק כשידוע שאחד רצה שיקבדוהו אצל קרוביו אף שהיו מחללי שבת רשאין לקוברו וכ"ש כשציוה שיקברוהו שם ואם אי אפשר להרחיק האדם כשר מהמחלל שבת בפרהסיא מצד דוחק המקום וכדומה יצטרכו לעשות גדר גבוה עשרה טפחים ביניהם. See Rav Heinemann Mah Nomar Hilchos Refuah (8:28)

they became *ma'aminim* in the Ribbono Shel Olam, then it became much easier for them to start doing *mitzvos* as well. In fact, many of them are already turning around. It could be that in the beginning, that was the same goal that Rabbi Rice had – make the Yidden *ma'aminim* in the Ribbono Shel Olam. Maybe because of that credit, the Conservative and Reform didn't have such a strong foothold at that time before the war. Maybe for that reason the Ribbono Shel Olam sent these cicadas as a *siman* that there is a Hashgacha Pratis on this town because this is clearly שלא כדרך הארץ.

One thing you can see from the cicadas is that when they are at the height of their season – this is the third time I will see them since I came here in '67, they weren't as strong in Yeshiva but much stronger in town – you cannot even talk to someone else in the street because they make so much noise. They can't utter any sounds, rather the sound comes from the flapping of their wings. They are about an inch or so long and hardly make any sound individually, but there are so many of them that you cannot even hear yourself talking unless you shout. I never really understood what Chazal say that there was a lot of noise at Makkas Arbeh until I experienced this myself. However, the cicadas are not Arbeh – the Arbeh ate everything up[13] while the cicadas don't bite, sting, or eat anything. They are here for maybe two weeks. There are different types of cicadas which emerge, so the entire season is about six weeks, but then they burrow back into the trees and into the ground not to emerge again for another 17 years. What is their purpose? One *tachlis* is that you see the Hashgacha Pratis that the Ribbono Shel Olam runs the world. People say they come out every 17 years so it's not such a miracle – people also said that even though the Mabul was *hashgacha* it really occurs every

---

[13] Shemos (10:15) - וַיְכַס אֶת־עֵין כָּל־הָאָרֶץ וַתֶּחְשַׁךְ הָאָרֶץ וַיֹּאכַל אֶת־כָּל־עֵשֶׂב הָאָרֶץ וְאֵת כָּל־פְּרִי הָעֵץ אֲשֶׁר הוֹתִיר הַבָּרָד וְלֹא־נוֹתַר כָּל־יֶרֶק בָּעֵץ וּבְעֵשֶׂב הַשָּׂדֶה בְּכָל־אֶרֶץ מִצְרָיִם

1,656 years.[14] They thought that was the natural way of the world, so they wanted to create a place where they could take refuge. The Tiferes Yonasan says they tried to take refuge on the moon because they thought the Earth wasn't a safe place.[15] Whatever their *cheshbon* was, Rashi explains that they wanted to stop the flood from happening.[16] For people who are not *ma'aminim*, the cicadas are not going to help make them into *ma'aminim*. However, for people who are *ma'aminim*, they can see the Hashgacha Pratis here which is unusual and doesn't happen as much in other places – for whatever *zechus* we have to experience the יָד חֲזָקָה וּזְרֹעַ נְטוּיָה. I can understand polar bears live in the polar region, and that certain animals are native to certain countries, as ostriches come from Australia, and Rashi says horses come from Egypt,[17] and lions come from Africa. However, to see that

---

[14] Bereishis Rabba (38:6) - דָּבָר אַחֵר, וּדְבָרִים אֲחָדִים, שֶׁאָמְרוּ דְּבָרִים חַדִּים, אָמְרוּ אַחַת לְאֶלֶף וְתרנ"ו שָׁנָה הָרָקִיעַ מִתְמוֹטֵט בּוֹאוּ וְנַעֲשֶׂה סָמוֹכוֹת, אֶחָד מִן הַצָּפוֹן, וְאֶחָד מִן הַדָּרוֹם, וְאֶחָד מִן הַמַּעֲרָב, וְזֶה שֶׁכָּאן סוֹמְכוֹ מִן הַמִּזְרָח, הֲדָא הוּא דִכְתִיב: וַיְהִי כָל הָאָרֶץ שָׂפָה אֶחָת וּדְבָרִים אֲחָדִים

[15] Tiferes Yonasan (Noach 8a) - אם אפשר להביא כל עופפות למעלה מהאויר העב הלזה יכול לילך ברוח מעלה מעלה עד הכדור הירחי כי הרוח יגביה אותו תמיד לילך ולמעלה הרוח הולך וחזק וכבר חברו בזה חבורים איך לעשות ספינה כזה לילך לכדור ירחי אבל העיקר שיגיע תחלה ספינה זו למעלה מאויר העכור הזה וזה היה כוונת דור הפלגה ג"כ שבקשו לקבוע מושבם בכדור ירחי ששם יהיו נצולים ממבול וחשבו לעשות ע"י ספינה הנ"ל אפס כיצד יגביהו אותה הספינה למעלה מאויר העכור ווזלה חשבו לבנות מגדל גבוה כל כך עד למעלה מאויר ההוא ומשם יכלו להשתמש בספינה הנ"ל לשוט באויר עד כדור הירחי

[16] Rashi Bereishis (11:1) - ודברים אחדים. בָּאוּ בְעֵצָה אַחַת וְאָמְרוּ לֹא כָּל הֵימֶנּוּ שֶׁיָּבֹר לוֹ אֶת הָעֶלְיוֹנִים, נַעֲלֶה לָרָקִיעַ וְנַעֲשֶׂה עִמּוֹ מִלְחָמָה. דָּבָר אַחֵר עַל יְחִידוֹ שֶׁל עוֹלָם. דָּבָר אַחֵר וּדְבָרִים אֲחָדִים אָמְרוּ אַחַת לְאֶלֶף ותרנ"ו שָׁנִים הָרָקִיעַ מִתְמוֹטֵט כְּשֵׁם שֶׁעָשָׂה בִּימֵי הַמַּבּוּל, בֹּאוּ וְנַעֲשֶׂה לוֹ סְמִיכוֹת

[17] Rashi Devarim (17:16) - לא ירבה לו סוסים. אֶלָּא כְּדֵי מֶרְכַּבְתּוֹ, שֶׁלֹּא ישיב את העם מצרימה, שֶׁהַסּוּסִים בָּאִים מִשָּׁם, כְּמָה שֶׁנֶּאֱמַר בִּשְׁלֹמֹה (מלכים א י') וַתַּעֲלֶה וַתֵּצֵא מֶרְכָּבָה מִמִּצְרַיִם בְּשֵׁשׁ מֵאוֹת כֶּסֶף וְסוּס בַּחֲמִשִּׁים וּמֵאָה and Rashi Sanhedrin (21b) - הסוסים באים ממצרים לארץ

the single city of Baltimore is particularly affected by cicadas, and they are already much calmer by Yeshiva, is very unusual. It's not as if you can take cicadas to Detroit and they will multiply over there every 17 years. It doesn't happen. It's *Hashgacha Min Hashamayim*. You will see that the cicadas crawl out of their shells to fly out, and those shells are left all over. It looks like an empty shell that had an insect. They have red eyes – it's very unusual. Besides all this, the mere fact that they come up every 17 years in itself is a *siman* of Hashhgacha Pratis. We human beings who have brains and intellect, when we go to sleep and have to get up at a certain time in the morning, we have to set our alarm clock or appoint someone to wake us up in order to make sure we get up on time. These cicadas, if they have a brain, it is definitely much smaller than that of human beings. Their intellect is way below that of human beings, and they get up from their sleep every 17 years exactly without any alarm clocks and without anyone waking them up. מה גדלו מעשך ה. But the truth be told, we see this Hashgacha all the time even without cicadas. Who tells the grass to start growing in the Spring? Who tells the trees to bear fruit in the summer? They also have no alarm clocks and the trees dutifully shed their leaves in the Fall and regrow them in the Spring without any brains. It's clearly Hashgacha Min Hashamayim.

(5781) - It says by the *tzefardim*,[18] וַיִּצְעַק מֹשֶׁה אֶל־ה' עַל־דְּבַר הַצְפַרְדְּעִים אֲשֶׁר־שָׂם לְפַרְעֹה. Pharaoh says, "Please get these *tzefardim* away from me."[19] It doesn't use the lashon of וַיִּצְעַק except by *tzefardim*. The reason is because the frogs made a

---

ישראל וצריך לשלוח שלוחים לקנות לו סוסים ועוברים בלא תוסיפו לראותם עוד עד עולם (שמות יד:יג)

[18] Shemos (8:8) - וַיֵּצֵא מֹשֶׁה וְאַהֲרֹן מֵעִם פַּרְעֹה וַיִּצְעַק מֹשֶׁה אֶל־ה' עַל־דְּבַר הַצְפַרְדְּעִים אֲשֶׁר־שָׂם לְפַרְעֹה

[19] Shemos (8:4) - וַיִּקְרָא פַרְעֹה לְמֹשֶׁה וּלְאַהֲרֹן וַיֹּאמֶר הַעְתִּירוּ אֶל־ה' וְיָסֵר הַצְפַרְדְּעִים מִמֶּנִּי וּמֵעַמִּי וַאֲשַׁלְּחָה אֶת־הָעָם וְיִזְבְּחוּ לַה'

lot of noise with their croaking, as it says in Rashi[20] that they croaked in their stomachs, and certainly when they weren't in the stomachs. Since you need to hear yourself speak when *davening*,[21] Moshe Rabbeinu had to shout in order to hear his *tefillos*.[22] At the height of the cicada period, when two people speak to each other in the street one person cannot hear the other unless he shouts. Last year because of covid, all the *shuls* were closed. The Vaad HaRabbonim forbade even outside *minyanim*. Then after the situation improved, they permitted outside *minyanim*. Then after it improved even more, they permitted *minyanim* in the *shuls* (with masks). Still, there were people who were very cautious and continued the outside *minyanim* until today (Rosh Chodesh Sivan 5781). Maybe this is a *siman min hashamayim* that if outside one cannot *daven* and hear the *tefillah* that he is saying because of the cicadas, then it is time to come back to the shuls. Chazal[23] say כָּל הַקּוֹבֵעַ מָקוֹם לִתְפִלָּתוֹ אֱלֹקֵי אַבְרָהָם בְּעֶזְרוֹ – an outside *minyan* is not considered a *kevius makom* for

---

[20] Rashi Shemos (7:29) - ובכה ובעמך. בְּתוֹךְ מְעֵיהֶם נִכְנָסִין וּמְקַרְקְרִין

[21] Shulchan Aruch OC (185:2) - צריך שישמיע לאזניו מה שמוציא בשפתיו ואם לא השמיע לאזניו יצא ובלבד שיוציא בשפתיו and Shulchan Aruch OC (62:3) - צריך להשמיע לאזנו מה שמוציא בפיו ואם לא השמיע לאזנו יצא ובלבד שיוציא בשפתיו and Shulchan Aruch OC (206:2) כל אלו הברכו' צריך שלא יפסיק בין ברכ' לאכיל': הגה יותר מכדי דיבור וצריך להשמיע לאזניו ואם לא השמיע יצא ובלבד שיוציא בשפתיו

[22] Nachalas Tzvi (Vaera p. 151) and Sifsei Chachamim Shemos (8:6) - מקשים העולם למה שינה הכתוב בצפרדעים ויצעק משה אל ה', ובשאר מכות כתיב ויעתר משה אל ה'. ויש לומר, משום דאמרינן המתפלל צריך להשמיע לאזניו מה שמוציא מפיו, וכאן היו הצפרדעים צועקים כמו שפירש רש"י בסמוך, והוצרך להרים קולו בתפלתו כדי שישמיע לאזניו את תפלתו

[23] Berachos (6b) - אָמַר רַבִּי חֶלְבּוֹ, אָמַר רַב הוּנָא: כָּל הַקּוֹבֵעַ מָקוֹם לִתְפִלָּתוֹ אֱלֹקֵי אַבְרָהָם בְּעֶזְרוֹ and Shulchan Aruch OC (90:19) - יקבע מקום לתפלתו שלא ישנהו אם לא לצורך ואין די במה שיקבע לו ב"ה להתפלל אלא גם בב"ה שקבוע בה צריך שיהיה לו מקום קבוע

tefillah because it is very difficult to *daven* with *kavana* in the rain, in the freezing cold, in the blistering heat, and with harsh winds blowing, all of which did not affect us in a *shul*. Therefore, it is considered more of a *makom kavuah*. (However, if the place has a bigger *kedusha*, for instance in the courtyard of the Beis HaMikdash or by the Kosel, it is preferred to *daven* there over a place that has a roof but is not in a *makom kadosh*.) A Sukkah is a דירת עראי even though it may have brick walls because the *sechach* lets the rain through.[24] Certainly when we have all these problems with outdoor *minyanim* that it's not considered the ultimate הַקּוֹבֵעַ מָקוֹם לִתְפִלָּתוֹ.

Q1. Are the cicadas kosher?

A: There is no Mesorah on the cicadas to be able to eat them, but even if there was a Mesorah on them they would be *treif* because the Torah says you are allowed to eat הַשֶּׁרֶץ הַשֹּׁרֵץ עַל־הָאָרֶץ.[25] This insect is שֹּׁרֵץ עַל־הָאָרֶץ. If someone would eat one cicada, he would get 6x *malkus*. The Gemara[26] says אכל פוטיתא – someone who eats a frog gets 4x of *malkus*,[27] נמלה gets 5x, and צרעה לוקה שש. Rashi[28] explains that there are two

---

[24] Tosafos Sukkah (2a) - וי"ל דנהי דלא חיישינן בדפנות אי עביד להו קבע מ"מ בסככה שעיקר הסוכה על שם הסכך לא מיתכשרה עד דעביד לה עראי

[25] Vayikra (11:41) - וְכָל־הַשֶּׁרֶץ הַשֹּׁרֵץ עַל־הָאָרֶץ שֶׁקֶץ הוּא לֹא יֵאָכֵל

[26] Makkos (16b) - אמר אביי אכל פוטיתא לוקה ארבעה נמלה לוקה חמש משום שרץ השורץ על הארץ צרעה לוקה שש משום (דברים יד, יט) שרץ העוף

[27] Rashi Makkos (16b) - לוקה ארבעה - שני לאוין כתובין בשרץ המים אחד בתורת כהנים (יא) ואחד במשנה תורה (יד) ושני לאוין כתובין בשרץ סתם (ולא) תשקצו את נפשותיכם בכל השרץ השורץ ולא תטמאו בהם ומשמע בין שרץ המים בין שרץ הארץ הרי ד

[28] Rashi Makkos (16b) - צרעה לוקה שש - חמש משום שרץ הארץ ואחד משום שרץ העוף דכתיב במשנה תורה (יד) וכל שרץ העוף טמא הוא לכם לא יאכלו אבל לא תשקצו את נפשותיכם בבהמה ובעוף וגו' הכתוב

pesukim by any שרץ that they are forbidden to eat, there is another two איסורים of שרץ על הארץ, and more for שרץ העוף. This insect is a שרץ העוף since it flies, and it is also שרץ על הארץ since it walks on the ground. You would get 6 x 39 *malkus* for eating one, which is about 234 or so. Whatever the number is, it's not *geshmak*. There are certain types of locusts which are kosher, but we are not experts in them. There are four conditions to be able to eat any particular locust.[29] They must have four wings, כנפיו חופין את רובו – which these cicadas do, קרצולים to jump with, like grasshoppers – but cicadas do not jump. Grasshoppers have large feet to jump with which cicadas do not.[30] Finally, it must be שמו חגב – it must be called a *chagav* – and that is where the Mesorah comes in because the Sefardim eat certain types of grasshoppers, but if you don't have a *kabbalah* regarding what is considered a *chagav* or not then you cannot eat it. I once opened a can of string beans which had a *hechsher*, and it had a grasshopper inside. Evidently the *hechsher* felt this grasshopper was considered a *chagav*.

Q2. Why can't we rely on someone else's Mesorah for what a *chagav* is?

בפרשת קדושים תהיו אינו מן המנין דלאו בשרץ כתיב ואע"ג דכתיב ביה אשר תרמש האדמה לשון בריות גדולות הוא ושרץ לשון קטנה ונמוכה שנכרת בהלוכה בקושי ונראית כרוחשת

[29] Chullin (59a) and Shulchan Aruch YD (85:1) - סימני חגבים כל שיש לו ד' רגלים וד' כנפים וכנפיו חופין את רוב אורך גופו ורוב היקפו ויש לו שני כרעים לנתר (פי' לקפץ ולהעתיק ממקום למקום) בהם ואפילו אין לו עכשיו ועתיד לגדלם לאחר זמן ואע"פ שיש בו כל הסימנים הללו אינו מותר אלא אם כן שמו חגב או שיש להם מסורת ששמו חגב

[30] Rashi Chullin (59a) - ובחגבים - זהו סימן טהרתם כל שיש לו ארבע רגלים וארבע כנפים ויש לו קרצולים הם שני רגלים ארוכין לבד הארבעה והם סמוך לצוארו ממעל לרגליו לנתר בהם כשהוא רוצה לקפץ וכנפיו חופין את רובו והן ד' סימנים:

A: We are allowed to rely on someone else's Mesorah, but למעשה Ashkenaz Jews don't eat grasshoppers.[31] I'm not sure if the Sefardim eat grasshoppers today either, but if they have a Mesorah for it then they may the grasshoppers. If you are allowed to eat them then you would say a Shehakol on them.

Q3. Should we be careful about not stepping on the cicadas on Shabbos?

A: Yes, you should be careful not to step on them on Shabbos because they are all over,[32] and it is possible to be careful not to step on them. Some of them may be on the ground, but most of them are in the bushes and trees. Just as you cannot step on ants on Shabbos, you are not allowed to

---

[31] Aruch Hashulchan YD (85:5) - אמרו חז"ל [נ"ט.] דלסימנים אלו נצרך ג"כ שיהא שמו חגב וכתב הטור דלכך אין לאוכלם אפילו יש להם כל הסימנים אא"כ יש על מין זה מסורת ששמו חגב ולשון הרמב"ם כן הוא ואע"פ שראשו ארוך ויש לו זנב אם היה שמו חגב טהור עכ"ל משמע מדבריו דא"צ שמו חגב רק בארוך ראש ויש זנב אבל בראש קצר ואין לו זנב א"צ לשמו חגב ומסוגית הש"ס [ס"ה:] יש ג"כ ללמוד כן ומ"מ כתב המגיד משנה דכוונתו לאו בדווקא ובכל ענין צריך לשמו חגב ע"ש וצ"ע וכ"כ הטור והש"ע והצייד נאמן לומר ששמו חגב ע"פ מסורת שלו [עפמ"ג במ"ז] ועכשיו אנו נוהגין שלא לאכול שום חגב אפילו בכל הסימנים ואפילו ידוע ששמו חגב ומימינו לא שמענו שיהא מקום שאוכלין בו חגבים

[32] Shulchan Aruch OC (316:9) - פרעוש הנקרא ברגות בלשון ערב אסור לצודו אא"כ הוא על בשרו ועוקצו ואסור להרגו: הגה ואף לא ימלילנו בידו שמא יהרגנו אלא יטלנו בידו ויזרקנו and Mishna Berura (316:38) - ואסור להרגו - הטעם דמחלקינן בין פרעוש לכנה הוא דכל מלאכות דשבת ממשכן ילפינן להן וילפינן מיתת כל בע"ח לחיוב משחיטת אילים מאדמים שהיו במשכן בשביל עורותיהן ולאו דוקא ע"י שחיטה דה"ה ע"י הכאה וחניקה או נחירה וכל כי האי גוונא כיון שבא עי"ז נטילת נשמה חייב ואמרינן מה אילים מאדמים שפרים ורבים אף כל שפרים ורבים לאפוקי כנה דאינה באה מזכר ונקבה אלא באה מן הזיעה לא חשיבא בריה אבל פרעוש אע"פ שגם היא אינה פרה ורבה מ"מ כיון שהווייתה מן העפר יש בה חיות כאלו נברא מזכר ונקבה וחייב עליה משום נטילת נשמה ואפילו אם הפרעוש עוקצו אסור להרגו

step on these insects either. If it is impossible not to step on them when walking outside on Shabbos, then you should stay home. If it is a *shaas hadechak gadol* then maybe there could be a *heter*, but one should not step on them.[33]

Q4. What about if I'm in the Bais Midrash and need to get to the dining room for Shabbos Seudah?

A: So then don't eat and stay in the Bais Midrash all Shabbos. If you will transgress an איסור by walking outside on Shabbos, then you cannot go out. If it's a question of *pikuach nefesh* then that's a different *shailah*, but otherwise it is forbidden to step on insects because of *netilas neshama.* It may only be an איסור דרבנן since stepping on this insect is a מלאכה שאינו צריכה לגופו, but it's still אסור מדרבנן.[34]

Q5. Is it forbidden to step on the shells of the cicadas?

---

[33] משום מלאכה שאינה צריכה לגופו ופסיק רישא דלא ניחא ליה, ואולי לא ימותו מיד והוי רק גרמא, ואולי לא ימותו כלל

[34] Shulchan Aruch OC (316:8) - שמונה שרצים האמורים בתורה הצדן והחובל בהם אע"פ שלא יצא מהם דם אלא נצרר תחת העור חייב ושאר שרצים אינו חייב החובל בהם אא"כ יצא מהם דם והצדן לצורך חייב שלא לצורך או סתם פטור אבל אסור ולהרמב"ם חייב and Mishna Berura (316:33) - (לג) שלא לצורך - כגון לשחק וכה"ג ופטור משום דהוה ליה מלאכה שאין צריך לגופה. הצד דגים מן הנהר אפילו נתנו תיכף בתוך ספל של מים שלא ימות חייב משום צידה ואם הניחו עד שמת חייב גם משום נטילת נשמה ולאו דוקא מת אלא אפילו אם הניחו עד שיבש כרוחב סלע בין סנפיריו ועדיין הוא מפרכס והחזירו בתוך המים חייב ג"כ משום נטילת נשמה דשוב אינו יכול לחיות [ואמרינן בגמרא דלאו דוקא יבש ממש אלא כשזב ריר משם ונמשך האצבע שם כשמניחו עליו] וא"כ צריך ליזהר שלא יצוה לא"י ליטול דג מן החבית של מים ולהניחו ביבשה אע"פ שירא שמא ימות ויפסדו המים דלא מקילינן איסור דאורייתא ע"י א"י במקום הפסד אם לא שיצוהו ליתן אותו תיכף בתוך בריכה אחרת של מים וטלטול בע"ח שהוא איסור דרבנן מקילינן ע"י א"י בזה and Mishna Berura (316:34) - ולהרמב"ם חייב - אפילו שלא לצורך כל שנתכוין למלאכה דס"ל מלאכה שאינו צריך לגופה חייב עליה ורוב הפוסקים פוסקים כדעה הראשונה דפטור מחטאת משום דבעינן מלאכת מחשבת ואסור מדרבנן

A: There is no problem with stepping on the shells, rather it's only a problem to step on them when they are alive. Have you ever seen a dead fly on the ground? Unless you kill it, they just go somewhere right before they die. All animals are like that – mice, stray cats, etc. It's a *chiddush* when you see a dead cat lying on the ground unless it got into an accident or another animal attacked it. When an animal dies a normal death then it goes into a hiding place somewhere and then whatever happens to them happens. You don't see them anymore. In the summer if you keep your windows open then the room will fill up with many flies. What happens to all those flies? The average life of a fly is two days, so what happens to them. The Ribbono Shel Olam has a whole ecological system worked out that the birds eat them or whatever other cleanup system is in place. When a tree is uprooted and falls down, termites will eventually come to eat it up and there will no longer be any more tree left. There is a cleanup system the Ribbono Shel Olam put into the world, so we don't really see dead animals too much. In fact, they were looking for dead elephants – the lifespan of an elephant is about 70 years – and in Africa there are so many of them. The tusks of an elephant are worth a lot of money because in the past the ivory would be used to make the keys on a piano. Entrepreneurs wanted to hunt down where these dead elephants were so they would be able take their tusks when they die. They couldn't find them, so they put a radio on an old elephant in order to track where this elephant goes to die, and then they would be able to find the rest of the dead elephants. They found it dead in the middle of a field, but they couldn't find the rest of the dead elephants. That's one of the things which the Ribbono Shel Olam made – that dead animals are gone.

Q6. Should I make a *beracha* עוֹשֶׂה מַעֲשֵׂה בְרֵאשִׁית when seeing the cicadas for the first time in 17 years?

A: It doesn't seem that Chazal were *mesaken* a *beracha* on that. It says that when you see a big river then you say עוֹשֶׂה

מַעֲשֵׂה בְרֵאשִׁית,[35] but if you see a small river then you don't say עוֹשֶׂה מַעֲשֵׂה בְרֵאשִׁית.[36] Why? Because we are not sure that the small river was there from מעשה בראשית.[37] When you see a big mountain then you know it was there from מעשה בראשית, but if it's not a big mountain then it may be that it was not created in the time of מעשה בראשית.[38] Mountains come down and go up all the time from the rain and the weather. New mountain are being formed on a pretty consistent basis, so you need to make sure it was there from מעשה בראשית. For instance, if you see the Mississippi River, which I believe is the third largest river in the world, then you can assume it was there from מעשה בראשית. I'm sure the cicadas were there since מעשה בראשית since they are a *briah*, but they are different than rivers and mountains.

Q7. If it flies at you on Shabbos, can you swat it out of your face?

A: They don't usually fly into your face, rather they generally fly on your clothes. They are considered *muktzah*,[39] but you can shake your clothes to get them off.

---

[35] Shulchan Aruch OC (228:1) - על ימים ונהרות הרים וגבעות ומדבריות אומר ברוך אתה יי אמ"ה עושה מעשה בראשית

[36] Shulchan Aruch OC (228:2) - לא על כל הנהרות מברך אלא על ארבע נהרות דכתיבי בקרא כמו חדקל ופרת והוא שראה אותם במקום שלא נשתנה מהלכם ע"י אדם and Mishna Berura (228:4) - כמו חדקל ופרת - לאו דוקא אלו אלא ה"ה כל הנהרות שהן גדולות כמו אלו הד' נהרות ושיהיו ידועים שהם מימי בראשית כמו אלו ולא נתהוו אח"כ מברך

[37] Mishna Berura (228:5) - במקום שלא נשתנה וכו' - פי' דבמקום שהפרו ושינו מהלכו של הנהר לדרך אחרת אין מברכין מאותו המקום והלאה דשם לאו מעשה בראשית הוא ועיין בא"ר שמצדד לומר דאם ספק לו אם נשתנו ג"כ לא יברך

[38] Shulchan Aruch OC (228:3) - ולא על כל הרים וגבעות מברך אלא דוקא על הרים וגבעות המשונים וניכרת גבורת הבורא בהם

[39] Shulchan Aruch OC (308:39) - אסור לטלטל בהמה וחיה ועוף ואע"פ כן מותר לכפות את הסל לפני האפרוחים כדי שיעלו וירדו בו and Mishna Berura (308:146) - אסור ובעודם עליו אסור לטלטלו

Nonetheless, they are harmless – you can just leave them there anyway. So far no one has got hurt from them.

Q8. Should one avoid stepping on them during the week?

A: As I said, they are harmless so there is no reason to kill them. You don't need to specifically go out of your way not to step on them, but there is an *inyan* of רַחֲמָיו עַל־כָּל־מַעֲשָׂיו – the Ribbono Shel Olam has mercy on everything He created.[40] When the עגל came to Rebbi to cry that they were going to *shecht* it, he was punished for not having *rachmanus* on it.[41] Therefore, to kill the insects for no reason should be avoided, but you are not obligated to go out of your way to make sure you don't step on them.

Q9. Is there is איסור of *tzar baalei chaim* for insects?

A: It's an interesting thing – we think in terms of ourselves all the time. We wouldn't like some giant to step on us and crush us. It would be very painful. However, we don't know for sure whether insects have any feelings. We know that animals have feelings to some degree, though not the to the same degree as human beings, so the *tzaar* is different. There was a whole *shailah* one time about the milk that one of the stomachs of the animals sometimes gets twisted which

---

לטלטל וכו' - דהם בכלל מוקצה כעצים ואבנים דהא לא חזו. ואפילו אם יכול להגיע להפסד על ידם כגון שהעוף פורח ע"ג הכלים ויכול לשברם אפ"ה אסור לתפסם בידים ואפילו אם הוא מורגל בבית מכבר דתו אין בו משום חשש צידה כמבואר בסימן שט"ז אפ"ה ליטלם בידים אסור משום מוקצה אלא יפריחנה מעליהם וכמבואר בסימן של"ד במ"א בסק"ג דאיסור טלטול מוקצה הוא אפילו במקום הפסד

40 Tehillim (145:9) - טוֹב־ה לַכֹּל וְרַחֲמָיו עַל־כָּל־מַעֲשָׂיו

41 Bava Metzia (85a) - ע"י מעשה באו מאי היא דההוא עגלא דהוו קא ממטו ליה לשחיטה אזל תליא לרישיה בכנפיה דרבי וקא בכי אמר ליה זיל לכך נוצרת אמרי הואיל ולא קא מרחם ליתו עליה יסורין וע"י מעשה הלכו יומא חד הוה קא כנשא אמתיה דרבי ביתא הוה שדיא בני כרכושתא וקא כנשא להו אמר לה שבקינהו כתיב (תהלים קמה, ט) ורחמיו על כל מעשיו אמרי הואיל ומרחם נרחם עליה

prevents the food from going through, making the animal die. Therefore, they sew the stomach into the side of the animal to fix this, which makes the animal a *treif*ah since they make holes in the stomach. The milk from this animal is also milk from a *treif*a. That *shailah* surfaced maybe ten years ago (around 5754), and some vets claimed that they don't make holes in the stomach while others said they do make holes in the stomach. It wasn't clear, so I went down to the cow hospital to see exactly how they do this operation. Do you think the vet surgeon wears scrubs when they do an operation on a cow? I'll tell you this: the cow hospital was one corner of a barn. The vet gave the animal some hay to eat, he split the animal down the whole side while it was munching on the hay, turned around the stomach and sewed it into the side of the animal. The animal was still munching away at the hay and didn't move at all. The surgeon sewed up the rest of the animal and that was the end of the operation. There was no anesthesia – nothing – and when the animal was finished eating it went back to be with the rest of the animals. Evidently it was not in any big pain as it did not kick or yell the entire time. It seems they don't feel pain the way we do. As a matter of fact, when a cow used to get bloated then it would die because the food wouldn't go through. They used to just take a knife and stick it straight through the skin into the stomach, then all the air and whatever was in the stomach would go outside the animal and release the pressure so that the animal could live. You would think it would get infected with all the dirt from the stomach coming out, but nothing happened. They are different than human beings. Even though animals do have feelings, it is not the same as human beings. In fact, scientists say that ruminating animals don't have feelings as much as non-ruminating animals. Meaning, animals which chew their cud don't have as many feelings as those which are non-ruminating, so a horse would feel much more than a cow. Therefore, when you step on a roach, whether it feels pain or not is something we don't know. They don't have the same nervous system or brain as we do. It's all completely different – they are a different *briah*.

Q10. If someone enjoys killing the cicadas, is that considered *tzaar baalei chaim*?

A: The Noda B'Yehuda says there is no *tzaar baalei chaim* for killing an animal because the animal will die anyway and endure that *tzaar*. The *shailah* was whether you are allowed to go hunting for enjoyment. In the times of the Noda B'Yehuda, the way they hunted was using a bow and arrow. If you are a skilled marksman then you'll get the animal with the arrow, and that's the thrill to show that you can shoot an animal. Are you allowed to do that? The Noda B'Yehuda says that since the whole *briah* was given to mankind to benefit from, we are allowed to do what we want with them since the time of the Mabul – just as we are allowed to kill an animal to enjoy eating its flesh, we are also allowed to kill an animal for the enjoyment of going hunting.[42] However, he says at the end of the *teshuva* that hunting is the practice of Esav HaRasha and is not the *yiddishe* thing to do.[43] Therefore, one should not hunt, even though it is not forbidden due to *tzaar baalei chaim* since the animal will

---

[42] Noda B'Yehuda YD (2:10) - ואמנם אין לנו להאריך בזה כי כבר האריך מהרא"י בפסקים וכתבים סימן ק"ה שכל דבר שיש בו צורך להאדם לית ביה משום צעב"ח וגם לא שייך צעב"ח אלא לצערו ולהניחו בחיים אבל להמית בהמות וחיות וכל מיני בעלי חיים לית ביה משום צעב"ח וכן מוכח בחולין דף ז' ע"ב עקרנא להו איכא צעב"ח קטלנא להו איכא משום בל תשחית הרי אף שהשיב לו על עקרנא דאיכא צעב"ח אעפ"כ אמר קטלנא להו. וא"כ אין בנדון שאלתו משום צעב"ח, ומשום בל תשחית ודאי ליכא דהרי נהנה בעור וגם אינו עושה דרך השחתה.

[43] Noda B'Yehuda YD (2:10) - ואמנם מאד אני תמה על גוף הדבר ולא מצינו איש ציד רק בנמרוד ובעשו ואין זה דרכי בני אברהם יצחק ויעקב ופוק חזי לומר תבלה ותחדש כתב מהרי"ו בפסקיו הביאו רמ"א בא"ח סוף סימן רכ"ג שאין לומר כן על הנעשה מעורות בהמה משום ורחמיו על כל מעשיו, ואף שרמ"א כתב עליו שהוא טעם חלוש היינו מצד שאינו חיוב שבשבילו ימיתו בהמה וכמה עורות יש שכבר מוכן וכמה מתים מאליהם ויכולים להשתמש בעורותיהם ועם כל זה סיים רמ"א שרבים מקפידים על זה, ואיך ימית איש ישראלי בידים בעלי חיים בלי שום צורך רק לגמור חמדת זמנו להתעסק בצידה

have that *tzaar* of dying anyway. If a person enjoys killing the cicadas, then it would be permitted – but the Noda B'Yehuda would say it's not a *yiddishe* thing to do.

Index

Index

Made in the USA
Middletown, DE
20 May 2025